Harbinger

Oberleutnant-Zur-See Peterson and the crew of the Zeppelin L32 have the distinction of being the first men to bombard Havering from the air. On the night of the 23rd September 1916, this 650ft long leviathan dropped 15 bombs across Hornchurch and Upminster. Four fell on Suttons Farm, one of which caused a crater 21ft wide by 4ft deep opposite the Good Intent Public House. Two fell on Argents Farm, seven on Tylers Hall Farm and two on Upminster Common. This was but a taste of what the area would endure a quarter of a century hence, at the hand of the same enemy.

There were to be no celebrations aboard the L32 however, for 35 minutes later it fell in flames at Great Burstead, shot down by 2nd Lieut. F Sowrey, flying from Suttons Farm, Hornchurch.

Falling to earth from the burning Zeppelin, the last impression Peterson was to make on this country's soil was to be his own.

1

Rear Cover: Disguised as a German, a Home Guardsman is threatened with the
bayonet of his comrade during manoeuvres staged in Gerpins Gravel Pits, Rainham.

HITLER

V

HAVERING

1939 - 1945

Researched and compiled by Peter Watt

Published by

CARLTON ARMITAGE PRESS

30 Romford Road
Aveley
Essex

© Peter Watt, 1994.

I.S.B.N. 0 9524032 0 X

Printed in Great Britain by
The Balkerne Press

Contents

Acknowledgements & Sources

Romford Central Library.

Public Records Office (Kew).

The Essex Police Museum.

The Essex Records Office (Chelmsford).

Home Guard photographs reproduced by permission of the Trustees of the Essex Regiment Museum (The Leggett Collection)

The Trustees of the Mass-Observation Archive, University of Sussex. Repoduced by permission of Curtis Brown Group Ltd, London

Royal Commission on the Historical Monuments of England.

The Hornchurch & District Historical Society.

British Gas plc (North Thames).

Imperial War Museum.

U.S. National Archive.

Romford Recorder

Romford Times

Individuals (alphabetical)

Fred Barnes
S. G. Champion
Mrs. Cook
Elmer Coton
Margaret Eldred
Patricia Eldred
Joy Eldridge
Brian Evans
Fred Feather
Alfred Gregory
Reginald Harris
Eric Hayward
Mrs. Hesford
Ian Holt
Ian Hook
A. F. Kilby (deceased)
Mrs. A. Levack
M. O. Diarist No. (M5370)
Wilfred Mott
Don Paterson
Roger Pickett
Glyn Richards (deceased)
Joyce Russell
Margaret Skinner
David Smith
J. L. Stevens
J. D. Watt
Ron Wingrave
Mrs. W. Wunderly

C ould it really have happened here? Did a bomb disturb the tranquillity of this leafy avenue? Is it possible a Nazi warplane fell in flames upon these flats? Can a rocket from the stratosphere have fallen on those semi-detached suburban homes?

To the casual observer there seems little to evoke the dark years between 1939-1945. Visually, the scars have all but healed, with little or no sign of the devastation that once prevailed. It is all too easy to pass by the site of a direct hit, in ignorance of the tragedy and sorrow it entailed. In one blinding flash, three generations lost and a family tree truncated forever. For those fated to lose a limb or their sight the results were all too permanent and would have to be borne to the grave. Scars to the mind, engraved by the horror of war, could be just as long lasting. How many nightmares, even today, still revert to events of half a century ago?

This is the record of one borough's ordeal, and the effect one man had upon it,

' HITLER V HAVERING '.

To be precise and to assuage the pedantic, I should obviously point out that Havering as a borough did not exist in the war years, but was split between the then Borough of Romford and Hornchurch Urban District Council. The close co-operation between the two districts during the war years was an important factor in enabling their merger some years later. Of course many of the bombs that fell showed scant regard for local boundaries and caused destruction straddling both districts in an egalitarian and dispassionate fashion.

A common topic of discussion as the war clouds loomed in 1939 was that of the likely fate of the Havering area should the storm break. Opinion was divided. There was the cheery optimist, who having seen it through the last war felt sure we should do so again. Then there was the pessimist, with visions of apocalyptic dimensions. In reality Havering possessed a number of factors that might make it a target, if only by default. By far the most important target was Hornchurch Aerodrome which was of great strategic military importance. Just to the west was Dagenham, where nestled many a potential industrial target. Here Ford Motor Co. manufactured military vehicles and engines, Briggs Motor Bodies made armoured vehicles, bombs, shells and rockets and Sterling Engineering Co. produced sub-machine guns and radar equipment. A combination of industries that might well attract the attention of the Luftwaffe. Also to the west of Havering lay the outer ring of London's defences, consisting of barrage balloons and anti-aircraft guns and when confronted with these, many less stalwart bomber crews might be tempted to drop their load and head for home. All these factors undoubtedly played a part, but despite widespread belief held at the time that the enemy had been aiming at 'such and such a building', the sad truth of the matter was that the inaccurate nature of bombing at the time meant that Havering was often the 'best they could do' when aiming for London as a whole. In the latter years of the war the indiscriminate nature of the V1 flying bomb and the V2 rocket made any area in the South East of England a potential target and Havering would gain its fair share in this lottery.

The frequency and persistence of raids during the period of the 'Blitz' has the regrettable consequence that it is virtually impossible to give adequate coverage to each bomb that fell upon Havering soil. Even attempts to be selective by merely reporting incidents where there was loss of life is defeated by the sheer volume of fatalities. The necessary brevity accorded to each would thus devalue each individual loss, which in reality were distinct and unique tales of grief and suffering. The only rational conclusion is to restrict reports to the 'highlights' which should perhaps more accurately be described as 'lowlights'. Throughout the war years all occurrences however serious were referred to as 'incidents' and I have maintained its usage throughout.

To what extent have these events been recorded before? The usual oracle of information, the local newspaper was severely restricted by censorship from revealing much of what took place at the time. One can imagine the chagrin of editors when faced with stories which in peacetime would have made the national press for days on end, being forbad from even mentioning the place in which they occurred. The stock description was 'somewhere in the South East of England'. These restrictions were to deny the enemy gleaning information as to the accuracy and efficacy of their bombing. The members of the press could appreciate this and respected the restrictions, but sometimes they were able to convey the information they wished to impart by subtle innuendo. For instance when one local paper wished to convey the location of one incident to its readership it referred to, "bomb damage at a famous hospital, named after a famous Queen*. It is likely even the Germans might have been able to work that one out, had they been scouring our local press for news. With such restrictions placed on the press most facts had to be gained by word of mouth. This inevitably

left many hungry for news. It was only when hostilities ceased that Glyn Richards, editor of the Romford Recorder, was able to publish his excellent little book 'Ordeai in Romford'. Even in getting this published he had to overcome a great deal of bureaucracy and red tape. Hornchurch, Rainham and Upminster were left undocumented however, and so maybe this will redress the balance some fifty years on. I have tried to restrict the detail of this book to cover the effect the war had on the civilian population and hence military installations such as Hornchurch Aerodrome are treated as just another potential target. Hornchurch Aerodrome attributed the area the greatest importance it has ever held in any modern conflict and the valour of the pilots who flew from there has consequently been extremely well documented. For this reason only aircraft that crashed in the area and so affected the civilians on the ground are included.

If an excuse is needed for documenting those far off black years, it is that we should not forget the terrible sacrifice paid by many, not in the course of some military exploit, but in simple pursuit of everyday life, on what became known as the 'Home Front' . It is a sobering fact that up until September 1942 the number of British women and children killed exceeded the total number of deaths in the armed forces.

* Victoria Hospital.

The A.R.P. Control Room at Langtons, Hornchurch. Steel-helmeted personnel take part in an exercise as the war clouds gathered in mid 1939. Notice the Boy Scout runners ready for action in the background.

Phoney War

The morning of Sunday, September 3rd saw the last precious hours of peace ebb away. The British ultimatum to Hitler expired at 11.00 a.m. and at 11.15 a.m. a sombre and saddened Neville Chamberlain addressed the nation by radio.

"I am speaking to you from the Cabinet Room at No.10 Downing Street. This morning, the British Ambassador in Berlin handed the German Government a final note, stating that unless the British Government heard from them by 11 o'clock that they were prepared at once to withdraw their troops from Poland, a state of war would exist between us. I have to tell you now that no such undertaking has been received, and that consequently this country is at war with Germany."

Barely had the Prime Minister finished speaking, and his audience digested the enormity of his words, than the air raid sirens sounded their dreadful wail. Eyes all over Havering gazed aloft in fearful anticipation of the waves of German aircraft they expected to bring death and destruction any second. Would they drop high explosives bombs or incendiaries, or maybe the even more dreadful gas? For 77 year old Mrs. Emily Bone of 9 Garbutt Road, Upminster, the strain was all too much. The former cook to the Joslin family of Hoppy Hall, was preparing her midday meal, when suddenly, on hearing the siren, she was seized by a stroke and died a short time later. Hers and everyone else's fears were without foundation, for the cause of this first scare was a solitary French aircraft which had over-flown an observation post at Maidstone. It would be nearly a year before the sirens of Havering signalled the actual arrival of the Nazi menace.

Thus was ushered in the period quickly dubbed the 'phoney war' for its seeming lack of action. If there was little action in the air or on land however, there was never any such respite at sea. At the outbreak of war, 39 of the German fleet of 58 U-Boats were at sea. At midday they received a communication by radio to open hostilities. Shortly after 9.00 p.m. the Captain of U-30 caught sight of what he mistakenly identified as an auxiliary cruiser. Accordingly, he fired two torpedoes, both of which struck the target, which turned out to be the Donaldson-Atlantic liner 'Athena' bound for Canada. The liner sank with the loss of 112 lives including 28 American citizens. On board was Mr. F. Milbourne, his wife and their two young children, Margaret aged eight and John aged four. They had left their home in Sycamore Avenue, Upminster to sail to Windsor, Ontario. All were thankfully rescued and returned with the other survivors to Glasgow and safety.

So even though there had been no direct attack on Havering, Hitler had already succeeded in casting a dark shadow over its borders. A far darker shadow was self inflicted - the 'Black-Out'. It had long been appreciated that one of the greatest protections against the threat of air attack after nightfall would be the black-out. It pre-empted the outbreak of war by two days in response to Hitler's invasion of Poland and the possibility of a surprise attack upon this country by the Luftwaffe. For London, and hence Havering, there was one fundamental failing with any such attempt to hide its location beneath a cloak of darkness. This was that with even the dimmest of starlight, the twists and turns of the River Thames shone like a silvered path to the heart of the City. The blackout was nonetheless rigorously enforced which resulted in the A.R.P. wardens becoming thoroughly disliked for their seeming glee in tracking down the most petty breaches of the regulations. Numerous prosecutions ensued, but not all officialdom was hard of heart, as demonstrated on one occasion when Ada Leeworthy of 3 Station Parade, Harold Wood, was summonsed for showing a light in the blackout. When the bench heard that she had been carrying her baby at the time and must have caught the light switch as she went downstairs and also that her husband was in the Army, so that she was dependent on the allowance, they fined her ten shillings to set an example, but paid the fine themselves.

What made the A.R.P. wardens so universally unpopular with the population was that there was little to keep them active. A snippet of conversation overheard and jotted down, reflects the humour and feeling of the time.

Romford Workman 1 :

"I see Harry's joined the A.R.P."

Romford Workman 2 :

"What's that, 'anging round pubs'"

It could not be appreciated at the time that this period of tranquillity was something to be savoured, for once the storm broke, minor gripes would seem as nothing to the hardships that had to be endured. Then no longer were the A.R.P. services scorned, for theirs was to be a perilous and thankless task. For the time being however, an uneasy peace persisted.

Sandbags, sandbags and more sandbags!

One practical A.R.P. step that could be undertaken immediately was the protection of strategic sites with sandbags. In the week following the outbreak of war over 100,000 bags were filled in Romford alone. Of these some were used in protecting St. Michael's Hall Gidea Park , **(Above)**, which had been converted into a first-aid post. A further 40,000 bags were piled around Victoria Hospital. **(Right)**

My First Three Weeks of War

Diary of a Romford Girl, Aged 17.

Originally written for Mass Observation, an organization established to record people's everyday experiences, this diary gives an atmospheric insight into the way world events dramatically engulfed ordinary people's lives, the mundane mingling with the international crisis. Not having been written from a post-war perspective, it escapes contamination by the sureties of hindsight, instead each page was penned with trepidation as to what the next day would bring.

❖ **Sept 1st Friday.**

When I arrived at the Senior Girls School where I am pupil-teaching, the staff were deep in conversation about the international situation. The general feeling was optimistic. There was a murmur of assent all round when the history mistress affirmed that, "This evacuation business was a brilliant propaganda stroke on the part of Chamberlain. He only did it to fool Hitler into submission. No possibility of war now."

Yesterday (Thursday), we installed a wireless set in the staff-room, and our head mistress decided that someone was to be in the room all the time, in readiness for any special radio message. At eleven this morning, as I was only observing a lesson, I decided to go to the staff room to see if anyone was there. There were three others there, and together we listened to the announcement that "serious developments in the international situation" had occurred. As the details of the Poland air-raids were unfolded, one of the staff, an intending missionary, kept muttering to herself, and clicking her tongue. All four of us knew it was virtually war.

At break, everyone was asking everyone else, "Has there been any more news?" At the dinner table, anecdotes of A.R.P., evacuation and the last war were exchanged, and now and again, someone would say "I can't believe it's here."

After dinner we listened to another news bulletin. Our head mistress, and the headmaster of the joint boys' school were present - no man had ever before been in our staff room before. Everyone was terribly grave, and most eyes were on the ceiling. When a child knocked on the door, we switched off the radio, because we did not want the pupils to learn the news just yet. A few of the bigger girls did get to know, however. One class (13-14 year-olds) was particularly ill-behaved. Afterwards I asked them why they were so naughty.

"Well Miss," was the reply, "you see we might not be here in a week."

At 4.15, we all said prolonged goodbyes, in case we weren't here next week. Many of us decided not to prepare Monday's lessons. Actually, I think I was the least upset, but I was the only one who had not experienced the last war.

After tea, a friend called at our house, for me to go to supper with her. I was about to go, when my mother arrived, and unconditionally refused to let me go.

"You are not to go away from home," she declared dramatically, "If we die, we all die together."

So I spent the evening at home, reading. The conditions were not exactly pleasant. My father insists upon listening to every news bulletin and our makeshift black-out arrangements involve the use of of a light so small that it strains the eyes. It's only ten, but I'm going to bed.

❖ Sept 2nd Saturday.

A telegram arrived, with arrangements for my sister's evacuation, so I had to go out and find her. When I returned, a boyfriend was waiting for me, and he suggested a visit to the cinema, "to get away from all this." After tea, we went to my father's shop where it took me ten minutes to persuade my mother that I would be safe, and even then I had to promise to be in by ten.

The cinema was almost full, and the audience was very worked up. It cheered and booed wildly in the appropriate places, and roared with laughter at the topical allusions in the film. They were more subdued while the news reel was showing, but Chamberlain earned a hearty cheer, and Mussolini was in for some heated hissing.

We had to leave early, to satisfy my waiting mother. The black-out was much more successful than yesterday. (Yesterday several houses in our street ignored the existence of a blackout.) We could see nothing at all, except the buses, which were half lighted. I couldn't even see my companion. There were a good few people about - we heard them!

Thought for the day.........What an anti-climax it would be if there was no war!

❖ Sept 3rd Sunday.

What a storm it was last night! I lay awake, wondering whether the flashes were of lightning or gunfire, until well into the morning. My small sister kept calling out, "Are they here?"

In the morning, however, the weather was good. My mother considered the news much more cheerful. She didn't think a war would be needed at all

At eleven fifteen, I was playing the piano in the front room, when suddenly my mother burst in, shouting "Stop that noise!" and then flung open the window, letting in the scream of the air-raid siren, and the scuffling noise of neighbours in a hurry. Immediately, my father assumed the role of the administrative head of the house, issuing commands and advice:

''All get your gas-masks!........Steady no panicking!....... Every man for himself! ....Keep in the passage!''

My small sister (11) began to sob;- ''Will it be alright?'', she kept querying.

My mother was frightened, but was trying to take hold of herself. My heart beat hard for the first few seconds, and then it calmed down. I think my brother and elder sister felt much the same as I did. We gathered in the passage (we have no shelter) and sat on the stairs.

After a few minutes, we decided that it was either a false alarm or a trial, so we went to the front gate (all except my mother and small sister, who kept calling to us to come back.) and remained there until the ''All Clear'' was given. A few babies were crying and air-raid wardens with gas-masks and crash helmets, were running up and down. After the all clear we learnt for the first time about the **Declaration of a State of War**. Most people were glad. ''High time someone showed Hitler he wasn't such a god as he made out'', was a typical comment.

After dinner, we made more lasting black-out arrangements, and gathered into one place, all the ''War-time accessories,'' such as torches, five pails and black paper, that we could lay our hands on.

At tea time, a boy friend came to see me. He is a refugee, and was very worried as to his position as an alien. He expressed willingness to enter National Service, or the Army, or whatever they asked of him. He was I think, sincerely grateful to England for its protection, and wanted to prove it actively.

The black-out curtains made the room very stuffy, and the light bad. We went into town to see what was going on. Evidently others had come out for similar reasons, so every street corner was ornamented with little groups of people; almost everyone carried a gas mask. One in six of the men was not in civilian clothes.

Before we went to bed, we put warm coats where they could easily be found in case of emergency.

❖ Sept 4th Monday.

At 3 o'clock this morning, my mother ran into our room and cried, "They're here"

Immediately my small sister began to cry. We slipped into our warm coats and ran downstairs. We were all quite calm, and joked and munched apples until the ''All Clear'' was sounded. Then my parents had tea, while we went back to bed.

In the morning, we were amazed that there had been no air-raid, and glad that we had not accepted the standing offer of any of our neighbours to use their shelters. Incidentally, one issue of the war, is that we are now on speaking terms with our next-door neighbours, with whom we have been on bad terms for at least 17 years.

❖ Sept 5th Tuesday.

Today, I merely wandered about, at home and in the town, with nothing to do, feeling too restless to read. All my friends have evacuated, or else joined the army. On the streets I didn't carry my gas-mask, but I was in a 2% minority. I do however, wear an identity disk on a chain, as instructed on the wireless.

In the evening, a friend of my mother's came round. She believed that her husband had been on the 'Athena', and was afraid to go home, in case a telegram was waiting for her. She was terribly upset, and her hand shook as she held her cigarette. During the news bulletin, she burst out crying, and clung to my mother like a child.

❖ Sept 6th Wednesday.

We took the air-raid very calmly this morning. When we heard the sirens, we dressed, came down and had breakfast, and then sat in the dining room, listening to the wireless. After a time, we got fed up, so my father and I went into the street. There were people at every front gate.

When we heard gun-fire, we went in, and sat in the passage. My mother was nervous, and hadn't dressed. The rest of us soon became bored again, sitting on the stairs and just waiting, so we went into the back garden to see how people were enjoying sitting in their shelters. None of them were in use.

As soon as the "All Clear" was given, my father and sister rushed off to work. I got ready at my leisure, and followed my father to his shop. The air was saturated with rumour. One person told me that 14 German planes were shot down at Sheerness, another that the German plane that was shot down at Chingford (alternative reports said at Goodmayes, Ilford, Gidea Park and Woolwich) contained three German officers. One was dead, and the other two had been taken to the police station, where they were divulging Hitler's secrets, in the hope of gaining their freedom.

I served in my fathers shop all day. Every third person asked for candles or nightlights ; every fourth for sugar ; every sixth for black paper. We soon sold out of these things, as did every other shop in Romford, and it became clear that people were wandering from shop to shop, getting a pound of sugar here, a pound there, a candle here, a nightlight there, just where, and as cheaply as they could.

Everyone who came into the shop made some comment on this morning's air-raid. Customers were far too talkative, we simply could not get rid of them. Old women told in high, cracked voices, what happened in the last war, what happened this morning, and what would no doubt happen in a few days time.

We closed the shop at 6.30, because of black-out regulations.

In the evening, the lady whose husband was on the "Athena" visited us again. She had no news, but she had calmed herself, and we were able to learn more details. Her husband is a Civil Servant, and he received a letter, sealed and marked "Strictly Private", instructing him to go to Glasgow, where he would receive orders of how to reach Canada. He arrived just in time time to catch the "Athena", but his movements were so secret that he was not allowed to write and say which boat he got on. The woman assumes it is the "Athena". We feel infinitely sorry for her, but fear that her husband is lost.

❖ Sept 7th Thursday.

I served in the shop again today, and the first person who came in was the woman whose husband was feared drowned. All smiles, she waved a letter before us, and explained incoherently that he had written to say he just missed the boat. So that was one tragedy with a happy ending.

Sugar, candles and nightlights continue to be in demand..........people won't believe that we haven't any.

"I'm sorry", I say. "We're right out of candles."

"Haven't you any small ones either?"

"We have no candles at all."

"Haven't you any pink ones left?" etc. etc.

In the afternoon, I went to the Town Hall, to sign on for full-time A.R.P work. I might as well do this. I can't possibly continue with my studies, under the circumstances.

There was a lot of red tape at the Town Hall, but eventually, I managed to encounter the right person, and was handed a form, which I duly filled out. People were joining up by the hundred. By the evening, they had signed on all the volunteers that were needed, and had closed their door to recruits.

On the way home, I passed a house from which an insufficiently obscured light shone through the blackness like the sun. The people living across the road began to shout, "Turn 'Em Out!.......Switch off them lights", and as I turned the corner, I saw that their shouts had effect, and the lights were properly covered. No need for the police!

❖ Sept 8th Friday.

A joyful postcard announced that High School Term's commencement is postponed indefinitely. I have framed it, and hung it on the wall.

ALEXANDER KORDA
presents his mightiest spectacle

A. E. W. MASON'S

THE FOUR FEATHERS
IN TECHNICOLOR

Directed by ZOLTAN KORDA
with JOHN CLEMENTS • RALPH RICHARDSON
C. AUBREY SMITH • JUNE DUPREZ

CERT 'A'

HAVANA
PHONE ROMFORD 300

SUNDAY, SEPT. 3rd — GEORGE FORMBY in KEEP FIT (U) — NAN GREY in RECKLESS LIVING (U)

MONDAY, SEPTEMBER 4th, FOR SIX DAYS
JOHN CLEMENTS — RALPH RICHARDSON — JUNE DUPREZ
THE FOUR FEATHERS

1.0   3.45   6.80   9.15   (A)
—ALSO—
THE CRIME REPORTER in CONSIDER YOUR VERDICT (A)

❖ Sept 9th Sat.

The black-out arrangements in our front room are not a success. They consist of our old curtains, mounted on black cloth, and although no light shines through, chinks of light escape at the sides. So I spent the entire morning edging each pane of glass with 2" of black paper........and I haven't finished even now.

In the afternoon, I went to the cinema. Today is the first time they have opened since the outbreak of war. The house was packed and the audience wild and appreciative. In "Consider Your Verdict", which was excellent, the audience roared with laughter at the slightest humour, and openly mocked all sentiment and melodrama. The other film, "The Four Feathers", seemed to carry the audience much better, although, personally, I disliked it so much that I didn't sit through it. Every time an enemy was stabbed in the chest, a yell of delight escaped the audience. When the British flag was hoisted, everyone cheered. They were taken hold of by an hysterical patriotism, which was really repulsive.

In the evening, I went in search of the Fallen Aeroplane, reputed to have been brought down near here. (See Sept 6th).

❖ Sept 10th Sunday.

I went to see a friend in Gidea Park. We agreed that, while at first the war had, if nothing else, been a break from routine, an extra excitement, but that now, what with black-outs and evacuation, it was boring, depressing and nerve-racking, and the sooner it was over the better.

When I reached home, there was devil to pay. Why was I late? I would never be allowed out in the evening again. I was a naughty girl. And why hadn't I taken my gas-mask with me? I would never be allowed out if I didn't take my gas-mask, etc..etc....   Bed will be a welcome relief.

❖ Sept 11th Monday.

In the evening, I went to supper with my friend, the Jewish refugee boy, whose 20th birthday it is today. He was feeling very depressed, he kept comparing this birthday with his nineteenth, (he was fairly well-off in Germany), and he kept wondering what his 21st would be like. He was worrying about his mother in Germany too, as he was unable to communicate with her.

As usual, I had to be in early, nine o'clock was the set time. By 8.30, it was so dark that nothing at all was visible: we had to feel our way along.

❖ Sept 12th Tuesday.

I served in the shop during the morning. It was very depressing; we've sold out of so many goods; and so many others have gone up, that no customer went away completely satisfied. Many indeed, mutter under their breath about "Not letting the poor live in these hard times." etc..etc.. But what can we do?

❖ Sept 13th Wednesday.

I went to the library in the morning. The librarian said they had been very busy since the war. On the way home, I looked around the Romford Market. It was very miserable, compared with normal times. Only Romford residents were allowed to pitch a stall, which meant that more than half the square was empty. Every other stall sold gas-mask bags. there were half-a-dozen men selling the repulsive pamphlet "Hitler's Last Will", and doing excellent business too.

All sorts of black-out commodities were thrust in one's face. One elderly man is making a small fortune, by selling tin shades for electric lamps. He and his wife make them at home, thousands a day.

❖ Sept 15th Friday.

Doesn't this eternal waiting-for-something to happen get on peoples nerves! Today, as I was serving in the shop, I heard the barman in the pub opposite shout, "Time Please" and immediately one fat old woman, completely tipsy, gave him a clout on the head. In doing so she slipped on the step leading into the street, and fell. Commotion followed. A crowd collected, and policemen were called. And as the old woman was hurried away, under escort, one observer on the outskirts of the crowd whispered to her friend, "Cor, I thought we was going to 'ave some excitement."

❖ Sept 16th Saturday.

In the evening, we listened, of course to Bandwagon. It wasn't so much the actual fact of Bandwagon's return that caught our enthusiasm; it was rather its significance as a long-awaited advance in the B.B.C.'s war policy. I don't know how good the thing was, but it made us laugh. I think we laugh more easily in these strained times. Even my highbrow sister, who always sneers contemptuously at variety programs, almost went into hysterics over the joke about the budgerigars at Berchtesgaden. Only my mother, for whose benefit alone we usually switch on variety, refused to be amused.

"I'm not in the mood for laughing", she grumbled, "Who can listen to this rubbish when real trouble is going on all round us? I've no patience with it."

But it certainly put the rest of us into a good mood, and we sat up late, swapping Hitler stories, and "talking war".

❖ Sept 17th Sunday.

When I dragged myself downstairs this morning, (even in a life of leisure Sunday is a difficult day for tearing oneself out of bed), I was greeted with the cheerful cry from my sister,

"Poland is already divided in two. It's all over."

When I asked her where she had gleaned this information, she replied that my father had told her. Eventually we both concluded that it was one of my father's characteristic exaggerations, so we decided to wait for the 12 o'clock news. At twelve we switched on. When it was over we realized just how serious the position had become.

"The whole things a farce!" said my father, for the 48th time. Now whether bad news has an effect on my inside, I don't know, but the fact remains that ever since the news this morning, I have felt acutely bilious.

❖ Sept 18th Monday.

I served in the shop during the morning. The situation is impossible. All prices have risen, and no customer accepts the rise without question. We have hardly any stock, and have to refuse five out of six customers. They all complain. Many make little "scenes". They accuse us of profiteering; threaten us too. But we can do nothing.

❖ Sept 22nd Friday.

This morning, we had a delivery of candles. Not ordinary wax candles, but smelly, tallow ones, wrapped up in tissue paper, and about half the size of the others. Still, they were candles, and, joyfully, we crossed out ' no candles' on the notice that we put on the counter, and added

> **WE HAVE NO**
> *Nightlights*
> *Pixie-Lamps*
> *Drawing-Pins*
> *Candles*
> *or*
> *Black-Paper*

"Candles, Three for a Penny".

We felt very pleased with ourselves. It was a pleasure to say,

"Yes, madam, we have candles today."

In the evening, as usual, I went to the Post-Office at about 9:30, and on my way back, I met the 'Reason Why Young Girls Are Not Allowed Out During a Black-Out'. However, a timely allusion by me to the British Police, caused his immediate dissolution into the darkness.

"Romford's A.R.P. nerve centre. The control room and report centre underneath the Town Hall where messages are received from wardens' posts outside. This picture shows volunteers plotting details of incidents that were staged during an A.R.P exercise"

The War Comes To Rainham?

22nd May 1940

*D*espite the obvious signs of war such as the balloon barrage overhead, the piles of protective sandbags, the taped windows and the omnipresent military uniforms, the Spring of 1940 still saw no direct attack having affected Havering. Rather foolishly Chamberlain felt moved to remark that "Hitler seemed to have missed the bus". Then on the 10th May 1940 the Germans unleashed their devastating Blitzkrieg on the Low Countries. By the 22nd May the Germans had smashed their way through the crumbling Allied forces. In four days time the order would be given to initiate 'Operation Dynamo', the evacuation of our men from Dunkirk. It was in this highly charged atmosphere, with attacks on the mainland expected at any moment, that a confused message was sent from Essex County Control to the Regional Control at Cambridge. It helps to convey the tension of the time.

The message read as follows:-

"SPECIAL REPORT........STOP...........REPORTED THAT A BOMB........!!!!!!!!!****?????......."

At this point the regional telephonist fainted, apparently at the first mention of the word bomb. A relief had to be found before the end of the message could be sent.

"DROPPED NORTH OF GRAYS APPARENTLY BETWEEN ORSETT AND BULPHAN ....STOP......NOW REPORTED THAT EXPLOSION WAS FRIENDLY AEROPLANE CRASHED AT RAINHAM......STOP......REPORTED FROM ANOTHER SOURCE THAT PLANE DOWN IN BERWICK ROAD RAINHAM .... STOP......... MAKE UNKNOWN.......STOP"

Essex County Control. 22/5/40

Despite being fired upon by both German and British guns on the same night, Pilot Officer Coton survived to swap the controls of his outdated Hampden for that of a Manchester, pictured here, after it had undertaken its first bombing mission. **(Inset)** Fifty-three years on and Pilot Officer Coton has become Wing Commander E. Coton (retired). He is seen here holding a shell case from a local gun site, which notionally might have been one fired at him that fateful May night in 1940.

The Pilot's Story

*T*he unfortunate plane in question was a Hampden bomber, No. L4067 of 144 Squadron, from Hemswell, Lincolnshire. The story starts the previous evening when Pilot Officer Elmer Coton, along with his crew of three, took off from their base, at the start of a mission to bomb munition trains in Germany. The weather, which had been fine to begin with, slowly deteriorated, and by the time they were approaching the target it had begun to rain.

Flying at an altitude of 6000 feet they were within range of the German flak, which worryingly began to burst all around them. Luck having deserted the poor crew, a shell exploded close to their plane. The port wing was badly damaged and both the rudder and ailerons disabled. It seemed certain that the aircraft and crew would not see England again that night or for many nights to come. Pilot Officer Coton gave the order for the rest of the crew to bale out, whilst somewhere in the vicinity of Krefeld. Pilot Officer Jones and Corporal Smith were taken prisoner shortly after landing, though tragically the fourth member of the crew, Sergeant Cyril Shewry, was shot on descent.

The plane was not quite finished however, for when down to no more than 1000 feet P/O Coton, found he could regain some control of his shattered aircraft by pushing the throttle through its gate to give maximum power. Intended only to be used sparingly and for short periods, this facility would quickly wreck the engines if used for long periods and it was not long therefore until one of the engines started to glow in the darkness. This was not his only problem, for without the navigator he could no longer be certain of his location and so simply pointed the aircraft in what he felt was the right direction and hoped for the best.

Climbing slowly all the while, he limped homewards, until, by his reckoning, somewhere over The Wash, with the fuel gauge on empty. Then suddenly the beam of a searchlight illuminated his aircraft, but far from being over The Wash, he was instead heading up the Thames Estuary. Once challenged, the proper procedure was to fire off flares, correctly coded for that day, to show that one was 'friendly'. Unfortunately the navigator knew the 'colour for the day' and he was somewhere in Germany, and anyway it was all the pilot could do to keep the plane in the air.

With so few controls intact there was no chance of making or even attempting a landing and so having made it back over land he decided it was at last time to throw in his hand and bail out. At that moment the British guns opened fire at his aircraft.

Parachuting down in the night sky, he watched his departing plane in the beam of the searchlight, as it flew on for a short distance, finally crashing in Berwick Road, Rainham. His own landing, in a ploughed field, was far from light, and he would later discover that a bone in his foot was broken. Quickly, he was confronted with an angry mob, who completely misinterpreting the situation, mistook him for a German, and nearly lynched him.

A fortnights leave and Pilot Officer Coton was back in the war. A war he was to survive, flying with distinction in Wellingtons, Manchesters and Lancasters. Rising to the rank of Wing Commander he was awarded the D.F.C. and Bar, along with the A.F.C., and subsequently went on to become Chief Experimental Test Pilot at Farnborough. He now lives in retirement in Sussex.

YEAR 1940		AIRCRAFT		PILOT, OR 1ST PILOT	2ND PILOT, PUPIL OR PASSENGER	DUTY (INCLUDING RESULTS AND REMARKS)
MONTH	DATE	Type	No.			
MAY	21	HAMPDEN	L4067	SELF P/O JONES	SGT SHEWRY CPL SMITH	OPS. CREW ABANDONED near KREFELD SELF near HORNCHURCH
				Sum	MAY	40 HAMPDEN
				Unit 144		
				Date 1. 6. 40		
				Sig.		

An extract from Pilot Officer Coton's Log Book for May 1940. The necessarily concise entry understates the drama of the occasion.

The Gunner's Story

*T*hat night, Reginald Harris, a gunner with 170 Battalion of the 61st Middlesex Regiment, was standing on ground defence behind No.3 gun at Hornchurch Aerodrome, from where he would have an excellent view of that night's proceedings. The gun was one of four 4.5 inch guns stationed there during this period. Coincidentally, earlier that same night at 00:32 a German aircraft, with its navigation lights switched on, had bombed Felixstowe. Therefore the Guns Operation Room at Vange issued the order to fire at any aircraft not showing the 'colour of the day' or morse signal. At 03:45 the searchlights picked up an aircraft displaying navigation lights only and so the order was given to open fire. One salvo (four shells) was fired simultaneously. Three of the shells appeared to burst right underneath the 'enemy' bomber, the fourth failing to go off came down embarrassingly close to an Anti-Aircraft battery the other side of the river. From his vantage point Reg Harris saw something fall across the beam of the searchlight and concluded it was possibly one of the crew bailing out. Then to his excitement, he witnessed the plane crash land in Rainham, only about a mile from where he was stationed. With other members of the gun crew he rushed to get a look at their quarry. They were first to arrive on the scene and found that the plane had landed, virtually intact, at the edge of a row of bungalows. In the darkness they fumbled about, still unaware that what they were looking at was in fact a British plane. Just as they were starting to tear pieces off as souvenirs out of the darkness came their commanding officer, Major Sergeant, with a brusque, ''Who the hell are you?''

Politely informed of their mistake they were dispatched back from whence they had come. The Captain who had given the order to fire, one Captain Fox, was later severely reprimanded for having fired at a British aircraft.

This was the first 'incident to directly involve Havering and unfortunately was an inauspicious and ignominious opening of 'hostilities'. Such is war.

Reg Harris (right) and fellow gunner, Vic Parsons, pose for a photograph against the perimeter fence of Hornchurch Aerodrome.

Local residents were also curious to see what all the noise and commotion was about. The plane had actually come to rest on a vacant plot of land on the corner of Berwick Road and Abbey Wood Lane. Alfred Gregory, then 19 years of age, ventured out with his father to view the crashed aircraft. When they arrived at the scene the plane was fully ablaze to the extent that they were unsure whether any crew members were possibly in the flames. As they stood there gaping, live machine-gun bullets popped and cracked in the fire, only afterwards did it occur to them just how lucky they had been not to have been struck by one of these stray rounds. The following morning, Alfred's younger sister, Joyce, also visited the site and retrieved several fragments of aircraft as souvenirs, only to have them later confiscated by her father. One of her other brother's, Johnnie, also collected some strange and dangerous debris, for alarmingly his hand turned a peculiar colour and the skin peeled off. Here we see Alfred Gregory and his sister Joyce, as they pose for a photograph in front of a bungalow subsequently built upon the crash site.

On the 17th June 1940 Churchill broadcast to the nation, stating that the Battle of France was over and that the Battle of Britain was about to begin. His message was "Let us so bear ourselves that if the British Empire and Commonwealth last for a thousand years, men will still say, "This was their finest hour." His powerful oratory captured the spirit, hearts and imagination of the population as they awaited the onset of the epic and bloody struggle.

Hitler appreciated that he would have to defeat the R.A.F. before his plans for invasion could be realized and he entrusted Goering with the task of annihilating our air defences. Starting on 10th August 1940, Goering was permitted six short weeks to gain mastery of the skies. Thus the most powerful airforce the world had ever known was turned against Britain. With defending fighters outnumbered 4 to 1, the odds were against us.

Situated on the gateway to London, Hornchurch could expect to bear much of the brunt of this forthcoming attack. Hornchurch, the fighter airfield, was unique at the start of the war, insofar as having been equipped entirely with the modern Spitfire fighter. In France a lesson had been painfully learnt, for many of the vital Allied airfields had been captured by enemy parachutists and to add insult to injury, were now to be used as staging posts for the attack on Britain. To prevent Hornchurch falling in the same manner it was enclosed within fortifications of pill-boxes and barbed wire and supplemented with armoured cars and Bofors guns. A searchlight was also located on the boundary to illuminate enemy positions if an attempt was made to land by night. Should the unthinkable happen and events demand the evacuation of the airfield, plans were laid for the demolition of the 72,000 gallon fuel dump and over a million rounds of .303 ammunition.

Day after day British radar picked up huge number of enemy aircraft formating over the coast of France. It was apparent from the beginning that the airfields were to be the targets of the Luftwaffe. On the 12th August Manston and Hawkinge were bombed, on the 16th it was the turn of North Weald, Debden and Biggin Hill. On the 24th the usual build up of planes was detected, but this time there was one all important difference. The W.A.A.F's in the Operation Room at Hornchurch watched the plots on the Operation Table as they inexorably drew close and closer. As their range narrowed there could be no doubting their intended target for that day, Hornchurch! All available planes were scrambled to meet this attacking force of bombers and their accompanying fighters. At a little after 4:00 p.m. the first of the bombs started to whistle their way towards Hornchurch soil. Such was the spirited defence however, that only a few bombs fell upon the airfield itself. Although undoubtedly of great relief to the R.A.F., it was not necessarily such good news for the surrounding residents, who regrettably became the unintended recipients of the German aggression. Somewhere in excess of eighty bombs fell across South Hornchurch and Rainham, resulting in the destruction of ten homes, fortunately with no loss of life, although John Richard Lewis of Hillview Avenue, who happened to be at the Airfield during the attack, has the dubious honour of being the first civilian to be killed in Havering.

An eye witness of the attack on Hornchurch takes up the story;

"The bomber formation came towards the town in front of us, and the sky was thick with bursting shells, while the din of the anti-aircraft guns was terrific. The firing was extremely accurate, yet with amazing luck the Germans maintained their close formations. At times they were lost among huge clouds of exploding anti-aircraft shells, and it seemed impossible they would survive the barrage, as the bombers came over their objective clusters of bombs rained down and we watched them explode with deafening concussion. As the bombs contacted the earth huge columns of smoke shot high in the air and slowly sank. And the whole time the anti-aircraft guns were pounding away. As soon as they had deposited their deadly cargo, the bombers, followed by the gun-fire, wheeled to the right and came straight towards us as we crouched near a tree. At one time, as they were close above us, the sky over our heads was a white canopy of bursting shells''

Hornchurch had been bloodied, had survived, and was to see its aggressor summarily punished. One of the bombers, a Heinkel 111, was hit by anti-aircraft fire, disabling its port engine. This stricken machine became easy prey for two fighters of 615 Squadron. It made a crash landing, relatively intact, at Clay Tye Hill, North Ockendon. Two farmers, Mr. Pinchon and Mr. Pearson, had been watching the aerial spectacle from the relative safety of a ditch, when suddenly it became apparent to them that the bomber was coming down close to where they lay. As it came to rest they picked up the only weapons to hand, a spanner and a piece of iron, and cautiously approached the aircraft. The crew of five

were already emerging. Two of their number had been injured and needed to be helped clear by the other able bodied airmen. On seeing the approaching farmers, brandishing their rough and ready weapons, they put up their hands and surrendered without a struggle. Moments later, and probably self detonated, the aircraft blew up, scattering debris across the field and in the process setting fire to a hayrick. By this time all were at a safe distance and so no one was hurt in the explosion. Despite having surrendered so readily, the uninjured members of the crew behaved in a defiant and arrogant manner. They had witnessed the seemingly effortless overrun of France only weeks before and so believed Britain would succumb to the same fate within the space of two months and that they would once more be free. Five years in a prisoner of war camp may have given them time to revise their attitudes and opinions.

Throughout the raid, and in addition to the bombs, empty machine gun cartridges and shrapnel rained down on Havering, encouraging the more reckless residents to dart out from their places of sanctuary in order to pick up these souvenirs. For the first time in history the fate of a nation was being determined in the air, above the upturned faces of the civilian population below. The heavens were full of vapour trails, glistern barrage balloons, woolly anti-aircraft

Members of the Home Guard examine the remnants of Heinkel He 111 (A1+KT) which crashed at Clay Tye Hill, North Ockendon at 4:00 in the afternoon of 24th August 1940. Three of the five man crew wore iron crosses.

puffs and deadly shrapnel. One man, fascinated by the dog-fights overhead, stood in the street, (despite official warnings not to do so) and was hit in the mouth by a piece of shrapnel and had to be rushed to Oldchurch Hospital.

In their attack on Hornchurch Aerodrome that Saturday afternoon the Germans lost five of their aircraft in all. Undaunted the Luftwaffe returned on the 26th, 27th, 28th and 30th August, but these raids were either blunted or turned away entirely by the R.A.F.

Then on the 31st August 1940 Hornchurch Aerodrome suffered its worst hammering of the war. A force of twelve Junkers 88 and four Messerschmitt 110 flying in vee formation at 15,000 ft released their bomb load over the airfield. No. 54 Squadron were just taking off in their Spitfires when the bombs started to rain down amongst them. Flt. Lt. Deere had a 1000lb drop right in front of him, blowing his engine, port wing and tail clean away. He was flung into the air and crashed inverted onto the runway from 100ft where he slid along for 250 yds with his head scraping along the ground. With bombs still dropping all around, he was left hanging upside down in a pool of petrol. He was rescued from this predicament by Pilot Officer E.F. Edsall

who had also just crashed after losing one wing. In their bright 'Mae West' life-jackets they were spotted by a German fighter who dived to machine-gun them. They only just managed to reach the comparative safety of the hangar before he opened fire. Sergeant Davis, who had also just been taking off, was blasted two fields away, but was able to scrabble out of his wrecked plane unharmed. It was acknowledged by all concerned that they had had a miraculous escape. Despite some damage to the hangars the aerodrome remained serviceable. As was to be expected however, the damage was not confined to the aerodrome, the bombs dropping across Hornchurch and out into Romford, and in their wake lay the bodies of six civilians.

Apparently not satisfied with the result of their earlier raid, the Luftwaffe returned in force at 6:00 pm. This time their force consisted of 30 Dorniers 17's with fighter escort. They once again managed to penetrate the defences, but not without some loss to themselves. In the raid a further two parked and precious Spitfires were destroyed and an even more precious member of the ground crew killed.

On one of these raids, an R.A.F. pilot who had bailed out of his damaged aircraft drifted to earth by parachute. As he was floating down, an angry crowd

The scene in Benhurst Avenue, Elm Park, following a raid on Hornchurch Aerodrome on 26th August 1940.

25

The attack on Hornchurch Airfield of the 31st August trailed out over Hornchurch and Romford. This is what one bomb did to No. 3 Randall Road, Romford, shortly after 1 o'clock in the afternoon. Six civilians perished in Havering that day; two of them here in Randall Rd.

Forty six years on, and the town planners continued where the Luftwaffe had left off. To facilitate the construction of a section of the Romford ring-road, numerous houses in the area were demolished. Fortunately, unlike the Luftwaffe before them, the authorities saw fit to drop a note through their letterboxes of residents to inform them of the imminent destruction of their homes, and as a result failed to kill anyone. This photograph is taken from the middle of the ring-road shortly before its opening to traffic.

formed a reception committee, believing him to be an enemy pilot. He came to rest suspended from a high wall of a public house. Seeing an angry mob below, he called out several times to tell them he was British. The crowd either did not hear him or did not believe him and so surged forwards to attack the poor strung up airman. The police tried to intervene and a scuffle ensued, in which one policeman had the leg of his trousers torn off, before the injured pilot could be taken off in an R.A.F. vehicle to safety.

One man thought he heard an unexploded bomb fall in his back garden, but was too frightened to look, and so sought advice from the nearest air raid warden. The warden, believing it to be in the neighbouring district, disclaimed all responsibility for the 'bomb' and told him to go to the town hall. There he was told that they did not deal with unexploded bombs and he should go to the Auxiliary Fire Service for help. They thought it fell under the jurisdiction of the Police and so he dutifully sought their assistance. They in their turn, felt it a job for the military authorities who fortunately accepted that this matter fell within their province. However, upon close examination of his back garden it was found that there was no bomb at all, and yet he at least knew where to go should he receive one! The civil defence organization could not yet be accorded the label of a well oiled machine that subsequent sustained bombing would help it achieve.

For the next week intermittent raids on Hornchurch Aerodrome were attempted. These were not pressed home and apart from damage to surrounding houses, where casualties remained light, were largely ineffectual.

The 7th September 1940 was a turning point to rank alongside the foundering of the Spanish Armada in the stormy North Sea. The German formation that made their way up the Thames Estuary that Saturday afternoon did not divert, in their now customary fashion, to attack the fighter airfields, instead their course was unswerving and clear. For the first time London was to be their target. His objectivity clouded by thoughts of retribution for attacks on Berlin, Hitler made a fatal error of judgement in sparing the R.A.F. bases in favour of less strategic retaliatory action against the Capital. It was the prelude of an experience that was to become known universally and simply as the 'BLITZ'

Thankfully the residents of No. 6, The Farm Way, Elm Park, were in the safety of their shelter when a bomb demolished the side of their home on the 2nd Sept. 1940, and exposed to the world their taste in interior decor. The rest of the house was eventually demolished and the plot used for the siting of an emergency water supply for the duration of the war.

(Inset) As it is today, rebuilt and extended.

Captured German Target Photograph

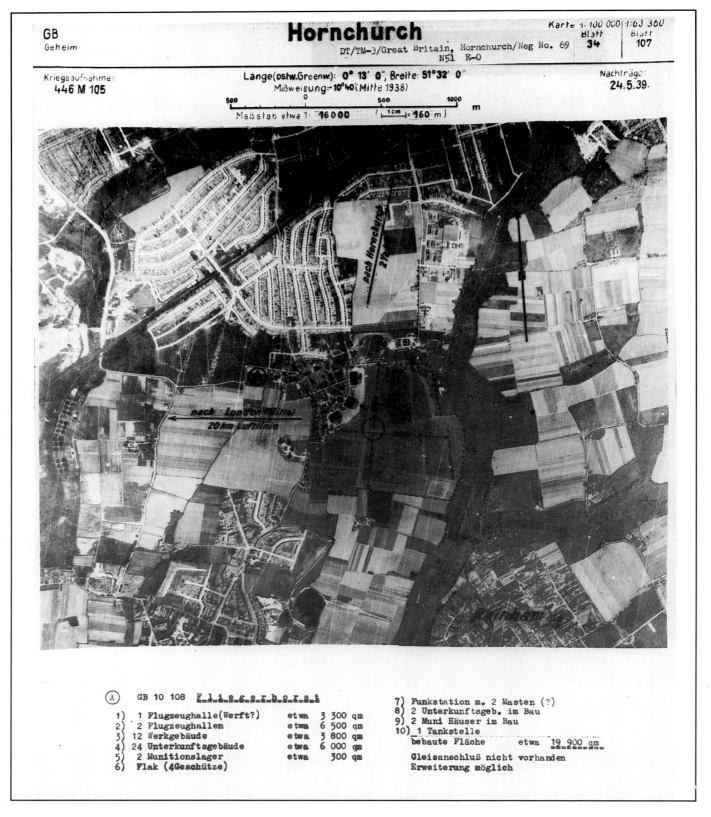

GB
Geheim

Hornchurch

DT/TM-3/Great Britain, Hornchurch/Neg No. 69
N51 E-0

Karte 1:100 000 | 1:63 360
Blatt 34 | Blatt 107

Kriegsaufnahme:
446 M 105

Länge(ostw.Greenw): 0° 13' 0", Breite: 51°32' 0"
Mißweisung: 10°40'(Mitte 1938)

Nachträge:
24.5.39.

Maßstab etwa 1: 16000 (1cm = 160 m)

(A) GB 10 108 Fliegerhorst

1) 1 Flugzeughalle(Werft?)   etwa 3 300 qm
2) 2 Flugzeughallen   etwa 6 500 qm
3) 12 Werkgebäude   etwa 3 800 qm
4) 24 Unterkunftsgebäude   etwa 6 000 qm
5) 2 Munitionslager   etwa   300 qm
6) Flak (4Geschütze)

7) Funkstation m. 2 Masten (?)
8) 2 Unterkunftsgeb. im Bau
9) 2 Muni Häuser im Bau
10) 1 Tankstelle
   bebaute Fläche   etwa   19 900 qm
   Gleisanschluß nicht vorhanden
   Erweiterung möglich

This photograph, perhaps like no other, justifies the title 'Hitler V Havering' (or at least Hitler V Hornchurch). This intriguing captured German target photograph of Hornchurch Aerodrome shows the extent to which the fighter base had been documented. It was taken on 24th May 1939, three months before the declaration of war, presumably clandestinely, by an ostensibly civilian German aeroplane.

Translated Key GB 10 108

1) 1 Aircraft Hangar (Repairs?) 3,300 sq m
2) 2 Aircraft Hangars   6,500 sq m
3) 12 Workshops   3,800 sq m
4) 24 Personnel Buildings   6,000 sq m
5) 2 Ammo Dumps   300 sq m
6) Anti-Aircraft (4 guns)

Air Force Station

7) Radio Transmitter. 2 masts (?)
8) Accommodation under construction.
9) Munitions building under construction.
10) Underground refuelling station.
Railway siding not in existence
Runway extension possible.

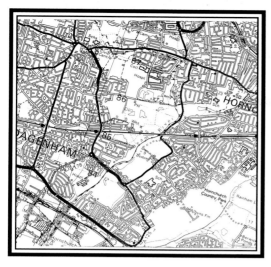

Luftwaffe Reconnaissance Photograph No. 1

In order to assess the efficacy of their raids on Hornchurch Aerodrome during August 1940, the Germans undertook several photographic reconnaissance missions. This first shot was taken in early September 1940. The aerodrome is situated in the bottom right hand corner. Notice the attempt to camouflage its true identity by painting fake tar 'hedge' lines across the grass runway. When one realises that the German navigators probably had on their lap, a copy of the target map seen opposite, it seems perhaps a little futile, and indeed, this minor subterfuge was not persevered with for long. It is just possible to discern some of the first bomb craters along the Ingrebourne Valley adjacent to the Aerodrome. The first of many.

Captured for posterity at the same time are South Hornchurch, Elm, Park and Dagenham. Your home as the Germans saw it, some fifty-four years ago.

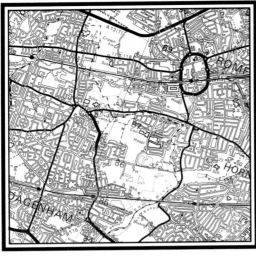

Luftwaffe Reconnaissance Photograph No. 2

The aircraft which took the previous photograph (Frame No. 040) was travelling in a northerly direction and so Frame No. 042 reveals the wartime streets of Hornchurch and Romford down below.

At the centre of the picture is Central Park, Dagenham. The unusual criss cross pattern are anti-invasion defences, designed to prevent enemy planes landing there in a surprise attack.

Could you possibly have been gazing up at the German aircraft that took this photograph? Where were you on the morning of 2nd September 1940?

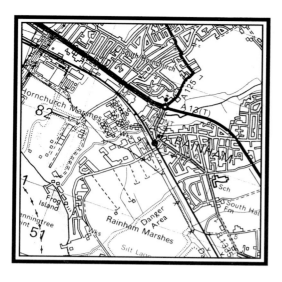

Luftwaffe Reconnaissance Photograph No. 3

In this photograph we see South Hornchurch, Rainham, and the Murex plant on the Riverside. Once again it is possible to make out the bomb craters along the Ingrebourne Valley and also a distinct stick of bomb craters north of Wennington Road, near South Hall Farm.

What is more fascinating about this photograph is that some unknown German hand has pencilled a circle around Chandlers Corner, Rainham and also drawn a box encapsulating the bridge on the A13 that straddles the River Beam, near Fords Works. But why? It seems unlikely that these would have been targets for bombing. Could it be possible that these were strategic sites of interest come the invasion? Alas we shall probably never know.

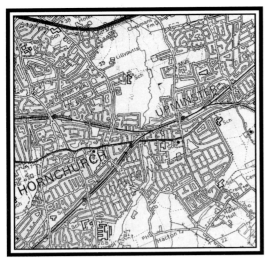

Luftwaffe Reconnaissance Photograph No. 4

This final photograph provides us with coverage of the rest of Hornchurch, including Upminster.

Obviously these photographs were never intended to be seen by the residents of the subject matter, (i.e. the inhabitants of Havering), but here they are after having gone a somewhat convoluted route. Originally taken by the Luftwaffe, they were flown back to Germany for further examination and analysis. For five years, there they remained, until the final defeat of the Nazi regime. The American military were quick to round up much of the German intelligence material and these photographs were caught within their efficient dragnet. They were crated up and brought back to Britain before being shipped off to the United States. It is from there, half a century later, that they made their final leg of their tortuous journey back to this borough and subsequent inclusion within the pages of this book.

All that remains of a house in Park lane, Hornchurch, after a direct hit by a bomb on 31st August 1940. The occupants escaped injury.

Not so fortunate were the residents of 117 Park lane, Hornchurch, when a bomb hit their house in the same daylight raid. Both Kathleen and Letitia Bouchard were killed in the explosion.

Shop fronts in High Street, Hornchurch, blown in by a bomb which fell on the pavement during the daylight raid on Hornchurch Aerodrome of 2nd September 1940.

Hornchurch High Street 1994. Who among today's shoppers is aware of the fate that would have awaited them had they been window shopping fifty-four years previously.

As the last German bomber left the shores of England on the evening of the 7th September 1940, they left in their wake a scene of destruction, on a scale unprecedented in the history of this island. The combined payload of some 300 enemy bombers had rained down upon London Docks and as a result darkness never fell that evening. Instead, looking westward from Havering, a glorious sunset was to be seen, one which refused to set. It was of course the fires in the docks, raging out of control. The wind was from the west that Saturday evening, with it came the smoke of the fires and drifting down from the sky fluttered the charred remains of some of the commodities burning in the giant warehouses of the docks. One soldier, stationed at the Ayletts gun battery at Rainham, remembers burnt remnants of CRS sugar packets falling like black snow, whilst another young resident recalls seeing blueprints fluttering from the sky, presumably from some office now caught in the conflagration. Guided by these beacons, the Luftwaffe returned that night to deposit still more explosives and incendiaries into the bubbling cauldron below. It was not realized at the time, but this was the start of a period of near continuous bombardment that was to persist into the spring of 1941, nine months of agony.

Initially, both day and night raids were attempted, but as the losses from the daylight raids continued to mount the Luftwaffe were forced to retreat to the cloak of darkness for their protection. Our defences, so gallant by day were rendered ineffectual by night. This left the Luftwaffe with the mastery and freedom of the air during the hours of darkness. The Ack-ack batteries could put up a morale boosting barrage, but in reality they had very little prospect of hitting anything, save possibly the population below.

For some the mere anxiety of potential air attacks proved too much on its own. Such is the sad case of two spinsters found lying side by side in their gas filled bedroom. The two women, Miss Matilda Jennings, aged 60, and Miss Nellie Hopton, aged 54, of Fitzilian Avenue, Harold Wood, left separate suicide notes stating, ''We cannot go on living in constant terror.''

From the start of the Blitz and for the rest of the first month, it was indeed a time of constant terror, the sirens sounding every night and the Luftwaffe never failing to deliver their bomb load. Then on the 16th September something new arrived. Swishing out of the night sky over Rainham, came two parachutes. These were not Nazi paratroopers, but were something of far greater potential danger. In fact they were not animate at all, for they were two parachute mines, the first night such weapons had been used against land targets in England. The Germans had two sizes of mines, Luftmine A weighing in at 500kg, 5ft 8 inches long, and the Luftmine B of 1000kg and 8ft 8 inches long. To slow this giant of a mine down, a 27ft diameter parachute deployed shortly after it left the aircraft. Without the parachute the mine would have buried itself deep into the ground and lessened the blast, hence the need to slow its descent. If it worked as intended it would come to rest above ground at which point a 25 second clockwork fuse would be activated and carnage result. Fortunately Rainham was spared this first night. They fell at the rear of the Starch Works in Ferry Lane where on this occasion only slight damage was caused. The following evening another fell in Rainham, to the west of Moor Hall. Five seconds past, ten seconds, fifteen, twenty, twenty-five, thirty, one minute, ten minutes.....this example seem as though it was not going to explode and would have to be defused instead. A sentry was duly posted to guard

The Blitz

the area until the qualified personnel were available. One would imagine that the mere sight of this new monster weapon would deter anybody from approaching, but not so one stealthy and determined local labourer. Apparently having successfully evaded the sentry, he proceeded to relieve the mine of its now redundant parachute. Whether he was incredibly brave, stupid, drunk or a kleptomaniac is not entirely clear. Probably a mixture of all four! Parachute silk (if only imitation), may have been a highly prized commodity in ration bound Britain, yet it still seems to have been an extremely risky venture to meddle with an object of such unknown quantity. The parachute mine never possessed the mystique attributed to the later V-1's and V-2's but in hindsight it was to prove the most deadly weapon of the war.

An unexploded parachute mine bereft of parachute. It's innocuous appearance as it lies peacefully in farmland should not deceive. It was an evil killer of frightening potential. Time would show it in its true light. It would eventually kill 72 citizens of the Havering area.

Tragedy in Havering Drive, Romford.

At ten to midnight on the 20th September a lone German Bomber passed over Romford in a north westerly direction. Down below at No. 42 Havering Drive, Mr. & Mrs. Rycraft and their two sons, Gerald (19) and Peter (15), were in the comfort of their own home. Despite possessing their own Anderson shelter, and having used it in previous raids, they had decided to spend that night indoors. One of the main reasons was that Gerald was over 6 feet tall and so found it very difficult to get comfortable within the confined space of the shelter. Aboard the bomber, with one small pull of a lever, a stick of five bombs was released and the die cast. Now the crew had no more control of the bombs eventual destinations than did the population below. The first bomb fell near shops in Carlton Road, a thousand yards from Havering Drive .... the second, 250 yards ominously nearer, in Kingston Road .... another 250 yards and a bomb exploded in Main Road. With the same regular spacing the next bomb fell upon a detached house in Oaklands Avenue, where by good fortune the family were away. If one plots these progressive explosions on a map it will come as no surprise that the next bomb was destined to fall at No. 42, Havering Drive, instantaneously killing three members of the Rycraft family. The remaining youngest member, Peter, was extracted from the rubble alive, but died from his injuries in hospital soon after. The shelter was undamaged. A family tragedy, the likes of which was to be all too frequently repeated in the months to follow.

The four members of the Rycraft family were wiped out when they chose to stay in the comfort of their home, No. 42 Havering Drive, rather than face a night in their damp and cramped Anderson Shelter.

This photograph of an incendiary fire at No. 44 Victoria Road, Romford, in September 1940 was taken purely by the light of the flames.

Fifty-four years on and the shop is no longer a tobacconist, but instead sells items of a rather more exotic nature. Gloria, of Gloria's Lingerie, poses for this comparison photograph.

(Above) A grotesquely twisted gas main rears out of a bomb crater in Dagenham Road, in front of Romford Cemetery.
(Inset) Bomb crater, what bomb crater?

At quarter past ten on the night of September 10th a bomb fell in Hill Grove / Cedric Avenue, Romford. This was the result. Residents of the demolished house on the left were in the safety of their shelter and were unharmed, as were four people still in the damaged house on the right. Notice how the overturned car has had its number plate obscured by the censor, to prevent the Germans gleaning the merest hint of the location.

The Largest Crater In Essex

The following night a parachute mine fell in the back gardens of houses bounded by Carlton Road and Stanley Avenue. It is believed the parachute did not open, for the mine penetrated deep into the ground before exploding. The resultant crater was the largest in Essex throughout the duration of the war. It narrowly missed dozens of Anderson shelters, many of which were left teetering on the brink of this colossal cavity. No one had anticipated that craters of this magnitude were possible from just one bomb. A fourteen-year-old boy, Kenneth Hall was asleep alone in a shelter when the mine fell close by. The shelter was torn away from his sleeping figure which was then showered with earth until he was left buried beneath 6ft of earth, only two feet from the edge of the crater. Entombed, he frantically scooped away at the earth with his hands trying to fight his way out, but to no avail as the earth kept falling back on him. With the shelter blown away he could easily have been left for dead by the A.R.P. Rescue Squads, but by a stroke of luck they located him and successfully rescued him from what was nearly an early grave. He was suffering from cuts and shock, however it is hard to imagine a closer brush with death than this young lad had experienced. Elsewhere another shelter was buckled by the force of the blast and the great weight of soil which descended upon it. Once again the other occupants were brought out alive although in this case they required hospitalization. There may have been a vast amount of damage, but it is certain that if this mine had exploded on the surface the scene would have been dramatically worse. As it was there were over 100 houses damaged, many beyond repair, and at least eight serious casualties. Even windows in South Street over a mile away were broken by the explosion.

Any mention of parachute mines in the press was strictly prohibited and so there were cryptic references to 'bombs of a particularly large size' and it would be four years before the culprit of many of these explosions could be accurately revealed. It is not surprising therefore that the general population came to refer to parachute mines incorrectly as 'land mines'.

The huge crater caused by the Carlton Road-Stanley Avenue parachute mine on the night of September 21st 1940. Its immense size can be gauged by the tiny human figures on the rim of the crater. In the background can be seen the rear of battered houses in Carlton Road.

Another shot of the havoc caused by the Stanley Avenue / Carlton Road parachute mine. This shot is taken from the rim of the crater, looking towards houses in Stanley Avenue, where residents are busy sifting through the remnants of their homes and possessions.

The same houses viewed from the front. This photo was captured the following day as furniture is being removed from the damaged property

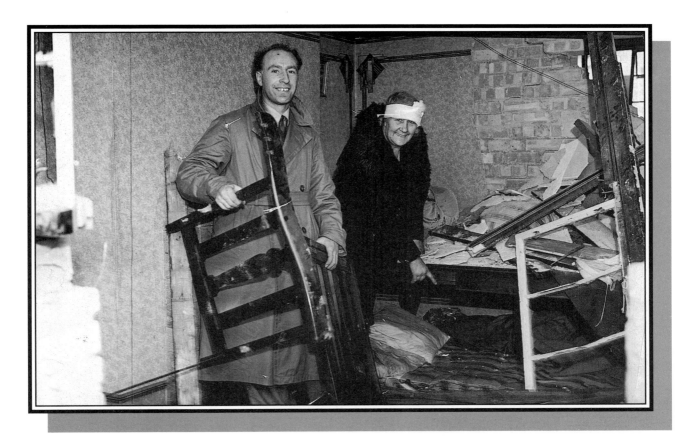

The Carlton Road / Stanley Avenue parachute mine fell thirty yards away from the Kirk household, partially demolishing their home. Mrs. Kirk and her daughter were asleep on a mattress under the dining room table, while her son slept nearby in an armchair. Debris fell on to the table under which Mrs. and Miss Kirk were sleeping and the chair on which Mr. Kirk was sitting was smashed. Amazingly none of the three was badly hurt, the only slight injury being to Mrs. Kirk's head. Commenting on her experience afterwards, Mrs. Kirk said: "This sort of thing will never beat us. We have got to go through with it to the bitter end. I felt shaky at first, but I am quite cheerful about the whole matter now."

Danger U.X.B.

Amongst the many places hit the next night was Oldchurch Hospital where an oil-incendiary bomb fell outside one of the blocks. All the patients in the wing escaped injury and were hurriedly evacuated to another part of the hospital. Ironically one of the patients under bombardment was a young German airman who was recovering in hospital from injuries sustained on being shot down in a recent raid.

On the 23rd September another parachute mine failed to explode. This one fell in Birkbeck Road, Romford, shortly before midnight. With the example of Carlton Road / Stanley Avenue incident still fresh in peoples minds it was decided to evacuate everyone within a quarter mile radius, some one thousand people. The authorities succeeded in the mammoth logistical feat of providing shelter and food for this vast army of evacuees. The following morning naval bomb disposal squad arrived and undertook the extremely risky job of removing the fuses and detonators. This they carried out successfully, though this did not render it innocuous, for it still contained a ton of high explosive, which could be detonated by concussion from another bomb or even a shell splinter. Unfortunately the bomb disposal squad were too hard pressed elsewhere to remove the mine straight away and this dictated that the 1000 residents would not be able to return to their homes for the foreseeable future. When the Borough Surveyor, Mr. Appleby, heard of the situation and that the army of evacuees might not be able to return to their homes for up to a week, always presuming the mine did not explode in the meantime, he resolved to take action. He asked the leaders of two rescue squads if they would try to raise a band of men willing to undertake the hazardous task of removing the mine to a place of safety. Back came the message "Every man has volunteered and is ready for action." Using ropes and planks, they winched the monster on to a lorry. That completed the first stage of the job; the second was to convey the mine to Bedfords Park without mishap. A route was planned that would limit the damage should the unthinkable happen. The unthinkable did not occur, the mine arriving safely at the park where the military detonated it on 5th October. The evacuated families were then allowed back, having spent some uncomfortable and sleepless nights away from home, but nonetheless thankful they still had homes to go to.

(**Above**) The crooked remains of No. 151 & 153 Corbets Tey, Road, Upminster, after a bomb demolished four of the neighbouring houses on the night of 23rd September 1940. Amazingly all the residents escaped with their lives. The houses were rebuilt after the war, though to a slightly differing design.

A grave-digger is presented with an unfamiliar task; crater filling, following the fall of a bomb in front of St. Andrew's Church, Hornchurch on the 20th September 1940.

(**Above**) It was Upminster's turn again on the 24th September 1940 when a bomb demolished four cottages in St. Mary's Lane. There were two fatal casualties, Mr. & Mrs. Mortlock, both aged 70.

(**Left**) The cottages were replaced by a row of post war bungalows

(**Below**) The censor apparently decided that the press photograph, shown above, showed too much damage to be good for public morale and so he marked the back with his ubiquitous rubber stamp.

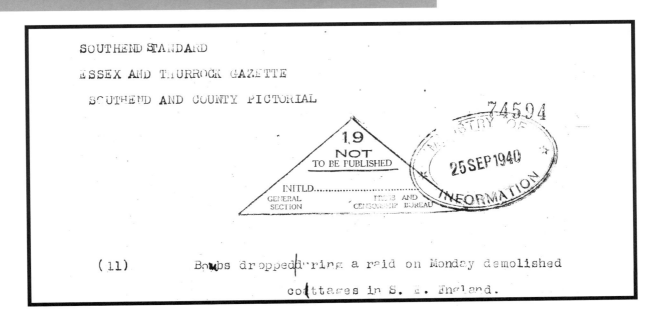

SOUTHEND STANDARD

ESSEX AND THURROCK GAZETTE

SOUTHEND AND COUNTY PICTORIAL

1.9
NOT
TO BE PUBLISHED

INITLD.............
GENERAL
SECTION

PRESS AND
CENSORSHIP BUREAU

74594

25 SEP 1940

(11)   Bombs dropped during a raid on Monday demolished
cottages in S. E. England.

A Pair of Mines for Havering Village

The following month on the 16th October six parachute mines were dropped over a wide area. The most common enemy bomber, the He 111, the workhorse of the Luftwaffe, was only able to carry two mines at one time. These were slung under each wing and in order not to destable the aircraft they were released virtually simultaneously. The nett result of this was that the parachute mines tended to fall in pairs. One of these pairs drifted down Havering Village's way. The late Mr. A.F. Kilby, a then warden, had a keen recollection of events that night.

"One night that stands out in my memory was when with two others, outside the warden's post, we were looking skywards shortly after the warning sirens had gone when in the general light provided by searchlights and incendiary bombs we saw a parachute swinging down towards us. Our mutual decision was to 'bash him' with our tin hats rapidly turned to thoughts of survival as we realised that 'he' was too long, too black, and too shiny to be anything but one of the new parachute mines our latest memo from headquarters warned us about. Simultaneously we dropped to the turf and the whole world about us turned red and a great roaring sound was followed by breaking glass and the thud of debris. It must have been only seconds but it seemed we lay there for ages, listening to bricks and tiles thumping into the soft earth and then came silence. Even the general din of the guns, the droning of the planes and the sound of exploding bombs all ceased at once. The three of us staggered to our feet and looked towards our post. The squat concrete building had survived the explosion, but immediately behind it the solidly built old wall and farm buildings beyond had vanished, while behind us over the village green were scattered large pieces of masonry and brick rubble, and we discovered at day break that some large lumps had gone through the stained glass windows of the church right on the other side of the green. Not one of us was scratched, yet all this debris had passed over our prone bodies as we lay only a few feet from the holocaust. We found a casualty in the vicarage nearby, a nasty leg injury, and a few minor cuts and bruises in the cottages round about. We were wondering why our colleagues further down the village had not appeared with assistance, when a special constable on a bicycle on his way to Romford for night duty, stooped and told us that a second mine had fallen further down the road, simultaneously with ours, and blown a bungalow away right to its foundations, adding hastily that there were no casualties as the widow occupant was in a shelter with a neighbour. He could see we were concerned as all three of us lived in that part of the village, and when the 'all-clear' siren went just afterwards we all dashed down the road on our bicycles to see how we had fared. Almost every roof and window went that night, yet mercifully the only other casualty was an old gentleman with a lost eye."

The badly shattered shell of Romford Stadium after a bomb fell there on October 9th, 1940

"Won't Anyone Save Us?"

*O*ne evening at the end of October 1940 we were sitting in our kitchen - I was reading, my mother was heating milk on a gas cooker. There was an air raid on, but there was no where else for us to go as our shelter had filled with water and we were unable to use it any more.

We heard the sound of a German plane and guns firing at it. My father decided to go into the garden to see where it was and then came in to say it had been hit and was coming down. As it did so it jettisoned its load of bombs and incendiaries and and as my father opened the door to check on the planes progress a 2000lb bomb exploded in front of our house.

We did not hear the bomb coming - I remember a roaring sound and everything went dark; a hole appeared in the side and rear wall walls of the kitchen: my mother screamed and shouted,

"Won't anyone save us?"

(She was constantly reminded of this for many years, my father thought it a huge joke).

My father, who was in the hall, shouted that the kitchen door was stuck and he would have to knock it down. The front door and stairs had been completely blown away . By this time, hot and cold water from the fractured tanks had started pouring through the damaged ceiling. We crawled through the hole into the garden. A huge sheet of flame from igniting gas came through the hole from which we had crawled. My father said we would have to go in next door's shelter. We had to negotiate round two incendiaries on the garden path - my mother in her shocked state, stepped over them and consequently set her nightdress on fire and burnt her legs. My mother had already been scalded by the hot milk she had been heating at the stove. An ambulance was summoned to take her to Oldchurch Hospital; this duly arrived but broke down on the way and it was two hours before she eventually got to hospital.

The bomb had fractured the main water pipe in the road and this cascaded everywhere. The crater extended over two pavements, the road and our front garden right up to the front door. The damage to the surrounding properties was considerable and the boulders strewn around the crater seemed enormous. I was dressed only in pyjamas and slippers and it was very difficult walking against the flow of water from the water main; it also started to rain to add to our misery. My father left me in the care of neighbours, standing on the corner of the road, not knowing where to go, whilst he went to a first aid post to get a head wound dressed. Later he found me in a public shelter near Elm Park Station - I was very wet and bedraggled so he borrowed a blanket into which I wrapped myself and he dried my clothing over a paraffin stove.

In the morning we went to a church in North Street, Hornchurch, which was being used as a reception centre for homeless families. I was given a pair of trousers, a coat (very thin), jumper, shoes and socks. My father was given £10 immediate clothing allowance and £20 for furniture. As we had no home it hardly mattered. After five days we had to leave and my father arranged that we should stay with his two sisters in Hornchurch. (We slept on the floor for two months).

We had been worried about our canary who had been buried under the kitchen debris but he was eventually rescued by the demolition squad some three days later. Fortunately he had enough food and water and had sung all day so his exact position was known. The larder door had fallen over his cage and this had sheltered him from the elements and debris which was constantly falling down. He was taken to the home of a PDSA Inspector and a week later my father and I went to collect him. On the way a German plane suddenly flew very low along the road and started machine gunning; my father pulled me to the side wall of a house for protection. Having just been bombed this was a somewhat unnerving experience.

Wartime experience of Mrs. J.L. Stevens then living at No. 79 Warren Drive, Elm Park.   30th Oct 1940.

A Night Out In The Blitz

Arthur was in bed with tonsillitis.

The Doctor examined him. He said it may be a case of diphtheria. He took a swab of the throat and asked Bert and myself to take it to Rush Green Isolation Hospital. We could hardly refuse, so wrapping ourselves in scarves and raincoats we set out at about 8.45 pm.

It was very black out, but almost immediately the sky was lit up by gunflashes, which together with the crashing of shells and the drone of enemy planes, made us scurry for shelter. We soon found an arrow painted in white on the pavement, which told us a Public Shelter was near at hand. Following the direction of the arrow, we found ourselves walking along a cinder path by the side of the Cinema. After walking about 100 yds. without finding the shelter, we began to shout and whistle, but no answer being forthcoming we walked on. Then something loomed out of the darkness, turning out to be a corrugated iron shed. It wasn't much, but it was better than nothing. There we crouched for several minutes until it quietened down, then anxious to get on the move, we made a dash for the 'Bell & Gate', where the buses stopped. After a short wait a bus came along. The conductor told us he was not going to our destination, but said he would drop us at the nearest point, which was Roneo Corner, Romford. This was something, so we boarded it and within twenty minutes we had alighted at Roneo Corner.

There our troubles began. The guns opened up and a plane droned over. Luckily we were between an A.R.P. Wardens Post and a Public Lavatory and so were quite well sheltered. In the Wardens Post we enquired the way to the 'Coopers Arms' which is quite near the Hospital. We were told that it was about a mile down the road, but there was little chance of getting a bus. With this piece of 'encouraging' news we duly set out once more. After unsuccessfully trying to stop several private cars for a lift, we started the lonely walk.

By the time we reached the 'Coopers Arms', the guns were kicking up 'Hell's Delight', so we decided to go inside for a drink. Inside it was more cheery. Parties of men were playing cards and darts. We finished our drinks and reluctantly made our way to the door. Just as we were about to leave, there came two terrific whistles. We dived flat against the bar, while others fell to the floor or ducked beneath tables. The bombs landed but there were no explosions. Everyone got to their feet again and began to joke about the affair, one man going as far as to say it was miles away. Once again we went to the door and on leaving, saw how near the bombs had been. A house opposite had been struck by an oil bomb. Smoke began to ooze through the tiles, and a cascade of sparks was falling into the road, whilst the stench of oil was everywhere. This was the sort of target the bombers revelled in, so once again we thought the best policy was shelter. Seeing a white concrete building next to the Public House, we made for it in the hope that it was a shelter. We were out in double quick time on discovering that it was a petrol station.

Setting off once more towards the Hospital, we hadn't gone far when the guns started once more. A passer-by told us there was a surface shelter a little further on. This was found quite easily, so standing just inside the entrance we waited for a lull. Everything seemed black and deserted. Then we made our second discovery. The shelter was in ruins and stood opposite several bombed houses. This made us move on again and being quite near to the Hospital, we made it non-stop. By this time the house that had been bombed was blazing fiercely.

We delivered the swab and started on the return journey. Bert tripped and fell flat, whilst I gave my shin a crack on some low railings, but apart from this everything went smoothly until we arrived back at Roneo Corner. This seemed to be an unlucky spot, for the guns started and we went into the Warden's Post once again. Then came a quiet period. We bade the Warden good night and left. We had taken only a few steps, when the guns restarted and feint cries came from the darkness. Thinking someone had been hit by shrapnel we drew the attention of a passer-by. He said it was a drunkard and so we left it at that. Several moments later a man stopped at the Wardens Post, having apparently fallen in the River Rom. Time and time again we tried to get on our way, but what with the guns and planes it was 11.00 pm. before we finally and thankfully arrived back home.

S. G. Champion. Collier Row October 1940

German Bomber Crashes In Flames

The Luftwaffe were not to be allowed to bomb with complete impunity, for on the night of 1st November 1940 an anti-aircraft shell scored a direct hit on a Heinkel 111 when directly over Hornchurch. Normally press reports were not allowed to mention exact locations, but in this case, as it represented a German failure, albeit with more English than German lives being lost, there was fulsome coverage in the papers, with places, names and times all freely given. The Romford Times gave this graphic account:-

Thousands of people over several miles heard the terrific whine as a stricken German Bomber crashed to earth at Hornchurch on Friday night. The plane, a Heinkel 111, crashed into some flats in Matlock Gardens. In a few seconds the flats were a raging inferno, while blazing wreckage from the machine was scattered over gardens. Before it crashed the Heinkel swooped very low across the district. As it screeched down not thirty feet above houses it was obvious it was out of control, flames were seen coming from it. Many people stated that they heard bombs dropped from this raider shortly before the crash, but none are reported in the immediate district. It crashed into the top of the flats with terrific force and was at once broken to pieces. It is believed that the petrol tank exploded. No bombs were on the plane when it crashed. A family of three were trapped in and killed in their shelter, while others were burned. .

The bodies of two airmen were recovered from the wrecked machine. Of the two others that baled out and surrendered, one was taken to Oldchurch Hospital and the other was handed over to the military.

The family killed in their shelter were Mr. William Bird, his wife Mrs. Margaret Bird, and their two year old daughter Joyce. Hornchurch A.R.P. and A.F.S men plunged into the blazing wreckage that covered the shelter in a vain effort to rescue them. The three people were suffocated by the intense heat and fumes.

In spite of the barrage and bursting machine-gun bullets from the Heinkel, a large crowd gathered to watch the rescue and fire-fighting work, and to collect souvenirs. Two flats were demolished and several others damaged by fire.

Part of the wreckage of the Heinkel 111 which was brought down at the rear of flats in Matlock Gardens, Hornchurch, on the night of 1st November 1940. Two of the crew had escaped by parachute, the other two crew members' charred and mutilated remains were extricated from their destroyed aircraft. Petrol from the plane spewed over an inhabited Anderson shelter and in the resultant fireball husband and wife, William and Margaret Bird, along with their two year old daughter, lost their lives.

Within a few minutes of the crash the services were on the spot, and the speed with which the men worked and the courage they showed, have won praise from all who were present. Among persons taken to Oldchurch Hospital suffering from burns were Mr. & Mrs. William Donald, of 24 Matlock Gardens. Their home was smashed, and burning petrol scattered over it. Mrs. Donald was soaked in burning petrol and ran from the flat, in which they had been sleeping, with her clothes blazing. Their son, Mr. A. Donald of 28 Matlock Gardens told of the lucky escape that he, his wife and eight month-old baby experienced. "As our baby has a cold", said Mr. Donald, "we were sleeping indoors. We were sleeping under a table in the the back downstairs room, and had armchairs all round us for added protection. Part of the plane wreckage smashed the french windows of this room, and flames came into the room right up to us. I grabbed the baby, and with my wife ran to the door but when I opened it flames shot in here too, while machine-gun bullets were bursting outside. We went to the front room, and escaped through a window, wearing only our night-clothes. If we had been sleeping in our shelter I doubt whether we should be here now. It was covered with burning wreckage, and I don't think we should have been able to escape."

Mr. Donald added that they came to Hornchurch after their home in East London was bombed.

It was not until 11:45 am. the next morning that both airmen who had baled out were accounted for. Officer Josef Haversteng, who was thought to be the observer, surrendered to the railway authorities at South Ockendon, who handed him on to the R.A.F.. Lieut. Hans Adalbert Tuffers, who was thought to be the pilot, had been hit in the leg, and so had to crawl to the Keeper's Lodge at Belhus Park to surrender. Mrs. Lowe who lived opposite the Keeper's Lodge was concerned that as the Keeper's wife was on her own, she would be frightened, and so in true British tradition she helped the wounded German into her own home, where she gave him a cup of tea. On returning, the keeper disarmed him of his handgun and kept it, quite unofficially, as a souvenir of Nazi Germany. The airman was subsequently taken to Oldchurch Hospital under police guard.

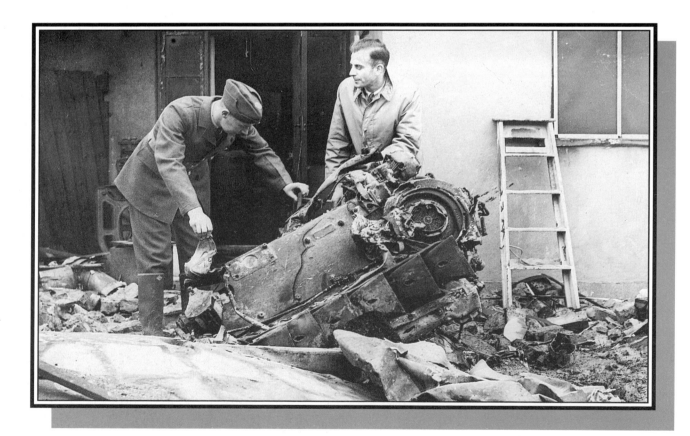

An engine from the wrecked Heinkel He111 bomber that crashed at the rear of flats in Matlock Gardens, Hornchurch, proves of interest to R.A.F personnel and civilian alike.

Bombs Under The Bed!

*O*ne morning, after a particularly heavy raid the night before, Eric Hayward and his pal set off from Ashmour Gardens, Romford, to go to School. They were slightly later than usual that morning and so decided it best to take a short cut across some open ground into Pettits Lane.

As they first entered the field to their delight they spotted an unexploded incendiary bomb and then another, in fact all around. Boys being boys, they were engrossed in their thrilling discovery and soon forgot all about heading for school.

They'd heard warnings to look out for incendiary bombs with exploding heads, but being a bit of a dare devil Eric's pal was the first to kick one.....nothing happened. Next he got hold of one and threw it down a grass hill....nothing happened. Getting more adventurous he threw one at another one.....and he hit it too. Eric dropped flat to the floor, because it was one with a black head on it, thought to signify an explosive warhead......nothing. Eventually they started to pick them up and soon had quite a considerable collection. These were definitely too good to waste, and so the decision was reached to take them back home for safe keeping.

So Eric headed for home with his armful of trophies. He turned into Ashmour Gardens and seeing there was nobody about, made a quick dash for home. When he reached his bungalow, he opened the front gate, went round the side and temporarily deposited his collection there. He then proceeded to knock at the front door, which his mother promptly opened.

"There's an unexploded bomb at the school mum"

"Oh! Is there?" she said, "Oh Dear! You'd better come in."

When things had settled down he nipped round the back of the bungalow, to the side gate, gathered up the incendiary bombs, and stealthily smuggled them up to his bedroom, where he hid them under his bed.

Half an hour went past, then suddenly there was a knock at the door. His mother opened the door, and sneaking a look round the corner, Eric could see a Policeman standing on the front step.

"Excuse me Madam" he said "but your son has been seen carrying bombs home"

"Eriiiiic", called his mother.

Sheepishly came the reply, "Yes?"

"Have you got any bombs?"

"Well yes"

"Where are they?", asked the policeman

"Under my bed", came the reply.

"I think I better take a look don't you madam?"

He cautiously approached the bedroom, looked in round the side of the door like a frightened rabbit, peeked under the bed and dashed out again, issuing nervous proclamations to stay clear and take cover.

About a half an hour later a lorry turned up with a couple of nonchalant soldiers on board. All they could do was laugh. They came in, casually picked the bombs up by their fins and threw them contemptuously into the back of their tipper lorry, which was fast filling up with incendiaries collected elsewhere in the vicinity.

That of course was not the end of the matter as far as the policeman was concerned. He demanded to know the name of Eric's accomplice and poor Eric was forced to squeal on his friend. Unfortunately for his pal, when the father heard of his son's exploits, he was in for a sound thrashing.

Young Eric at the tender age of twelve. And again today, posing for a photograph with an armful of incendiaries, something a policeman denied him over fifty years earlier.

49

Tribute to a 'Great Scout'

Whilst the Blitz continued unabated for night after night, with the Luftwaffe dropping conventional bombs, it was some time before any additional parachute mines fell in the area. When they did return, on a Friday night in mid-November, they brought with them their fearful devastation. Out of a pair that fell in the Ardleigh Green area, one came to rest in Redden Court road where it failed to explode, despite threatening to do so at any second. Its partner exploded in gardens at the rear of houses in Cecil Avenue, Ardleigh Green, where it made a huge crater, wrecking lives and homes over a wide area. Working in the dark and as the earth and air trembled with the concussion of heavy anti-aircraft fire and the explosion of bombs elsewhere, neighbours and the Rescue Squads strove to rescue victims trapped in the wreckage of their homes. A young scout Ronald Eke, 13, was one of the first to be located, his legs both severely crushed and

grim privilege to be able to help dig out two of the victims, one of them Scout Eke. Although his own injuries were very severe, and that he was suffering great pain there can be no doubt whatever, he managed to keep a firm hold on himself and gave valuable information not only about his own family, but also about the occupants of neighbouring houses. His extraction took a long time in the darkness and rain, yet he never complained, and only occasionally was a cry wrung from him when some movement in the debris sent a sharp pain through his already suffering frame. There is little romance of Scout stories in the ghastly tragedies such as occurred at Cecil Avenue, yet the heroism displayed by such boys as Eke is much more real, more valuable in the recording, more inspiring to his companions. I did not, of course, know at the time that he was a scout, but now that I know, I shall always remember him as a 'Great Scout'.''

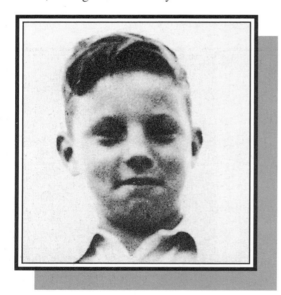

pinned beneath piles of masonry. Despite his injuries he gave the impression that he only had 'a few scratches' and insisted that the rescuers first locate his mother, Violet and father, Ronald. He could not know, but both were dead, killed outright under the rubble that had once made up No. 84 Cecil Avenue. When finally extricated he was rushed to hospital where he died whilst an operation to remove both his arms and legs was being performed. His gallantry was recognized by the grant of the Bronze Cross, the highest award the Scout Movement can give. A doctor present that dreadful evening gave this testimonial in a letter.

''I am glad to be able to testify to his personal courage and fortitude. I happened to be in Cecil Avenue shortly after the explosion and it was my

Next door to where poor Ronald lived and died was the Smith residence, and here too was brought bereavement and sorrow, when Mr. Alfred Smith and his 17 year old son were killed. At a neighbouring property Mrs. Roberts had just come to stay with her daughter and son-in-law and their six children, after having lost her husband and other daughter when bombed in East London. ''There was a lot of bangs going on and my daughter said we should all get under the bed. I said 'don't be silly they're only guns', but my daughter persuaded us all to get under the bed. Then there was a tremendous crash and the whole house crashed down on top of us. We were all eight under the bed and it saved us, as although we were under all that wreckage they managed to get us out alive.''

What appear to be just an ordinary pair of houses in Tawny Avenue, Upminster, have in fact their own unique story of courage and tragedy to tell. Back in the night of November 21st 1940 a bomb scored a direct hit on number 48, completely demolishing it. Next door Miss. Gilbert, her two brothers, her mother and aunt, Miss Pike, were all asleep. This is Miss. Gilbert's tale;

"I was sleeping in an upstairs bedroom when I was awakened by the ceiling crashing down on me. I struggled to my feet, ran out and met my two brothers. We went to the door of my aunt's room but it was jammed. We got a piece of timber and forced the door open. Then came a shock. Aunt's room wasn't there. It had completely collapsed. We thought she must certainly be dead.

Then we heard her shout to us and, looking down, saw her among the debris of the next door house. to our surprise she was alive and undismayed - working to try to release Mr. and Mrs. Clark, our neighbours"

Her aunt, Miss Pike, who was 62 years of age, had fallen with her room into the bomb crater, and yet, amazingly was unhurt. Alone she succeeded in releasing Mrs. Clark , and then helped the rescue squads release Mr. Clark. The other member of the household, 73 year-old Nelly Bellett, had died instantaneously when the bomb exploded in the room in which she was sleeping.

Original Caption : "HOME SWEET HOME...." - *Goering's Luftwaffe has failed to damp the spirits of Mr. and Mrs. Dick, despite the fact that their house has been wrecked by a bomb. Mr. & Mrs. Dick, together with their two children aged 2 years and eleven weeks, were in their Anderson shelter at the time, and suffered no injury at all. In fact, the children slept soundly all through the raid! When daylight came and salvage operations were possible, Mr. Dick recovered his concertina, and cheered everyone with music!*

Now I have no knowledge of where this is in Havering, except that it took place sometime in early October 1940. My reason for including this jolly little press photograph is that quite apart from this being an isolated event, it would seem people all across the district were striking up a tune, whilst sitting amongst the rubble of their homes. (see page 54, column 2)

'OUR BOMB' by Fred Barnes

We had spent 59 successive nights in the shelter, but then on the sixtieth night decided to stay indoors and take a chance, in return for a more comfortable night in bed. It was Sunday, 24th November 1940, and I was taking the luxury of a bath when the sirens sounded. Cutting short my ablutions, I went downstairs and started working on some papers which I had brought back from the office. Win Bishop was sitting by the electric fire, Monica and John were peacefully sleeping in and under a cot at the side of the room, Whilst Phyllis, who didn't like the sound of gunfire, was returning from the kitchen where she had been getting the supper drinks, when

'IT HAPPENED!'

For myself, apart from a whistling sound, I didn't hear a thing until, shaking my head which was resting on the table in front of the window, there was just the tinkle of broken glass somewhere reaching its final resting place, and I realised that Phyllis and Win were shouting something about "the fire". I had been blacked out, probably for something like half a minute, by the blast from a bomb which had landed just behind the house. Phyllis had been blown into the room through the doorway which she had just reached; the window had been blown in over my head and the black-out curtain (an old rubber ground sheet) was smouldering on the electric fire; and John and Monica were still sleeping peacefully in their beds! At least, I fervently hoped they were sleeping as, having first stamped out the smouldering ground sheet, I lifted up the somewhat limp bundles and thrust them hopefully into the arms of their respective mothers. They probably had also 'blacked out' , but they suffered no after effects, nor did any of us.

So far as is known , it was a 2000lb bomb, and although one description was an "aerial torpedo" it was probably a "mine" whose parachute had failed to open. It was certainly a big one, and apart from the eight houses in Cedric Avenue which were damaged beyond repair and eventually had to be demolished, nearly every house within a quarter-mile radius suffered broken windows and damaged roofs - it even broke a window as far away as the town hall. Our crater which was about 30 yards from

The rear of houses in Cedric Avenue, Romford, following the fall of what was probably a parachute mine, on 24th November 1940. Mr. Fred Barnes, who recollected events that night, lived in the house on the extreme left of the picture. Three members of the Atkinson family died in the house on the far right, whilst the two houses in the middle was the location for the feud over the garage wall, resolved only by the destruction of the garage and the death of one of the protagonists.

the back door, covered the whole width of the back garden of No. 10 and half that of No. 8; it was probably some 40 feet across and nearly as deep, in the shape of an inverted cone. The crater was large enough to take a house and in fact, when the houses were later demolished, the crater formed a handy repository for the debris.

When I had somewhat recovered from the initial shock, I went out into the hall to find that the whole of the rear of the house had gone and I could dimly see down the garden; the front door was hanging off its hinges and there was dust and debris everywhere. Our first thought was to get out in case the whole house collapsed, and so we picked our way down the front path hoping to find refuge in Wyn Bishop's bungalow at No. 1 opposite. At that moment I heard a plaintive plea for help and found the chap from No. 4 standing helplessly in the driveway with his face smothered in blood - apparently the blast had shattered his spectacles and temporarily blinded him. I told him to stay put and I would be back as soon as I had got the girls and children to safety.

We found we couldn't get into No. 1, which was shattered window-and roof-wise, as the front door had blown in and was jammed solid at an angle. So we wended our way down the road where the girls and the babies found sanctuary in the air raid shelter in the back of No. 9. The whole scene in Cedric Avenue was by this time something like Dante's Inferno. By this time the A.R.P. services had arrived and the road was full of fire engines, ambulances, rescue vehicles etc. with their crews milling around in organised chaos., with a background of wildly barking dogs (the St. Bernards from No.2, the bloodhound from No.8 and the Alsatian from No. 10 were all loose) and the high-pitched and continuous screaming of a woman trapped in the wreckage of No. 12. We learnt afterwards that she was the sole survivor of four, her husband, her sister and her brother-in-law all having been killed beside her. Mr. & Mrs. Barker at No. 10 were also killed, although their young son, who luckily was in the front of the house, survived.

[For a number of years Johnson at No. 8 and Barker at No. 10 had been indulging in a private ''war'' over Johnson's garage, the footings of the side wall of which were giving trouble. Barker refused Johnson access to put things right, so Johnson, when the Barkers were out, would nip over the fence and put a load of cement along the bottom of the garage boundary wall, which Barker would then wash out with a hose the moment he came home. This happened a number of times, and all hell was let loose on one occasion. Although I think they never actually came to blows, the shouting and dousing of each other with the hose caused quite an uproar; I refused to get involved in any way. The sad moral of the story is that the whole exercise was completely useless, as the bomb blew the whole garage down and killed Barker into the bargain]

Having seen the family into comparative safety, I wended my way back ''home'' and my first thought was to find my shoes -- I was wearing only slippers -- but could only manage to find one in the debris of what was left of the kitchen. Next (working according to the book) I tried to turn off the water, gas and electricity at the mains -- a useless exercise really in view of the wreckage and the water cascading from the tanks in the roof and from the fractured mains. I then scrambled out at the back and for the first time could see through the gloom where the bomb had actually fallen and what a mess it had made. At this stage, some shots rang out and my immediate reaction was to think, ''Oh God, what a time for the invasion to start!'' Actually, they were shooting the dogs which were still running amuck. I then heard some repeated pleas for help, and belatedly remembered the poor chap from No.4 who was still patiently standing where I had left him, and so I led him to one of the ambulances. He really was unlucky, as he had been bombed out of his house at the corner of Cedric Avenue and Mc Intosh Road by our September bombs, and now had an encore two months later.

The immediate labours of the evening being ended, I gathered some bedding from the cot, rescued the budgerigar who was cheeping a little mournfully in his battered cage hanging askew in a corner of the dining room, and went back to the family. On the way across the road, I bumped into Wilf Mott from the Town Hall, who seemed touchingly happy to see me and to shake me by the hand; apparently he had been on duty in the Report Centre, and had heard that a man and wife had been killed in Cedric Avenue, but their little boy was safe, from which he had assumed the worst. He insisted that we went home with him, which appealed to us more that going to a temporary Rest Centre, hence a little procession wound its way, with me carrying a roll of blankets in one hand and the budgie in its cage in the other, to Mott's house in Agar Way, where we eventually managed to get some uneasy sleep in hopeful safety under his dining room table.

I was up early next morning, as my father was coming up by train from Ipswich to spend a few days with us, and it was too late to stop him. I met him at the Station and played things on a low key in order not to alarm him too much. In fact, we had reached the Golden Lion corner before I thought thought it appropriate to say ''By the way, we haven't got a house -- we were bombed out last night.'' Sidney reacted so violently that he nearly fell under a passing bus, dropping the parcel of old gramophone records he was bringing up for me in the process, but he calmed down and we agreed that he would return that morning to Ipswich taking Phyllis and little John with him.

I went round to the office, where once again I was taken aback by the joyful and in some cases tearful welcome that I received; apparently the exaggerated report of my demise had also reached them. During the day I cycled round to Cedric Avenue (I borrowed a cycle, mine turned up later, a twisted mess under the bricks of the back wall) and for the first time, in daylight, saw the full extent of the damage. Apart from the crater which I have already described, the backs of all the houses had disappeared and the roof rafters, minus the tiles, were lopsided and sagging. Our stairs finished at the half-way landing, and the bath in which I had been sitting only a few hours before was hanging perilously outwards and full of bricks and rubble. All the boundary fences had been flattened, and my garage, lovingly built of asbestos sheeting on a timber frame, had virtually been blown to smithereens. The kitchen, in which Phyllis had been working literally seconds before the blast, was a complete shambles, with the gas oven battered and twisted, all the plaster stripped off the three remaining walls and the ceiling sagging. Some handles, minus their cups and jugs, were forlornly hanging on their hooks in the remains of the cupboard. Quite a lot of furniture had however survived, with scratches or minor damage, and was put back into service after cleaning up. Nevertheless, it was a sad sight to see our home, so laboriously and proudly built up, being loaded into a refuse van and taken away into temporary store until we found some other accommodation. At least there was the consolation that we had come through virtually without a scratch -- that was all that really mattered.

In those few seconds after the blast, a lot of minor, but quirkish, things were happening. For instance, one of the sheets of paper on which I had been working at the time had apparently been speared in mid-air by a drawing pin from the black-out curtain and neatly pinned to the wooden surround of the fireplace on the opposite side of the room. Years later, when we moved back after the end of the War, we discovered inside the piano a prized vase, broken into pieces unfortunately, which must have been shot into the air as the piano lid was blown open and then dropped inside before the lid came down again.

The chicken shed at the bottom of the garden had been blown to pieces (I'm afraid my carpentry hadn't allowed for high explosives!) but most of the half-a-dozen chickens were still forlornly wandering around in the vicinity, some with their feathers partly blown off, and others staggering round half blinded. This hurt me, and I gritted my teeth and wrung all their necks, leaving them in a pile ready to be collected later for the pot. This was a mistake, for having returned to the house I was so happy to unearth my piano accordion that I sat on a pile of rubble and played "Home Sweet Home" to the apparent gratification of the A.R.P. personnel; but when I returned my chickens had disappeared. This to me was equivalent to robbing a corpse and, temporarily at least, even my hatred for Hitler and his bombers was overshadowed by this unkind twist.

My homing instinct took me back several times before the house, together with the others in Cedric Avenue and four in Hill Grove, was demolished. Initially, I tried to keep alive the feint hope that, in some miraculous way, the rear wall could be rebuilt and a new roof put on, but that was soon dispelled by an ominous large whitewashed "D" for demolition, which quickly appeared on the front wall. I did salvage a few bits and pieces, including some plywood panels from the internal doors which I laboriously cut into a multitude of animals to make a Noah's Ark for John, and which still live in the summer house at Cedric Avenue, much appreciated after some fifty years by a succession of grandchildren.

For my part, I refused to let my little plot of England completely go, and fenced in the garden with barbed wire and built a little tool shed, turning the lawn into a potato patch. On weekends in summer I would cycle up with John on the crossbar and spend some hours "at home". Practically all the houses on our side of Cedric Avenue and most of those backing on us in Hill Grove having disappeared, my little "enclosure" was in the middle of a large wilderness of weeds, but it gave me comfort to have something tangible to anchor to in those traumatic years, even if people might think me a trifle mad to be sitting in the sun on a bomb site while flying bombs were passing overhead.

After the war, we were compensated in cash - my total claim at then current prices was under £200 and the house was rebuilt at a contract price of around £1,600

Is All Romford Rubble?

December saw the unwelcome reappearance of the parachute mine. Four fell on 8th December, together with a vile cocktail of incendiaries, oil bombs and conventional bombs. In terms of damage it was the worst of the war so far, with the majority of the destruction caused by just three mines. It was exactly 11 pm. when the first one fell on the A.R.P. Depot in Oldchurch Road, Romford. Unfortunately this meant that much of the rescue services vehicles and equipment which was needed to deal with other incidents was destroyed at the outset of the raid. The guard on the gate, Cyril Horsman, was the first to spot the mine. He caught a glimpse of it, by the light of the anti-aircraft gun flashes, as it floated down to earth, and immediately rushed to warn his colleagues in the control room. No sooner had he reached the partial sanctuary of the control room than the mine exploded, on the exact spot from where he had been gazing skywards seconds earlier. Lifted off his feet and flung across the room, the building collapsed around him and his colleagues, trapping and injuring many amongst the remains of the structure. The ambulances and Rescue vehicles, their fuel tanks ruptured in the blast, promptly burst into flames. The whole scene was one of devastation, soil from the crater merged with rubble from the buildings which in turn mingled with the twisted remnants of burning and exploding vans and cars.

The burning wreckage and fuel spewed over the wooden recreation room, igniting it instantaneously. Where moments before men had been enjoying a leisurely game of billiards, there was now a rapidly developing inferno. One of those inside was Mr. Finch ; ''I was knocked out by a falling beam and when I came to I found the place around me ablaze. I managed to fight my way out through the flames and wreckage without suffering serious injury. I was lucky not to get roasted alive.'' For those unlucky enough to be caught outside it proved fatal. John Pollard, a 48 year-old ambulance driver, was killed when walking between the canteen and the recreation room. Frederick Stevens, the five-year old son of the superintendent in charge of the depot was also mortally wounded. Perceiving him to be safer at the depot than at home, his father always brought his son with him when on duty. Under normal circumstances these unfortunate bodies would have been transported to the mortuary, but that too had been destroyed.

The second mine that night fell behind shops at the corner of South Street and the High Street, Romford. It partially demolished the telephone exchange in Exchange Street and so compounded the problems of the Report Centre by cutting off their means of communication. The mine actually fell directly on

An atmospheric and evocative picture of the destruction surrounding Exchange Street, Romford, the result of a parachute mine which fell on the night of 8th December 1940. The telephone exchange is on our left and the Brewery lurks amongst the smoke and mist in the background. One can almost smell the cordite and dust.

the Blacksmith's shop of Mr. S.H Bush, which when the dust eventually settled had completely vanished, leaving the surrounding area littered with horse shoes and ironmongery. The heart of any Blacksmith shop is the anvil and the tale of this one in particular has now become part of Romford folklore.

The Flight of the Anvil

From being at the epicentre of the explosion the anvil was thrown over coach buildings, over The White Hart Hotel, over a row of shops in the High Street and finally crashed through the roof of a concrete shelter in which seven people were sleeping. It came to rest in an empty bunk, causing only minor injuries! The same mine was responsible for damage to Romford Brewery and premises in South Street, where nearly every shop lost its window. Two shops were completely demolished, burying precious and rationed wartime goods under tons of rubble and dust and the normally secret world of banking was thrown open to the eyes of all when the rear of Barclays Bank was torn asunder.

A before and after shot. (**below**) In a prewar photograph the blacksmith and his two employees pose for the camera around the anvil.

And where it was to end up! (**right**) Embedded in a bunk, after crashing through the concrete roof of a shelter in which seven people were sleeping.

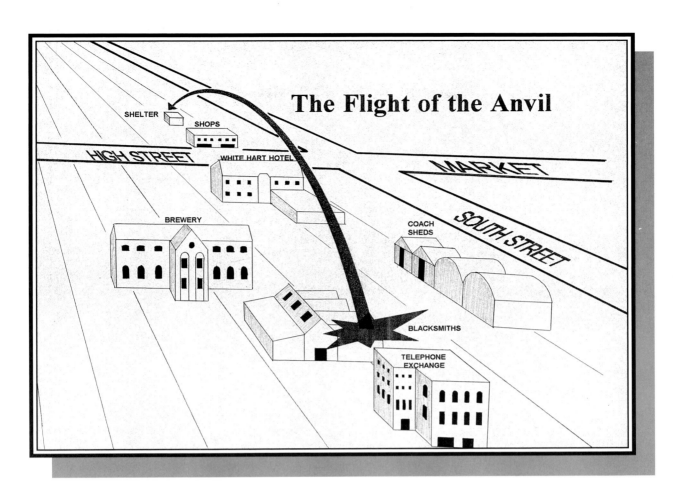

The Flight of the Anvil

SHELTER

SHOPS

HIGH STREET

WHITE HART HOTEL

MARKET

BREWERY

COACH SHEDS

SOUTH STREET

BLACKSMITHS

TELEPHONE EXCHANGE

(Below) Smoke still emanates from the ruins of a shattered Romford Brewery, blasted by the parachute mine of 8th December, 1940.

Romford Telephone Exchange, at the rear of South Street, was partially destroyed by one of the
parachute mines to fall on the night of December 8th, 1940. Forty-two year-old, Edward Fleming's lifeless body was discovered amongst the
rubble of the exchange, whilst Percy Vango also lay dead in South Street. **(Inset)** The rebuilt Telephone Exchange as it is today.

The twisted wreckage of a Vauxhall (?) car, impaled upon railings at the base of the Romford Telephone Exchange.

Bravery At The Gas Works

This was not the only drama of the night of 8th December, for unbeknown to all but the small band of men that worked there, some three bombs fell on Romford Gas Works. Two of the gigantic Gas Holders were holed and plumes of flaming gas threatened to engulf the entire plant in one great conflagration. Working frantically in this furnace, Mr. John Grayston, engineer of Romford Gas Co. and Bert Vincent Poole, shift foreman, attempted to shut the relevant valves and plug the gaping holes. With the ever present risk of further bombs falling and despite having their clothes set on fire on numerous occasions, they eventually succeeded in dousing the blaze and averted a possible disaster. In recognition of their heroism and devotion to duty they were each awarded the George Medal for gallantry.

A German Pays A Visit

Dacre Cottage, Paternoster Row, Noak Hill 16th January 1941; TAP TAP......TAPTAP.....

Mrs. Jane Hollick stirred from her slumber and listened. Had she heard a noise?....... She listened hard............nothing........and then, just as she had convinced herself that she was mistaken, there it went again. TAP TAP.........TAPTAP.....

It was a distinct knocking sound emanating from the rear of the house. Someone or something was knocking at her window. Looking at her alarm clock she observed that it was only half-past five in the morning. Who could it be at that hour? Perhaps it was her son Robert. She called out, "Is that you Bob?" ....Therecame no reply. A little anxiously she woke her still sleeping husband, Henry, who on quickly dressing, went to investigate. He too called out, and this time came the sound of a mans voice entirely unfamiliar to him, "Germany!.......Germany!"

Was this the invasion? Cautiously opening the door, there in the moonlight stood the bedraggled and bootless figure of a lone German airman, barely able to stand through the cold and an injured leg. He motioned he wanted to come inside. Mr. Hollick asked him what he wanted, but the airman could speak no English, although it was clear that this poor young man, bereft of his aircraft and unarmed, posed no threat. They helped him into their home and laid him on the comfort of their sofa. His limbs were stiff with the cold and so he was immediately proffered the ubiq-uitous 'British Cuppa'. Neither party being able to speak the others language, Mrs. Hollick's son, Herbert, ventured into French. By this means it was established that his name was Gefreiter Erich Hendur, aged 22. Plying him with cigarettes, Herbert further learnt that Erich was the sole survivor of a Dornier 17G which had crashed in flames near Harts Wood, Brentwood. (What young Erich could not have known was that his aircraft was one of two shot down that night by Pilot Officer Richard Stevens in his Hurricane of No. 151 Squadron). He told how he had landed by parachute three hours previously in a field not far from their cottage, and sure enough when Herbert went and looked, there lay his parachute. By this time the police had been summoned and the forlorn captured aviator was escorted to hospital in an ambulance. This was one of the few occasions when a Romford civilian met face to face the foe responsible for the Blitz, but Mrs. Hollick thought no ill of him, "He seemed a nice fellow and he was most grateful for what we had done for him."

Dacre Cottages, Paternoster Row, Noak Hill. 1994

Something's Coming Down!

Conventional bombing persisted but it was not until 19th March that the parachute mine returned with all the destruction that inevitably ensued. That night Upminster Road, Rainham was the luckless recipient. Six homes were razed to the ground and so widespread was the damage and confusion that for days it was still uncertain how many people remained buried. Slowly one grim find was made after another, until finally the death toll stood at twelve. In this part of Upminster Road, at the junction with Parsonage Road, the chalet bungalows were known by elegant sounding names rather than just plain numbers, but in the rubble of 'June Villa', Lucy and William Middleditch were to lose their lives and in the midst of 'Florence', lay Bertha and Ernest Jacobs and their three year old daughter Denice. Opposite the scene of the disaster was a small general store run by Mrs. Newbury, She was at the rear of the shop when suddenly a neighbour rushed in shouting, "something's coming down'. Unfortunately she took this to mean that a German pilot who had baled out was coming down and so consequently ran to the front to take a look. Just as she opened the door the parachute mine exploded.

Caught by the blast Mrs. Newbury was thrown bodily the whole length of the passage. "My chest seemed full of gas and dust from the explosion" she related. Not discouraged by the fact her little shop was a mass of wreckage, she vowed to be open for business the following day. Blown after her down the passage was a horseshoe from the door and not unnaturally she decided to keep this as a memento of her lucky survival.

The scene in Upminster Road today, 1994.

And Then Came Essex Road Night

Essex Road following the fall of parachute mine on 19th April 1941. The sheer scale of devastation is not immediately apparent until one realizes that two blocks of terraced houses on one side of the road are completely missing. In order to capture the whole scene of destruction, the photographer had to stand in a house in the next street. The death roll was for a long time uncertain, as it proved exceptionally difficult to ascertain the number of persons who occupied the demolished houses before the raid started. Eventually 38 victims were known to have been lost, unfortunately it was not possible to identify the remains of twelve of these bodies, which were subsequently buried in four mass graves in Romford Cemetery.

Saturday, 19th April 1941.

It was all the work of the Parachute mine, of which ten fell across the area that night. The first and by far the worst was that which fell in Essex Road, Collier Row, at twenty to ten that Saturday evening. Most people were not yet in the comparative safety of their shelters, the siren not long having sounded.

As the smoke and dust settled, gone was a complete row of terraced houses and then rising up from the ruins came a fearful sound, the countless and pitiful cries for help. The scene was appalling, by the flashes of the anti-aircraft gunfire could be seen the twisted limbs of victims poking from the debris, their smashed furniture strewn across the road, with their toys and crockery mingling with the bricks and tiles. The rescue squads were overwhelmed. Realizing that this was beyond their limited resources an immediate appeal for assistance was sent to Hornchurch and Brentwood, who were quick to respond.

With bombs still falling, the extraction of the dead and the still living began. The work continued through the night, all through Sunday, and even then in the afternoon of Monday, forty hours after the mine fell they heard the cries of a little girl. It was little Vera Carter, aged ten. As her tiny frame was

dug from the wreckage, she spoke to her rescuers saying, " I'm all right". Poor Vera was not all right, for shortly afterwards she lapsed into unconsciousness and died later that day in Oldchurch Hospital. She joined her mother and 38 residents of Essex Road who also died that fateful night.

Whether one attributes it to fate or luck, there were seemingly arbitrary survivors that night. Five members of the Limehouse family were killed, the only survivor was Joan. The reason she had outlived her mother and father, brother and two sisters? .... She had been on an errand to buy fish & chips for the family's supper.

Regrettably, it was never possible to identify the remains of twelve of the victims and so they were buried in four graves, at a mass funeral held at Romford cemetery the following week. There were many poignant incidents at the graveside, one such was where a woman mourner broke her wreath into four sections and laid a piece on each of the graves.

If this had been the only tragedy that night, it would have still have ranked as the worst night of the war but to this sad roll must go the names of six more who perished at the hand of a parachute mine in Hillfoot Avenue, Romford. That does not complete the death roll however, for in one of the most appalling catastrophes to engulf a household, nine members of the Gill family perished at 144 Brentwood Road, Hornchurch.

Fifty-five souls who had awoken that morning were dead before sunrise the next day. To put the night in prospective, nearly a fifth of those killed in Havering during the war died on that one terrible night in April.

One of the many tragedies that night was that of the Limehouse family, of 115 Essex Road. Only one member of the family, Joan, survived. The rest are not forgotten however, the grave in Romford Cemetery is still tended to this day.

REGISTER OF BURIALS in the BURIAL GROUND of ROMFORD, in the County of ESSEX.

No. of Entry.	NAME OF PERSON BURIED.	Place where Death occurred.	Date of Burial. 1941	By whom Ceremony performed.	Number of Grave.
15092	Unidentified Child (Male) and child (probably unborn)	Essex Road Romford	April 29	C. J. Haigh	LL 1667
15093	Unidentified Female	Essex Road Romford	April 29	C. J. Haigh	LL 1667
15094	Unidentified Male Child	Essex Road Romford	April 29	C. J. Haigh	LL 1667
15095	Unidentified Adult Female	Essex Road Romford	April 29	C. J. Haigh	LL 1668
15096	Unidentified Male	Essex Road Romford	April 29	C. J. Haigh	LL 1668
15097	Unidentified Male	Essex Road Romford	April 29	C. J. Haigh	LL 1668
15098	Unidentified Female	Essex Road Romford	April 29	C. J. Haigh	LL 1669
15099	Unidentified Female	Essex Road Romford	April 29	C. J. Haigh	LL 1669
16000	Unidentified Female	Essex Road Romford	April 29	C. J. Haigh	LL 1669
16001	Unidentified Female	Essex Road Romford	April 29	C. J. Haigh	LL 1670
16002	Unidentified Female	Essex Road Romford	April 29	C. J. Haigh	LL 1670
16003	Unidentified Male	Essex Road Romford	April 29	C. J. Haigh	LL 1670

Some of those that perished that night were to be denied even the dignity of their own marked grave. The remains of at least twelve bodies from Essex Road proved impossible to identify and so were buried in four unmarked graves in Romford Cemetery. The true horror that followed in the wake of bombing is brought home with shocking clarity by the hand written entry in the Register of Burials for Romford Cemetery, shown above.

Subsequent investigation would reveal an error in identification of two of the victims. The remains of the person buried as an unidentified male in grave LL1670 were on 30th May 1941 disinterred under a licence of the Home Secretary and returned the same day as those of Roy Stanley Wilson, aged 5 years, in grave No. KK1810. The remains previous thought to have been of Roy Stanley Wilson were then reburied as an unknown male child in grave LL1670.

Roll of Honour

GILL, George, age 64; of 144 Brentwood Road. Husband of Adelaide May Gill.   Died 19th April 1941.

GILL, Adelaide May, age 39; of 144 Brentwood Road. Wife of George Gill.   Died 19th April 1941.

GILL, Joyce Rosemary, age 11; of 144 Brentwood Road. Daughter of George and Adelaide Gill. Died 19th April 1941.

GILL, George John, age 9; of 144 Brentwood Road. Son of George and Adelaide Gill.   Died 19th April 1941.

GILL, John William, age 7; of 144 Brentwood Road. Son of George and Adelaide Gill.   Died 19th April 1941.

GILL, Mary Winifred, age 6; of 144 Brentwood Road. Daughter of George and Adelaide Gill. Died 19th April 1941.

GILL, Adelaide Doris, age 5; of 144 Brentwood Road. Daughter of George and Adelaide Gill. Died 19th April 1941.

GILL, Edward Richard, age 3; of 144 Brentwood Road. Son of George and Adelaide Gill.   Died 19th April 1941.

GILL, Pamela Mary, age 23 months; of 144 Brentwood Road. Daughter of George and Adelaide Gill. Died 19th April 1941.

(Above) The same night as a mine fell on Essex Road, one also fell in Hillfoot Avenue, Collier Row. Here, too, six unfortunates were to lose their lives.

(Inset) And as the scene looks today.

(Left) A direct hit on a shelter in Brentwood Road on the same night, killed nine members of the Gill family. To comment on this extract from the Roll of Honour seems superfluous. The names speak for themselves. Who could fail to be moved by the enormity of the tragedy that engulfed this one poor family.

A Church Is No More

Thankfully no more bombs fell for the next fortnight, but then on 11th May 1941 back came the parachute mine with vengeance. Of a pair that fell that night, the first came down shortly after midnight in Castellan Avenue, Gidea Park where it caused extensive damage. The home guard were first on the scene and helped extricate the injured and dazed people from their devastated homes. One girl was rescued after being found under debris on which a rescuer had been standing, though she subsequently made a good recovery. The only fatality was Mr. Walter Whittaker, of 59 Castellan Avenue, who was rescued from the wreckage of his home but later died from his injuries.

The second parachute mine scored a direct hit upon All Saint's Church, Squirrels Heath. Only a few hours previously, a party, with over 200 people present, was being held in the Church Hall, to raise funds for the Hall Debt Fund. As a churchwarden ruefully commented afterwards, "The proceeds were to raise funds to help extinguish the debt on the church but thanks to Hitler, when Sunday dawned, all that remained was the debt - the church and the Hall having both been extinguished!"

The explosion was followed by a fire which completed the work of destruction. Firemen worked vigorously to quell the fire to prevent it acting as a target for further bombers which were continually overhead. In the morning, members of the Boys Brigade helped locate some of the silver from the ruins, including the high altar crosses.

Opposite the church was the 'Squirrels Heath' public house where the ceilings were brought down, the windows blown in and the glasses smashed, but the following day the establishment was back in action, with the slogans "Open as Usual" and "Blasted but Game" defiantly chalked on the walls.

Parachute mines were not the only undesirable objects descending by parachute that night, for in Scotland, Rudolf Hess, the Deputy Fuhrer, had chosen to put in an appearance.

A few minor raids followed and then that was it......the end of 'The Blitz'. What had been the heaviest aerial bombardment in history had failed to break this island nation. Conversely, the Luftwaffe were not defeated and their reason for departure was far from clear. Then on 22nd June 1941 all became apparent. Hitler needed the Luftwaffe elsewhere, for in his infinite wisdom he had decided to attack Russia.

All that is left of All Saints' Church and Hall, at Squirrels Heath, after a direct hit by a parachute mine on May 10th, 1941. Despite the best efforts of the vicar to pay off the existing debt and raise funds for a new church it was never to be. He was however, successful in blocking plans to build a cinema on the site of the former church, though eventually a block of flats **(Right)** was built upon the consecrated ground. He was able to perform one last ceremony on the site though, a christening (see opposite page).

Baptised on a Bomb Site

(Above) The baptism was conducted by the former vicar of All Saints Church, the Rev. E. W. Gravett. Here we see the christening of Anthony Lawrence Hesford, then of 34 Compton Avenue, Gidea Park.

(Left) The little baby Anthony of 1943 matured into a man, and is now 51 years-old and working in Dubai.

A year after the church was destroyed, an open air church service was held on the bomb site, to commemorate the event. At the end of the service two babies were baptised. A brass band stood in for the organ, a table for the altar, and a glass bowl for the font. The service was packed, many could not recall ever having seen such a congregation when the church was standing.

(**Above**) Opposite All Saints Church was the "Squirrel's Head" pub. In spite of the damage it sustained, it was "Open as Usual" the following morning. The regulars never even missed a pint. Notice how the name of the pub has been blanked out for security.

(**Below**) The Pub may have been rebuilt, but the regulars still display a sense of history by posing for this comparison photograph.

The rear of houses in Castellan Avenue, Gidea Park, the result of a parachute mine that fell shortly after midnight on May 11th, 1941.

A local resident at the time was Glyn Richards, erstwhile Editor of the Romford Recorder and Captain in the Home Guard. His home was also damaged by the Castellan Avenue parachute mine and here he proudly displays an inscribed fragment of that mine, a treasured souvenir of an event of over half a century ago.

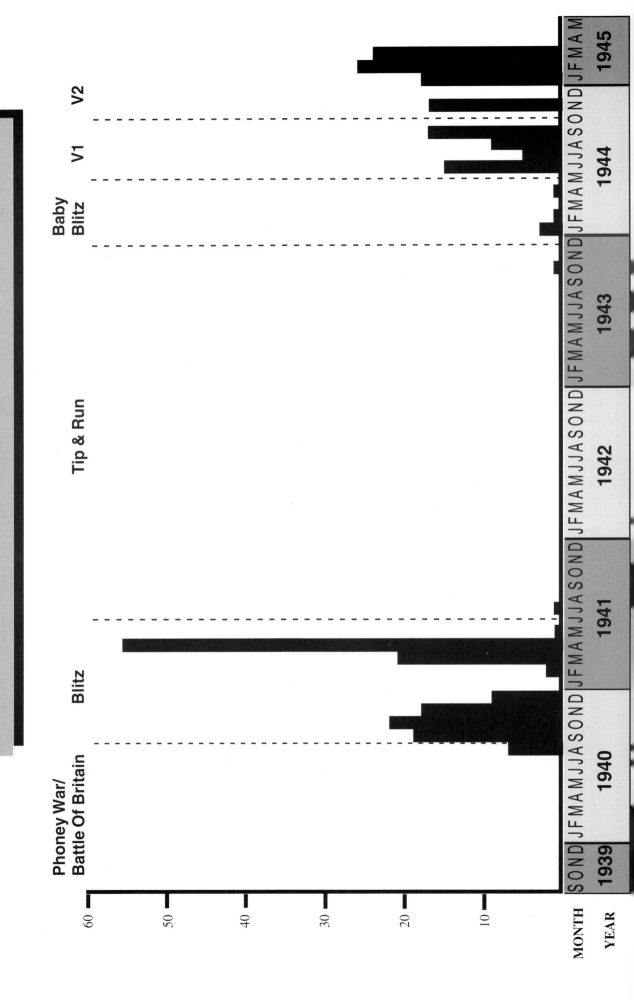

Number Of Fatalities In Havering For Each Month Of The War

68

Defence

Defence, a word on everyone's lips after the fall of France and the evacuation of our forces from Dunkirk in May 1940. Since the start of the war, Havering's population had been braced for air raids, but now there seemed the all too real possibility that for the first time since 1066 this 'Sceptred Isle' might be violated by an intruder. Only twenty-one miles of the English Channel stood between England and the Nazi hordes poised for attack on the French coast. Strategic military planning was turned on its head by the speed of events that had engulfed Europe. It was a time for improvisation and for policy making on the hoof.

A radio broadcast by Anthony Eden, the new Secretary of State for War, was made, appealing for recruits to form a volunteer home-defence force, of men in reserved occupations, or too old or young for military service. This force was to be known as the Local Defence Volunteers. In July this was changed, at Churchill's suggestion, to the far more effective and catchy title 'Home Guard'. Within a few minutes of the end of the broadcast, queues of eager volunteers had formed outside police stations the length and breadth of Havering. There was no doubting their enthusiasm, and indeed their patriotism, but what they lacked were supplies. To be distributed amongst the hundreds of volunteers were fifty rifles, five hundred rounds, fifty uniforms and fifteen armbands. Not much with which to defend an area of 40 square miles against crack fighting troops, who in such a short time had overwhelmed the combined French and British forces on mainland Europe. However, these volunteers were defending their homes, their loved ones and their way of life and consequently were resolute that Hitler should not pass. One elderly volunteer, a soldier from a previous century, who was nearer to ninety than eighty arrived brandishing an ancient shotgun, his services were gracefully declined though his weapon was retained. Another unorthodox means of obtaining arm-aments occurred when Glyn Richards (later to become Captain Richards), editor of the Romford Recorder, was covering a court case for his newspaper. The defendant was charged with possessing an unlicensed revolver and consequently heavily fined and the revolver confiscated by the court. After a discreet word with the judge, Glyn Richards was able to add another weapon to the Home Guard's limited armoury.

On the other side of the Channel someone else was also making plans.

"Since England, in spite of her hopeless military situation, shows no signs of being ready to come to an understanding, I have decided to prepare a landing operation against England, and if necessary carry it out. The aim of the operation will be to eliminate the English homeland as a base for the prosecution of the war against Germany, and if necessary to occupy it completely. I therefore order as follows: The landing will be in in the form of a surprise crossing on a wide front from Ramsgate to the area west of the Isle of Wight. Preparations for the entire operation must be completed by the middle of August. These preparations must also create such conditions as will make a landing in England possible, the English Air Force must be so reduced physically and morally that it is unable to deliver significant attack against the German crossing. The invasion will bear the name 'Sealion'."

Adolf Hitler. Directive No. 16   16th July 1940

German Troops, Prague 1939.

Local Defence Volunteers (Home Guard), Romford Market 1940.

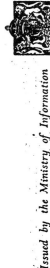

Issued by the Ministry of Information   *in co-operation with the War Office and the Ministry of Home Security*

Beating the INVADER

A MESSAGE FROM THE PRIME MINISTER

IF invasion comes, everyone—young or old, men and women—will be eager to play their part worthily. By far the greater part of the country will not be immediately involved. Even along our coasts, the greater part of the country will remain unaffected. But where the enemy lands, or tries to land, there will be most violent fighting. Not only will there be the battles when the enemy tries to come ashore, but afterwards there will fall upon his lodgments very heavy British counter-attacks, and all the time the lodgments will be under the heaviest attack by British bombers. The fewer civilians or non-combatants in these areas, the better—apart from essential workers who must remain. So if you are advised by the authorities to leave the place where you live, it is your duty to go elsewhere when you are told to leave. When the attack begins, it will be too late to go; and, unless you receive definite instructions to move, your duty then will be to stay where you are. You will have to get into the safest place you can find, and stay there until the battle is over. For all of you then the order and the duty will be: "STAND FIRM".

This also applies to people inland if any considerable number of parachutists or air-borne troops are landed in their neighbourhood. Above all, they must not cumber the roads. Like their fellow-countrymen on the coasts, they must "STAND FIRM". The Home Guard, supported by strong mobile columns wherever the enemy's numbers require it, will immediately come to grips with the invaders, and there is little doubt will soon destroy them.

Throughout the rest of the country where there is no fighting going on and no close cannon fire or rifle fire can be heard, everyone will govern his conduct by the second great order and duty, namely, "CARRY ON". It may easily be some weeks before the invader has been totally destroyed, that is to say, killed or captured to the last man who has landed on our shores. Meanwhile, all work must be continued to the utmost, and no time lost.

The following notes have been prepared to tell everyone in rather more detail what to do, and they should be carefully studied. Each man and woman should think out a clear plan of personal action in accordance with the general scheme.

Winston S. Churchill

STAND FIRM

1. What do I do if fighting breaks out in my neighbourhood?

Keep indoors or in your shelter until the battle is over. If you can have a trench ready in your garden or field, so much the better. You may want to use it for protection if your house is damaged. But if you are at work, or if you have special orders, carry on as long as possible and only take cover when danger approaches. If you are on your way to work, finish your journey if you can.

If you see an enemy tank, or a few enemy soldiers, do not assume that the enemy are in control of the area. What you have seen may be a party sent on in advance, or stragglers from the main body who can easily be rounded up.

CARRY ON

2. What do I do in areas which are some way from the fighting?

Stay in your district and carry on. Go to work whether in shop, field, factory or office. Do your shopping, send your children to school until you are told not to. Do not try to go and live somewhere else. Do not use the roads for any unnecessary journey; they must be left free for troop movements even a long way from the district where actual fighting is taking place.

3. Will certain roads and railways be reserved for the use of the Military, even in areas far from the scene of action?

Yes, certain roads will have to be reserved for important troop movements; but such reservations should be only temporary. As far as possible, bus companies and railways will try to maintain essential public services, though it may be necessary to cut these down. Bicyclists and pedestrians may use the roads for journeys to work, unless instructed not to do so.

ADVICE AND ORDERS

4. Whom shall I ask for advice?

The police and A.R.P. wardens.

5. From whom shall I take orders?

In most cases from the police and A.R.P. wardens. But there may be times when you will have to take orders from the military and the Home Guard in uniform.

6. Is there any means by which I can tell that an order is a true order and not faked?

You will generally know your policeman and your A.R.P. wardens by sight, and can trust them. With a bit of common sense you can tell if a soldier is really British or only pretending to be so. If in doubt ask a policeman, or ask a soldier whom you know personally.

INSTRUCTIONS

7. What does it mean when the church bells are rung?

It is a warning to the local garrison that troops have been seen landing from the air in the neighbourhood of the church in question. Church bells will *not* be rung all over the country as a general warning that invasion has taken place. The ringing of church bells in one place will not be taken up in neighbouring churches.

8. Will instructions be given over the wireless?

Yes; so far as possible. But remember that the enemy can overhear any wireless message, so that the wireless cannot be used for instructions which might give him valuable information.

9. In what other ways will instructions be given?

Through the Press; by loudspeaker vans; and perhaps by leaflets and posters. But remember that genuine Government leaflets will be given to you only by the policeman, your A.R.P. warden or your postman; while genuine posters and instructions will be put up only on Ministry of Information notice boards and official sites, such as police stations, post offices, A.R.P. posts, town halls and schools.

FOOD

10. Should I try to lay in extra food?

No. If you have already laid in a stock of food, keep it for a real emergency; but do not add to it. The Government has made arrangements for food supplies.

NEWS

11. Will normal news services continue?

Yes. Careful plans have been made to enable newspapers and wireless broadcasts to carry on, and in case of need there are emergency measures which will bring you the news. But if there should be some temporary breakdown in news supply, it is very important that you should not listen to rumours nor pass them on, but should wait till real news comes through again. Do not use the telephones or send telegrams if you can possibly avoid it.

MOTOR-CARS

12. Should I put my car, lorry or motor-bicycle out of action?

Yes, when you are told to do so by the police, A.R.P. wardens or military; or when it is obvious that there is an immediate risk of its being seized by the enemy—then disable and hide your bicycle and destroy your maps.

13. How should it be put out of action?

Remove distributor head and leads and either empty the tank or remove the carburettor. If you don't know how to do this, find out now from your nearest garage. In the case of diesel engines remove the injection pump and connection. The parts removed must be hidden well away from the vehicle.

THE ENEMY

14. Should I defend myself against the enemy?

The enemy is not likely to turn aside to attack separate houses. If small parties are going about threatening persons and property in an area not under enemy control and come your way, you have the right of every man and woman to do what you can to protect yourself, your family and your home.

GIVE ALL THE HELP YOU CAN TO OUR TROOPS

Do not tell the enemy anything   **Do not give him anything**

Do not tell the enemy anything   **Do not help him in any way**

(55001) Wt. 46381.F10/9 14/05/800 (2 kds.) 5.41 Hw. G.51

Meanwhile back in England countermeasures were being undertaken for just such an eventuality. It was anticipated that the enemy's principal objective in any attack would be the centre of Government in London. Defences were accordingly organised into (a) beach defences, designed to repel landings, and (b) in depth inland, designed to contain and delay the enemy until arrival of reinforcements. There was no reason to suppose that the enemy would employ tactics greatly different from those which were employed so successfully in France, namely rapid penetration by armoured fighting vehicles regardless of the flanks. One difference was, however, felt to exist. Even in the more open country of Northern France, the German tanks did not willingly leave the roads, and returned to them as soon as possible. In South East England the country was much closer and the roads narrower and less direct. Further, they nearly all converge on towns, small and large. The deduction made was that defence was best extended inland by holding these towns, which became known as 'nodal points'. Where does Havering fit in with this scheme? Well, for better or worse Romford was designated a Category A 'nodal point'. What did this mean? It meant that the Home Guard, together with available troops would have to hold the town for at least seven days if attacked. As Romford might well have been isolated or subjected to siege conditions, it was important that it was self-supporting after 'Action Stations'. This involved the storage of 2 gallons of water per head of the population, provision of food for the civil population and the Home Guard, and provision of treatment for the large number of casualties that were to be expected. It was also important that there was sufficient shelter space within the defence line, for as one major wrote at the time, "It was felt the military garrison might be defeated , as much by the efforts of the civil population to crowd the keep as by the enemy e.g. during bombings, difficulty was experienced in keeping civilians OUT of our pillboxes owing to lack of sufficient civilian shelters". The government distributed a leaflet to every home, ominously entitled 'IF THE INVADER COMES'. It urged everyone to stay put and avoid blocking the roads which would be needed for the military. Should the invasion have materialized Romford could have expected artillery bombardment, dive bombers attacks, as well as the inevitable murderous hand to hand street fighting. In order to slow any armoured column, concrete road blocks were located on strategic points on the roads. In addition the major roads were mined in approximately thirty locations and were to be detonated as enemy vehicles passed overhead.

The Hack, The Vicar and the German Parachutist.

On the 13th May 1940 the Government order was issued for the removal of "any sign which furnished any indication of the name, or direction, or distance of any place". The most obvious first step was to uproot all signposts, but to erase a town's identity completely was virtually impossible, as was to become all too apparent. Correspondence between a journalist of the Romford Times and the Vicar of St. Michael's Church, Gidea Park illustrates the magnitude of the problem. The journalist who wrote under the nom-de-plume of 'Mercury' had this to say. "I was responsible for much fluttering in clerical and council dovecots, last Wednesday, when I asked what was going to be done about war memorials, rolls of honour and gravestones, disclosing evidence of locality to parachutists. One immediate effect was the blotting out of the word 'Romford' on the town memorial in Laurie-Square. So far so good; but the cemetery problem still exists. As I said, districts are seldom on headstones nowadays, but there are a tidy few in the older part of Romford Cemetery which leave no mistake as to the locality."

"My dear Mercury", wrote the Vicar, "I agree with you today that you have certainly devoted space for many weeks in an endeavour to press home the necessity of making a clean sweep of all possible clues to locality in numberless and unthought of places. But, dear Mercury, it occurs to me that the scriptural exhortation, 'cast out first the beam that is in thine own eye', is most appropriate in this connection. A parachutist need not spend hours amongst tombstones and war memorials, all he need do today, tomorrow or the day after, is to walk into a local newsagents and ask for a copy of the local newspaper and he will be sold a copy of a newspaper bearing on the front page the name 'Romford' in bold letters and containing the name very many times on every page. WHAT IS MORE SIMPLE FOR THE PARACHUTIST? I beg to submit that your paper should now substitute the word 'local' for the name 'Romford' wherever this usually occurs. The churches have been exhorted to remove from their literature tables any matter bearing the name of the place in which the church is situated. To this I have rigorously complied, which means that I have withdrawn from public sale my parish magazine, it being available only to subscribers, but if the local newspaper bearing the name of the place in which it circulates can be offered publicly for sale, I might as well make it known that my parish magazine can be purchased at any local newsagents!"

Mercury replied, ''Does the vicar seriously suggest that a parachutist is going to take a stroll down town, call on the newsagent, buy the Romford Times and then sit down to read it? The vicar's proposal that the word 'local' should be used in this paper wherever a district name occurs would be carrying the new regulation to absurdity and would serve no useful purpose whatever. Utter chaos would reign in newspaper offices, trader's establishment and readers homes. Even in the present restricted size the name of a district appears in reports, headings, advertisements, etc., something like 400 times per issue! And that's not counting the small advertisements, whose number is legion! If we confined our activities to Romford only, it might be possible to erase the locality, but what about Hornchurch, Upminster, Rainham, Elm Park, Harold Wood, Collier Row and so forth? To put it in a nutshell Mr. Elvin, there is all the difference in the world between a memorial and a cemetery in a wide open space, to which the public have unrestrained access and a newspaper behind a counter in a shop which would be shut immediately a parachutist arrived. That is the legal ruling, and I think it's eminently sensible.''

Whilst this surreal correspondence was transpiring, a wholesale round up of aliens was being undertaken throughout the district. Police interned all male Germans and Austrians between the ages of 16 and 60 years of age. Certain areas of the British Isles were designated 'protected areas' and due to the sensitive nature of its Airfield, Hornchurch was included. No enemy alien, who had not been interned, was allowed in without special permission. So when a blonde, 30 year-old German woman, named Freda, was found within the area carrying a camera, she was immediately arrested and charged the following day with serious offences under the aliens order.

Tale in Memorial.

Romford's war memorial to the 'Great War', erected before people knew to number the wars, was to prove something of a problem during World War II. Who amongst the stonemasons that carved the proud but mournful monument, thought that one day they would be required to deface the word 'Romford'. For as the threat of invasion loomed menacingly up in 1940, the order was issued to strike out the town's name, lest it gave away the locality to Nazi parachutists. With post-war development the war memorial was moved from Laurie Square (now the underpass in front of Romford Library) and placed in Coronation Gardens, Main Road. The threat of parachutists having passed, the name of Romford was reinstated, together with the fallen of yet another generation.

Irony of Ironies

With unintended irony, in place of the war memorial in Laurie Square is a German sign post. Fortunately not a result of Nazi conquest, but a symbol of friendship between the Borough of Havering and the town of Ludwigshafen.

A salvo of anti-aircraft shells is fired off from Ayletts Gun Battery, Warwick Lane, Rainham. This was not an officially sanctioned photograph, but was instead clandestinely taken by one of the soldiers stationed on the gun-site. The only light source is the muzzle flashes from the guns themselves. Risking court-martial if discovered, our furtive photographer opened the shutter on his camera when the guns were about to fire and then closed it again as the shells winged their way to seek out the enemy high above in the night sky.

Mysterious Fires on Tylers Common

To deceive the enemy into dropping their bombs in open country, a ruse was devised involving decoy fires, code-named 'Starfish' sites. It was hoped that fires ignited on these sites during a raid, would lure the bombers away from their intended targets. Rainham Marshes was selected as a suitable decoy location for London, as the German aircraft would have to fly over it before siting the actual area under attack. The site at Rainham was ignited on the night of the last great Luftwaffe raid on London, May 10th 1941. Results were unimpressive, for it was lit at just after midnight, but by 3:40 a.m. no bombs had fallen on it whatsoever. Shortly after it was ignited, however, two parachute mines did fall on Romford, one in Castellan Avenue and one in Upper Brentwood Road, where it demolished All Saints Church. Could it be as a result of the deception plan? We shall never know.

Apart from this official site, other people felt moved to take matters into their own hands. A Home Guardsman began to have his suspicions. He spoke to his friend Arch Leggett on the subject:-

"Arch there's something funny going on at Tylers Common. Every time we have a hell of a raid here, a fire always starts on Tylers Common and we don't have any reporting of any bombing incident there. I'm going to ask Captain Deereburg, the platoon commander for that area."

He came in on the Saturday morning and I said,

"Deereburg I wanted a chat with you, there's something very peculiar about Tylers Common."

"What's peculiar", he said, "I've got a very good look out positioned there."

"Yes that's what I thought, but isn't it strange how there's been fires there when the raids have been at their worst."

He just burst out laughing.

I said, "Well come on, what's the big joke, share it with me?"

"We do that", he said, "to try and distract the Germans. This is open land, my home's not far away mind you, but it's open land and if they want to drop their bombs then that's the place to drop them, not on big conurbations of people."

"Oh I said it's done unofficially by the Home Guard then?"

"Not by the Home Guard", he said, "by Home Guardsmen, but not by the Home Guard."

Captain Glyn Richards   (Home Guard, Romford Sector)

Spies?

Romford is on the list of towns which restricts the entry of people who wish to enter the town for the purpose of "holidaymaking, recreation or pleasure, or as casual wayfarers".

Just within the borders of Romford and Chadwell Heath, buses, cars and cycles are stopped, and identity cards of passengers are examined. Only residents of Romford are are allowed to continue the journey. A lot of comment has been caused by the fact that pedestrians and train travellers are not challenged. Absurd situations arise from this. This morning, I travelled from Goodmayes to Romford by bus. As I asked for my ticket, the conductor said, "Do you live there?" "Yes", I replied. "Good for you. Otherwise they wouldn't let you go through." At the boundary, we were stopped by two policeman, who examined everybody's identity card. Three non-residents, realizing their position, left the bus before the police arrived, walked across the boundary, waited at the next bus stop, and remounted the same bus, the other side. Sitting next to me a woman of 35 years of age said, "It do seem a bit silly, don't it? They might be ordinary people, and they might be spies!"

Mass Observation 1939

The Germans are here?

One night when my father was away, my mother and I went to bed after the 'All Clear' had sounded. About 3 a.m. she woke me up to say she could hear people tramping up and down the street. She was too frightened to look out of the window in case the invasion had started and they were German soldiers. When she did look out of the window later she was surprised to see some British Soldiers further along the road and all the houses round us had their windows wide open. She discovered the soldiers were de-fusing a delayed action bomb and the neighbours had been housed for the night in a nearby school. Somehow we had been overlooked!

Mrs. J.L. Stevens, then living at No. 79 Warren Drive, Elm Park

Borough of Romford.

GAS MASKS FOR BABIES.

Demonstrations of how to use the Anti-Gas Protective Helmet for Babies under two years of age will be given for mothers in Romford as follows:—

OLDCHURCH HOSPITAL.
Wednesdays and
Fridays ... ... 11 a.m. to 12 noon
THE CLINIC, MARKS ROAD.
Mondays ... ... 10 a.m. to 12 noon
Tuesdays ... ... 10 a.m. to 12 noon
and 2 p.m. to 4 p.m.
Wednesdays ... ... 2 p.m. to 4 p.m.
Fridays ... ... 10 a.m. to 12 noon
Saturdays ... ... 10 a.m. to 12 noon
THE CLINIC, CHURCH HALL,
COLLIER ROW.
Mondays ... ... 2 p.m. to 4 p.m.
Wednesdays ... ... 10 a.m. to 12 noon
THE CLINIC, ST. MICHAEL'S HALL,
MAIN ROAD.
Thursdays ... ... 10 a.m. to 12 noon
THE CLINIC, MISSION HALL,
BIRKBECK ROAD.
Thursdays ... ... 2 p.m. to 4 p.m.
THE CLINIC, WEMBLEY HALL,
PRINCES ROAD.
Fridays ... ... 2 p.m. to 4 p.m.
It is important that mothers should know how to use this protective helmet and you should attend if possible for the demonstration.
This is a demonstration only.

Invasion Imminent

In the late afternoon of Saturday, September 7th 1940, the Germans began their first massive bombing raid on the Capital, carried out by 625 bombers and their 648 fighter escorts. By early evening the whole area of the docks was a great mass of flames, the glow of which was frighteningly apparent, even to the inhabitants of Havering. It was the greatest bombardment of the war so far and appeared to be the prelude to a German landing and therefore the Headquarters of the Home Forces issued the code word 'Cromwell', signifying 'invasion imminent'. Parachutists were expected at any moment, when from out of the sky came the first German. The start of the invasion? No, he was not part of the invasion and he would pose no further threat, for his parachute failed to open and he fell to his death in a field behind Franks Cottages, St. Mary's Lane, Upminster. Hans Mescheder, aged 20, was the gunner from a Messerschmitt 110, which went on to crash, at Park Corner Farm, Hacton Lane. In the atmosphere of high expectancy there were numerous false alarms, but the night passed without the arrival of the Nazi hordes. For the moment at least, there was not to be the sound of marching 'jackboots' along the streets of Havering

Home Guard Manoeuvres

By August 1941 the Home Guard had grown in numbers, equipment and confidence. "The Home Guard is warming up to its task. Training continues with unabated vigour to prepare the organization for the important role which it will play if invasion is attempted by the enemy."

They felt ready to display their prowess at a demonstration exercise staged in Gerpins Gravel Pits, Rainham. Part of the Home Guard played the part of the Germans and the other half showed just how they were to be swiftly dispatched.

(**Above**)   The Home Guard having successfully knocked out an 'enemy tank' at a road block, deal with the 'casualties and prisoners'.

(**Top Right**)   Let's hear it for the Home Guard! They've got the Hun on the Run!

(**Bottom Right**)   And if necessary, they know how to finish him off!

Further success. A 'Nazi' motorbike and sidecar, complete with its riders, are ensnared in a Home Guard ambush.

A Westland Lysander, seconded from the R.A.F. for the day, performs a low diving attack on a road block. Perhaps I am being too cynical, but it occurs to me that from the attitude of the aircraft and the angle of the control surfaces it looks certain to crash. Could it be that the photographer added a little dramatic enhancement in the dark room?

The valiant efforts of the 'few' in the Battle of Britain prevented the Luftwaffe from gaining air superiority, the prerequisite of any invasion. The weeks came and went and no invasion materialized, for by July 1941 Hitler's attention was focused elsewhere, on operation 'Barbarossa', the assault on Russia. Here the Nazi war machine was to meet its match. The men who might have stormed Romford's and Hornchurch's defences were instead dying by their thousand in the vast empty expanses of Russia.

The United States entered the war in December 1941 and with their entry came the hope that one day the roles might be reversed and that it would fall to the Allied forces to contemplate invasion of mainland Europe. It was to be two and a half long years before this dream could be fulfilled and in the intervening period this country experienced the greatest military build up in history. The Home Guard were not redundant however, for with this build up, a new threat was perceived. It was reasoned that when the Germans realised an invasion was about to commence, they might try a disruptive counter attack of their own in an effort to postpone or possibly avert the invasion altogether. The Home Guard were once more put on alert and a ban on entry into coastal areas imposed, the location of the majority of the build up. This coastal area took within its boundary the areas of Hornchurch and Brentwood and came into force in early April 1944. Henceforth, travelling between Romford and Hornchurch became the equivalent of crossing a frontier. You would be stopped by a policeman and asked to present your identity card and only allowed across if your reason was absolutely necessary. Crossing over the boundary was not allowed merely to go shopping or to visit a relative, there had to be some business necessity or personal emergency. Sporting fixtures were decimated as were all forms of socializing. Innumerable anomalies were bound to crop up, especially where the boundary ran along the middle of the road. There were so many people who forgot or neglected to carry their identity cards that a special session had to be held in Romford Court during June 1944 to deal with 81 summonses against the ban regulations. One of these unfortunates was Louisa Wiskin, of 25 Meadowside Road, Upminster, who had just left home to post a letter at the end of her road, when she was stopped and as she could not produce her card was duly fined ten shillings. Marion Leyland, of 35 Upminster Road, Rainham, was even more unlucky. She went to the police station to report that her gas meter had been broken into. When there she was asked to produce her identity card, but was unable to do so. A ten shilling fine was added to her misfortune!

Like the invasion before it, the German counter attack failed to materialize and D-day was able to proceed without sabotage or disruption. The border ban was lifted at the end of August 1944 by which time the Allied invasion was well under way. Once more people were free to visit their friends and relatives without fear of arrest. The raison d'etre for the Home Guard had thus thankfully disappeared and they were finally stood down in December 1944. They had evolved from a small force of poorly armed men into a formidable and well trained fighting force of some 5,000 men split between the two sectors that covered Havering. To many they remained an amusing 'Dads Army' who would have suffered grievously at the hands of the German Army. The only thing one can say for certain is that the invader never came, and there can have been few amongst the ranks of the Home Guard who were not profoundly grateful for this fact, whatever their state of readiness.

The Mine that Time Forgot?

As already stated, the major roads in Havering were mined in upwards of thirty locations. These were laid by the Royal Engineers and then handed over to the Home Guard, to be detonated in the event of a German armoured column passing overhead. As we have seen the Nazi hordes failed to materialize and so eventually it was decided that these mines should be cleared. This clearance operation once more fell within the jurisdiction of the Royal Engineers who successfully completed the procedure without incident. End of story? Well not quite. Due to an administrative error is was unclear whether <u>all</u> the mines had in fact been removed, as the original plans had been lost. Of particular concern were the series of mines laid at Gallows Corner Romford.

Nobody could be sure if they had all been removed or not. The decision was made to cut a trench right across the junction in the hope that this would reveal any remaining buried mines. This was duly undertaken and no such mines were located.

Conclusion; all the mines had been removed. Let us hope it was the right conclusion!

Bought By Hornchurch.
Sunk by a German U-Boat.

The Navy has signalled "ACTION." Day and night our ships plough the seas — seeking out and destroying the enemy. There's a signal for you, too— that signal is SAVE! Make your Warship Week a smash hit by investing for all you're worth in War Savings.

Go to a Post Office or your Bank or Stockbroker and invest your money in 3% Savings Bonds 1955-65, 2½% National War Bonds 1949-51, 3% Defence Bonds, or Savings Certificates : or deposit your savings in the Post Office Savings Bank. Buy Savings Stamps at 6d. and 2/6d. each from a Post Office, or your Savings Group.

INVEST ALL YOU CAN IN

3% Savings Bonds

2½% National War Bonds

3% Defence Bonds

Savings Certificates

Post Office Savings Bank

Feb. 7TH — 14TH
HORNCHURCH
OBJECTIVE £700,000
The cost of a Destroyer

Feb. 14TH — 21ST
ROMFORD
OBJECTIVE £400,000
The cost of a Destroyer

(Left) H.M.S Hurricane, the destroyer notionally bought by Hornchurch in the Warship Week of Feb 1942. Hornchurch's target had been to raise the overly ambitious sum of £700,000. In the event only £263,00 was raised approximately £3 per head. Romford was more successful raising £420,000, or £7 per head of population. The Hurricane was being constructed by Vickers Armstrong, Barrow, at the outbreak of war for the Brazilians, under the name 'Japarua'. The British Government purchased her in September 1939 and she was completed in June 1940. Unfortunately her stern was badly damaged in a subsequent air-raid whilst she was stilled berthed. Following this attack a new stern was fitted, and she was re-commissioned in December, 1941. With a complement of 145 sailors she took to the sea once more, only to be sunk on Christmas Eve 1943 by a submarine (either U275 or U415) in the North Atlantic, off the Azores.

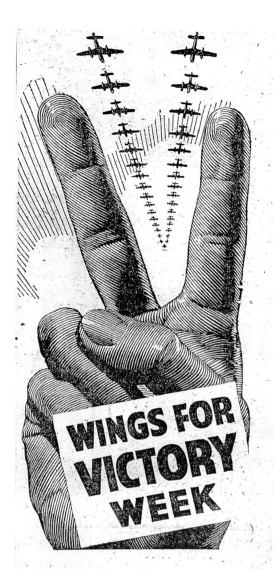

Day and night the R.A.F. reaches out after more and more targets; day and night we need more and more aircraft. We must provide them—through our work and savings—in our "Wings for Victory" Week. We have a special savings target to straddle—so that our district wins its "Victory Wings." Spend less — save more — and more. "Bank" at every turn—make our victory "roll" with savings. The sky's our limit.

PUT EVERYTHING INTO IT—

3% Savings Bonds
1960-70

2½% National War Bonds 1951-53

3% Defence Bonds

Savings Certificates

Savings Stamps

Post Office Savings Bank

Trustee Savings Bank

June 5th - 12th

HORNCHURCH

TARGET £250,000

The cost of fifty Typhoons

The Result of Wings For Victory Week 1943: Hornchurch supassed its target by raising £348,505 beating Romford' total of £341,000. Both impressive totals. In today's money the combined sum would be about £ 17 million.

URBAN DISTRICT COUNCIL OF HORNCHURCH.

EMERGENCY POWERS (DEFENCE) ACTS 1939 and 1940.

REQUISITION OF UNNECESSARY RAILINGS.

UNDER direction by the Minister of Supply all unnecessary iron or steel railings, posts, chains, bollards, gates, stiles, etc., in the Urban District of Hornchurch will shortly be removed and collected for use in the national war effort in iron and steel works and foundries.

NOTICE IS HEREBY GIVEN that on or before the 4th May, 1942, the work of removal will commence with the railings in the following streets and places :

Abbs Cross Lane	Fairview Avenue	Northwood venue
Acacia Avenue	Fanshawe Crescent	Oak Avenu
Acacia Drive	Farm Road, Rainham	Oak Glen
Albany Road	Farm Way	Oak Road
Aldborough Road	Fen Lane	Orchard Avenue
Allandale Road	Fernbank Avenue	Osborne Road
Allen Road	Findon Gardens	Park Drive
Ambleside Avenue	Fitzilian Avenue	Park Lane
Arbour Way	Ford Lane	Parkland Avenue
Ardleigh Green Road	Foxhall Road	Parkstone Avenue
Argyle Gardens	Front Lane	Parsonage Road
Ashburnham Gardens	Gaynes Park Road	Penerley Road
Ashley Gardens	Gaynes Road	Percival Road
Ashlyn Grove	Geoffrey Avenue	Pond Walk
Athelstan Road	Glanville Drive	Rainham Road
Avenue Road	Glebe Road	Randall Drive
Babington Road	Glebe Way	Ravenscourt Drive
Barton Road	Globe Road	Ravenscourt Grove
Bedford Gardens	Gordon Avenue	Rayburn Road
Beech Avenue	Great Gardens Road	Recreation Avenue
Beech Close	Grenfell Avenue	Redden Court Road
Belmont Avenue	Grey Towers Avenue	River Drive
Benhurst Avenue	Grosvenor Drive	Rockingham Avenue
Berther Road	Grosvenor Gardens	Rom. Crescent
Berwick Pond Road	Gubbins Lane	Rosebank Avenue
Berwick Road	Hacton Drive	Rosewood Avenue
Beverley Gardens	Hacton Lane	Rosslyn Avenue
Billet Lane	Hall Lane	Rothbury Avenue
Bird Lane	Hamilton Drive	Roxburgh Avenue
Boscombe Avenue	Hardley Crescent	Sandown Avenue
Boundary Road	Harrow Drive	Saunton Road
Bowden Drive	Harwood Avenue	Shepherds Hill
Brackendale Gardens	Harwood Hall Lane	Slewins Lane
Branfill Gardens	Haynes Road	Southend Arterial Road
Brentwood Road	Hazel Close	South End Road
Brian Close	Hazel Rise	South View Drive
Bridge Avenue	Hazelmere Gardens	Spencer Crescent
Briscoe Road	Helen Road	Springbank Avenue
Brookdale Avenue	Herbert Road	Springfield Gardens
Bruce Avenue	Highfield Crescent	Spring Gardens
Bryant Avenue	Highfield Road	Squirrels Heath Lane
Burn Way	High Street	Squirrels Heath Road
Butts Green Road	Hillview Avenue	Stafford Avenue
Calbourne Avenue	Holden Way	Standen Avenue
Carnforth Avenue	Hornchurch Road	Stanley Road
Cavenham Gardens	Howard Road	Stanley Road North
Cecil Avenue	Hubbard's Chase	Station Lane
Cedar Road	Hyland Close	Station Road (Harold
Champion Road	Hyland Way	Wood)
Chester Avenue	Ingrebourne Gardens	Station Road
Chestnut Avenue	Ingrebourne Road	(Upminster)
Chestnut Close	Kenilworth Gardens	St. Andrews Avenue
Chestnut Glen	Kinfauns Avenue	St. Georges Avenue
Church Lane, Gt. Warley	King Edward Avenue	St. Mary's Lane
	Kings Gardens	St. Nicholas Avenue
Church Road (Harold Wood)	Kingsley Gardens	Sunningdale Avenue
	Kyme Road	Sunnings Lane
Claremont Road	Laburnum Avenue	Sunnyside Gardens
Clay Tye Road	Laburnum Gardens	Suttons Avenue
Clydesdale Road	Laburnum Walk	Suttons Gardens
Coniston Avenue	Lake Avenue	Suttons Lane
Coronation Drive	Lambs Lane	Sylvan Avenue
Corbetts Avenue	Lancaster Drive	Tawney Avenue
Corbets Tey Road	Leasway	The Avenue
Courtenay Gardens	Lee Gardens Avenue	The Crescent
Cowper Road	Lewis Road	The Drive
Craigdale Road	Limerick Gardens	The Grove
Cranham Gardens	Link Way	The Shrubbery
Cranham Road	Little Gaynes Lane	Upper Brentwood
Cranston Park Avenue	Longfield Avenue	Road
Cromer Road	Maclennan Avenue	Upland Court Road
Crystal Avenue	Malvern Road	Upminster Road,
Curtis Road	Manor Avenue	Hornchurch
David Drive	Mansfield Gardens	Upminster Road,
Dawes Avenue	Maple Avenue	Rainham
Dennises Lane	Maple Close	Urban Avenue
Devonshire Road	Mavis Grove	Vaughan Avenue
Deyncourt Gardens	Maybank Avenue	Vicarage Road
Diban Avenue	Maybrick Road	Victor Gardens
Dorian Road	Maybush Road	Waldegrave Gardens
Dymoke Road	Maylands Avenue	Walden Way
East Close	Maywin Drive	Warley Street
East Hall Lane	Meadowside Road	Warren Drive
Eastern Avenue	Meadow Way	Wayside Avenue
Eastwood Drive	Melstock Avenue	Wennington Road
Edison Avenue	Melville Road	West Close
Ellis Avenue	Michael Gardens	Westland Avenue
Elm Avenue	Mill Park Avenue	Westmoreland Avenue
Elm Farm Road	Minster Way	Whitethorn Gardens
Elm Grove	Moor Lane	Willow Close
Elm Park Avenue	Morecambe Close	Windermere Avenue
Engayne Gardens	Nelmes Road	Wingletye Lane
Ernest Road	Nelmes Way	Winifred Avenue
Ethelburga Road	Norfolk Road	Woburn Avenue
Eyhurst Avenue	North Ockendon Road	Woodcote Avenue
Fairfield Avenue	North Street	Woodhall Crescent
Fairfield Close	Northumberland	Woodlands Avenue
Fairkytes Avenue	Avenue	Wykeham Avenue

It is hoped that owners will be prepared to make a free gift of their railings etc., to the nation, but property owners and others whose interests are affected by the removal and who desire to claim compensation may obtain the appropriate form from the undersigned.

Under the provisions of the Compensation (Defence) Act, 1939, no claim for compensation ordinarily can be entertained unless notice of claim has been given to the appropriate authority within a period of six months from the date of removal of the railings, etc.

Under the provisions of Regulation 50, paragraph (3A) of the Emergency Powers (Defence) General Regulations no person shall be liable, by virtue of any obligation imposed by any lease or other instrument affecting the land or by or under any enactment or otherwise to replace or provide a substitute for the thing severed, or to pay any sum by way of damages or penalty or to suffer any forfeiture in consequence of a failure to perform any such obligation, and any person who has guaranteed the performance of any such obligation shall be correspondingly relieved of his liability under the guarantee.

Council Offices,
Billet Lane,
Hornchurch.
28th April, 1942.

WILLIAM C. ALLEN,
Clerk of the Council.

A collection of another kind. The requisitioning of unnecessary railings to help the war effort.

THE GREAT ROMFORD RATION BOOK ROBBERY

Towards the end of the war, clothing rationing, based on a coupon system, was introduced. Inevitably a black market trade grew up, and Clothing Rationing books were changing hands at anything up to £5 each. The Food Office at "Normanhurst" on the corner of Main Road and Pettits Lane, had large cellars underneath and all the books from Romford and Hornchurch were stored there. Security was tight, the only door was locked and burglar-alarmed and two night-watchmen patrolled the premises and telephoned the Police at regular intervals to confirm everything was in order. Nevertheless, the thieves struck one night, entering the cellars via an outside lavatory. In making the elaborate safety arrangements, it had been completely overlooked that in the rambling building only a thin wooden floor lay between the outside convenience and the rear of the cellars. The thieves merely dropped through into the cellars from the outside of the building, and carried the parcels of books in sacks across the rear garden to a lorry parked in readiness in an access way off Pettits Lane. The crime was obviously highly organised and must have been based in some way on inside information. Ironically, while the thieves were busy working underneath, the night watchmen up above were cheerfully reporting to the Police that everything was in order! It was not until a Police Constable patrolling the outside of the building, in the early morning, nearly fell through the lavatory floor, that the crime was detected. By this time the thieves were miles away, leaving only a few empty sacks and some tyre tracks as evidence. Over 100,000 books were stolen, having a Black-Market value of about half a million pounds. Up-dated, this would amount to 12½ million pounds, and puts it in the same class as the Great Train Robbery. For security reasons, however, it did not receive the same publicity. Some months later, a few of the books were traced by their serial numbers to the Southend Area, but it was a cold trail, and the bulk was never recovered. Despite the efforts of the 'big brass' from Headquarters and Scotland Yard who swarmed over the Food Office, the culprits were never found.

Fred Barnes.

The wailing of the first siren on the bright sunny Sunday morning of 3rd September 1940, just eight minutes after Neville Chamberlain had announced, "....consequently this country is at war with Germany", caught many residents unprepared and resulted in frantic efforts to complete their shelters before the waves of expected German bombers appeared. One Upminster resident at the time remembers the last minute activity in her household.

"As a family, how unprepared we were! My brothers still in their pyjamas, anxiously grabbed their gas-masks when they heard the announcement. There followed a frantic digging in the back garden to prepare a hole for a shelter - but to our consternation a vital water pipe was uncovered and so another site had to be quickly chosen."

Some shelters had been delivered as early as April 1939, although many had shamefully been left unassembled and simply mouldered in a secluded part of the garden. Fortunately, the waves of German aircraft failed to materialize, the sirens having been a false alarm. In fact it was to be another ten months before the Luftwaffe appeared over the skies of Havering. This long lull gave both the local authority and private citizens the chance to prepare for the storm to come.

When the bombing did commence it was surprising how quickly people fell into the routine of taking shelter. "I would come from the train at Upminster station and as I reached the top of my road, the air raid warning would invariably be sounding. I would race for home to find mother calmly and carefully carrying a tray of food for us all to the shelter - as if it was the most natural thing to be doing. On one occasion we emerged from our shelter one winter's morning to find the previously bleak garden carpeted by a thick snowfall. The sudden discovery of a blanket of virgin white snow, which must have drifted down amongst the rain of shrapnel and bombs, seemed to accentuate the bizarre nature of the times. My mother remarked, "We must be mad living like this: rabbits coming out of their holes". One day I did not manage to reach home in time as the gunfire was heavy and seemed right overhead. I knocked at the nearest house of a person I knew only by sight, and asked if I could take shelter with her. We all (for she had several children) finished up under the stairs, until the danger seemed to have passed, when I thanked her and hurried home. Looking back on the scene - how strange it was that within minutes of walking along the road, there I was pressed close to a number of comparative strangers, but I was merely following my mother's instructions when she had said, "Never try to reach home in an air-raid, but knock at the nearest house and ask to be let in". I wonder if a mother would dare say such words to her teenage daughter today, and feel peace of mind?"

❑ The Anderson.

The most common type of domestic shelter was the 'Anderson', named after Sir John Anderson, the then Home Secretary. The Anderson was supplied free to all those earning under £250 per annum and at the cost of £7 to those whose earnings were higher. It consisted of six or more curved corrugated steel sheets which on arrival simply required bolting together to form an archway. This was then sunk 4ft into the ground and the top covered with at least fifteen inches of soil. If these construction methods were adhered to, the Anderson was capable of standing up to all but a direct hit. It had been designed to withstand a 500lb bomb falling twenty feet away or a 100lb bomb six feet away.

Shelters

Unfortunately this brilliant design suffered from one major drawback. In the majority of soil conditions if the shelter was sunk 4ft below ground there was an inevitable seepage of water and in time the shelter simply filled up. One Hornchurch Councillor commented at the time, ''When the history of the Anderson shelters comes to be written it would be shown to be one of the greatest hoaxes ever perpetrated. It was quite apparent that when it decided to distribute shelters the Government had no idea what the soil of districts such as Hornchurch was like.'' This was probably overstating the case, but the misery of trying to sleep in these damp conditions led many families to construct their Anderson shelters above ground. In many ways this was counterproductive for although it alleviated the problem of dampness it greatly reduced the shelter's strength and as a result led to many unnecessary shelter tragedies.

One of the first Anderson Shelters to be delivered is assembled by two Romford Schoolboys in a Lodge Avenue Garden

One enterprising Gidea Park householder got round the dampness problem by erecting his Anderson Shelter over the bed in his bedroom. He had good reason to, for his wife had just given birth to a beautiful baby girl. The photo shows the family on the bed under the shelter, gazing at the new arrival in her cot.

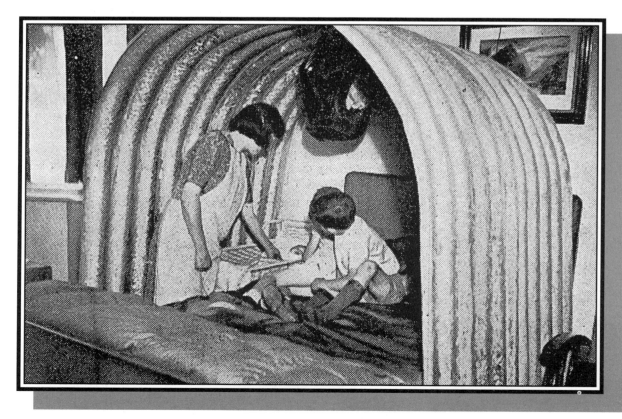

(Above) Close up of an Anderson Shelter to the rear of No's. 17 - 23 Oliver Road, South Hornchurch, after a parachute mine fell nearby on 21st January 1944. Notice how the corrugated sheeting has been peppered by small fragments of shrapnel and flattened by the blast.

(Below) A bomb dropped right next to this occupied Anderson Shelter in Albert Road, Romford, but fortunately the family of three was rescued alive.

Agnes makes a Complaint......

I'm so afraid for my daughter, she lives opposite. She's a cripple, she's had a T.B. hip, and had to have bone grafted on it, and all sorts of things, and she can hardly walk. And we had nowhere to go during the air raid. My shelter's full of water. I've been to the Town Hall...oh...four or five times. I'm getting fed up of going. It's so expensive too; 3d a time to get down there. I'd walk, only I'm not as strong as I used to be, not since I had an operation, it left me with a weak stomach. So, do you know, we had to stay here. I don't think it's fair, it isn't fair at all. She's a cripple, so she should be served first. I went to the town hall and they said I'd have to take my turn. Take my turn! It's not fair! It's full of water, you can't get inside it at all. I said to them, I said I wouldn't mind waiting, only the cart come along here several times a day, to pump out other people's water. They come next door, about a week ago, and stopped at the bottom of my garden. I went up to the man, and I said to him,

''I don't mind if you don't concrete it'' I said,

''So long as you pump it, so's we can use it.''

But ''no'' he said, he said he can't do anything until he's been told at the town hall. Came back here a few days ago, to do someone else's. Lovely concrete bottom they got next door, but they can't stop and do mine, Oh, dear no. So I went to the Town Hall, I was ever so upset, and I told them, I said,

''It isn't fair, especially when my daughters a cripple''.

She hasn't got one you see she's only been here a few weeks. So they said, well, they didn't know where the cart was, but if I could find it, I could have mine done. I went all round the streets looking for it, I did. I found one in the end, too, in a bit of waste land, but the men wouldn't come and do it. I went up there again, and was so upset, I broke down. It don't half make you feel a fool. Only there's such a stench from it, all the water just lying there. It's given me a sore throat. I wouldn't bother, only you read in the papers about everyone getting killed who stayed in the house. They put that in to warn you, and then they don't give you any way of going down there. It's a terrible thing not to have anywhere to go. I think they ought to look after cripples first. They did in London. It's only in Romford they do such things. I was so annoyed about my shelter. I'd thought of writing to Mr. Anderson about it...'Anderson Shelters', Indeed!

As soon as I heard the last air raid warning, I went over to fetch my daughter. My husbands away you see, so's hers. He was called up with the 24's. It was awful all those police whistles. We went next door, all of us. It was very nice of them only you don't like too, there was seven of them without us, and I believe the lodger had to stand outside, to make room for us. Then it wasn't very nice, because they wasn't dressed. They're very nice people, but very slow, and when we knocked on the their door, they was still dressing. I felt I wanted to be in their quick, and they was still putting their things on. Then you have to go right through their house and into the back garden before you get to the shelter, well, you could get hit before then, couldn't you? We stayed in the shelter the whole time. It wasn't half hot, with us all there. Began to stink it did.

Collier Row Woman, Aged 40.   Mass Observation June 1940

86

Gertrude has a grumble.....

You see, we haven't got a shelter. They wouldn't let us have one, because my husband doesn't pay insurance. Well that's absurd. We need one as much as the man next door. I don't suppose for a minute we earn more than he does. What happened was, the man came round here, and he said,

''Does your husband pay insurance?'' and I said ''No'' and he said,

''Well, I'm very sorry, but he can't have a shelter.''

I shouldn't have minded, but you see, I've taken in a little girl, and adopted her, and I don't think it's fair to her. She's a very nervy child, and she's my responsibility. I went to the Town Hall, and I asked them if I could have the one in the empty house a few doors away, and they said ''No'', and the very next day, a man from the other end of the road comes and takes it, without permission. I go and ask nicely, and they refuse. Yet a man without permission , but a lot of cheek, comes here and takes it. I shouldn't have minded if it wasn't for the little girl. Then to be told in the papers that we could have one, so I went there and showed them the bit in the News Chronicle, and they said,

''We're not responsible for what they put in the newspapers.''

Cheek of it, and only a young fellow too. They said I could be put on a waiting list 400 hundred long. Now I ask you, why is there a waiting list? Who are these four hundred? Newcomers, or what? Why should there be a waiting list? I've heard too, that there's piles of shelters by Romford Station that have been standing there for weeks, and the man who told me said I could use his name and address if I wanted to. I'm not going to leave it at that indeed I'm not. They said at the beginning I could buy one for £8. Well, where can I get £8 from? Why SHOULD I? I've as much right to a shelter as anyone else, especially when I've done my bit by taking in this little girl.

Collier Row Woman, Aged 45.   Mass Observation. June 1940

Irate mothers and children from Collier Row marched to Romford Town Hall to protest about the flooding of their garden shelters. October 1939

Banana Boxes

It was funny, I always said I'd never go down the shelter, we always said it wasn't much good, but there it was, all that we did was to go down there, as soon as we heard the siren, just as though we'd been doing it for years. It didn't take us long. We've a lot of things down there, we've got what they call 'banana boxes' all round there. They're cheaper than chairs, though there is a shilling on them. My chap said to me the other day, "Where are them boxes, we could get the shillings on them'', but I said nothing, and he never noticed what he was sitting on last night.

❏ APPLEBY DUMPLING

Another shelter design was that of the Appleby Shelter, known colloquially as 'Appleby Dumpling'. It had the appearance of a concrete igloo and took its name from the designer, Mr. F.V. Appleby, Romford's Borough Engineer and Surveyor. Unfor-

tunately this brilliant and dynamic man felt compelled to resign in January 1941 owing to petty departmental strife within the council. His design lived on however and gave a distinctive look to many wartime back gardens.

The blast from a rocket which fell in Collier Row Lane has sliced the top off this Appleby Dumpling some 30ft from the crater.

Intact Appleby Dumplings 30-60 yards from the same rocket crater.

❏ BRICK SURFACE SHELTERS

A design which tended to be widely despised was that of the 'domestic brick surface shelter'. It was essentially a windowless brick square with a concrete slab roof. Although vastly superior in terms of safety than a house, it was still above ground and thus particulaly susceptible to blast damage and it was this that made it so universally unpopular. Public shelters of the same type, but larger capacity were also built in large numbers, for people who had no garden in which to erect a shelter or for those caught away from home in a raid. Many still remain to this day in parks and schools, some having been converted to public toilets or secure storage for council property.

A destroyed brick surface shelter at the rear of houses in Hainault Road, Romford, following the fall of a V1 Flying Bomb close by.

The De-Angelis Shelter

The advertisement above portrays a cosy view of family life in a shelter. Unfortunately the harsh realities of war often impinged on this cheery scenario. **(See left)**

The shattered remnants of a "De-Angelis" shelter in Fairholme Avenue, situated twelve yards from where a rocket fell.

❑ WARDENS POSTS

For those on duty during a raid in some civil defence capacity, the dangers were still greater. Air-raid wardens, a target of derision during the inactivity of the 'Phoney War', were now in the front line and particularly vulnerable as they were expected to give a report on every bomb. which fell in their sector the moment it occurred. Each wardens post was provided with a concrete shelter, but even within its confines there was no guarantee of safety.

At a quarter to midnight on 20th October 1940, 34 year old, William Winn was killed whilst on duty in his concrete Wardens' Post at Wennington Road, Rainham, when a 50kg bomb exploded at the base of the outside wall.

❑ The Morrison

When it became apparent that many people were determined to stay in their homes what ever Hitler might send over, the Government introduced the indoor Morrison shelter. It too took its name from the Home Secretary, Herbert Morrison, the successor to Sir John Anderson. Made from angled steel it resembled a work bench with wire mesh sides and was designed to stand up under the weight of a collapsed house. Being introduced in the Autumn of 1941, after the end of the main Blitz, it saw most usage during the V1 and V2 campaigns in the latter stages of the war, when it was to prove itself over and over again. The one obvious disadvantage of the Morison was that if your house was unlucky enough to be demolished by a bomb, you might well survive the blast but then faced the very unenviable proposition of being entombed beneath the remains of your home awaiting rescue, possibly several hours later.

The Morrison Shelter

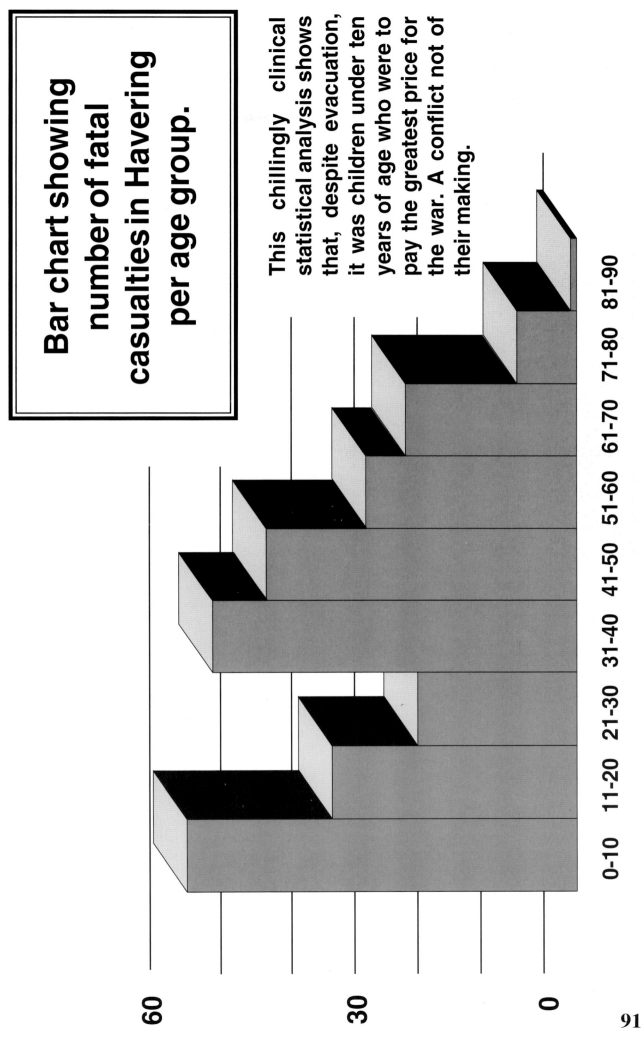

Bar chart showing number of fatal casualties in Havering per age group.

This chillingly clinical statistical analysis shows that, despite evacuation, it was children under ten years of age who were to pay the greatest price for the war. A conflict not of their making.

Age of Fatality

0-10   11-20   21-30   31-40   41-50   51-60   61-70   71-80   81-90

60

30

0

A Galvanised Bucket and a Song!

At the factory where I worked, shelters were available, if rather rudimentary. We sometimes had to spend long periods of time down there and if the call of nature became very strong it took quite a nerve to rise from the long bench seats to disappear behind a curtain and 'go' into a galvanised bucket, and one therefore, held on as long as possible.

On one occasion, a desperate female employee told her friends "I can't hold on any longer, please sing loudly while I'm behind the curtain." Suddenly, much to the surprise of the others, a small group started singing lustily. The only thing was we were unsure how long the song should last, so we kept adding another verse until she blushingly reappeared.

A cheerful band of school children, from Rainham and South Hornchurch, give the thumbs up to to the prospect of evacuation. This photograph was taken in June 1940, at Hornchurch Railway Station. Do you recognise anyone amongst this happy throng? Are you one of the evacuees?

Having shown all the damaged shelters, the question might be asked were they of any use at all. The answer has to be a resounding 'yes'. There were inevitably many who advocated remaining in the warmth of ones bed no matter how great the raid, with familiar fatalistic views that if a bomb had 'your name on it' , that was your lot no matter where you were. Others chose to remain indoors in a calculated act of defiance, in a mood of ''It'll take more than bloody Hitler to make me leave my bed.

However, if we dispense with emotion and look at the risks analytically, it was statistically far safer to take to any type of shelter in a raid than not to do so.

Of all the traces that remain of the war years, the shelter, in all its different guises, has been the most enduring. Scarcely a street exists in which one house does not still possess a shelter. Some of the types that were sunk in the ground have been completely covered over with soil and remain just a puzzling hump in the back garden, whilst others such as the Anderson have been converted into practical and robust potting sheds. Whatever their use they remain a physical reminder of a time when it was necessary to protect oneself from the threat of death that rained down nightly. A strange troglodyte existence, hiding from an unknown and unseen figure, trying to kill you from on high.

A perceptive Essex journalist wrote at the end of the war, that a British family discussing in the year 2000, what 1939-1945 was like, might well make the mistake of "exaggerating the dangers and under-estimating the discomforts."

We have not quite reached the millennium, though indeed his prophecy is probably already true, because for those too young to have experienced it at first hand, 'The War' and 'The Blitz' are virtually synonymous, with the common belief that the bombing was virtually continuous. To put the war years in perspective, of the 68 long months of its duration, Havering was under enemy bombardment for approximately 25 months. Thus it can be appreciated that between the major raids were long periods of relative tranquillity. The longest such period is that of the middle war years between June 1941 and Jan. 1944. With the might of the Luftwaffe committed to the monumental folly of Hitler's attack on the Soviet Union, Havering was subjected to only sporadic nuisance 'Tip & Run' raids by small numbers of aircraft. In the whole of this 2½ year period only two civilian lives would be lost (if 'only' can be used in this context), both of these deaths being caused by seemingly freak occurrences.

The first of these incidents was the sad loss of 12 year-old Francis Bixby of Margaret Road, Romford, on the 28th July 1941. Francis had lived with his grandmother for some years. At the outset of the raid she went downstairs to seek shelter, but her grandson, ignoring her pleas to the contrary, insisted on going to his bedroom to sleep. At quarter to three in the morning four bombs fell in Catherine Road and Hamilton Road, over one hundred yards from their home. His grandmother called upstairs for him to come down at once, as the bombs had fallen in the next road, but she got no answer. She thought he was larking around and so went upstairs to fetch her disobedient grandson. On entering his room she found him in his bed, under a huge piece of masonry, which had apparently been hurled the 100 yards from where the bombs fell, before finally crashing through the roof and bedroom ceiling. An ambulance was summoned, but Francis died shortly after admission to hospital.

The second death came over two years later, on the 18th October 1943. It was that of 41 year-old Frederick Mann (a well known garage proprietor), of 27 Rockingham Avenue, Hornchurch. A bomb fell in the middle of the Avenue opposite Mr. Mann's house. A small fragment of it penetrated the downstairs room in which he was sleeping, at the exact moment as he sat up in reaction to the noise, and hence he was caught in the upper part of his body. It is thought if he had remained recumbent he would have escaped injury. For a long while the small bomb splinter could not be found and so the police were called in to reconstruct the scene and ensure there was no foul play of any kind. Eventually the tiny fragment of the bomb was located in the centre of several pieces of cloth, "looking very much like a rag ball".

Perhaps the most dramatic and memorable attack of that year had occurred some seven months previously, at 7:30 in the morning of 12th March 1943. With the exception of the brief period of the Battle of Britain, it was rare for the civilian to see their attacker and visa versa, but on the morning of the 12th, both came as close as they possibly could without actually meeting. The attack was carried out by up to 24 FW 190's, principally fighter aircraft, but capable of carrying a 500kg bomb for ground attack. The main force of aircraft had flown up the Thames Estuary and then turned over Barking and Ilford where they deposited 16 of their bombs, before heading back to the coast over Romford at roof top height with their cannons blazing. One eye witness

saw a Nazi plane fly between his own and his neighbours house at the height of the bedroom window, whilst another householder declared that, as one bomber flew over his roof "the down draught was so severe that it practically swept the chimney". Anything that caught the Germans eye that morning was fired upon, this included trains, buses and commuters, who were forced to dive for cover as the area was spattered with bullets. One bus driver caught sight of an aircraft heading straight for him at little more than the height of his bus. At that moment the plane opened fire, but by good luck and the timely evasive weaving of his bus, all the bullets whistled harmlessly past. The giant gas holders at Romford Gas Works could take no such evasive manoeuvres and so were consequently peppered with bullets. Two of the holders were hit and immediately caught fire, with burning gas billowing out of the holes. The British claimed to have shot down six of the enemy planes that day, but post war reference to German records show that in fact only one aircraft was destroyed.

A gas-holder at Romford Gas Works, March 12th, 1943, following their straffing by several German Fw 190's. Using clay to plug the bullet holes, the asbestos suited figure successfully extinguished the fires.

The original caption for the photograph above was 'Courage on a gas-Holder'. In taking this comparison photograph it occurred to me that I should perhaps entitle this one, 'Cowardice on the gas-holder', as I am not too proud to admit that I found the height rather intimidating and that was with the holder at its lowest level. Harry Madgett (Site Foreman), immune to my foolishness, helps in the search for the illusive sign of wartime bullet holes.

The Strange Case of No. 23 Hawthorn Avenue, Rainham.

5:15 p.m. on 4th September 1942.

Boooommmmm!!! - the sound of the massive explosion that consumed No. 23 Hawthorn Avenue and three of the neighbouring houses, but why? There had not been a bomb dropped on Havering for over a year, so what was the cause of this strange explosion? A clue is to be found in the two men who died that day. They were Sergeant E.J. Hammond and Sapper J.M. Davies.

Our story reverts to 8th October 1940 when during the night the residents of the above address heard a bomb whistle towards their home - Thump!

In the morning the site was visited by members of the Surveyors Department who were puzzled at the small amount of damage surrounding the 8 foot diameter crater. The house in question had slightly moved on its damp-course and there were visible, but small, cracks in the wall of the house. It was reported to the Bomb Disposal Squad , and both they and the police came to the the conclusion that this was the work a small bomb which had exploded.

Rebuilt. No. 23 Hawthorn Avenue today. For nearly two years home to an unexploded 1000 kg bomb.

Throughout the Blitz of 1940 - 41 the hard pressed Bomb Disposal Squads found that the number of unexploded bombs requiring their attention steadily increased. On one night alone in November 1940, a stick of nineteen bombs fell across Romford, in a line from Crow Lane to Lodge Avenue, all failing to explode. It was a miraculous escape for the town. In an attempt to tackle this ever growing backlog, a system was devised whereby the bombs which were likely to cause the greatest disruption, should they explode, were given top priority, whilst those in outlying areas had to await less hectic times before being dealt with. By September 1942, the Luftwaffe had not dropped any type of bomb on Havering for over a year and this lull enabled the Disposal Squads to successfully clear the majority of U.X.B.'s in the area. A great deal of experience was gained in this period and thus it was determined that in many instances where it had previously been thought a bomb had exploded, there might, in fact, still be an U.X.B. It was not as obvious to tell whether a bomb had exploded, or not, as one might think. Dropped from a great height as they were, a bomb, weighing anything from 50kg to 2500kg, which failed to explode on impact, might penetrate tens of feet into soft ground. As it travelled through the earth it was quite common for the bomb to veer off at a tangent and so upon investigation of the hole it was virtually impossible to see the offending missile. It was therefore feasible to mistake the disturbance of a large U.X.B. entering the ground for that of the crater of a far smaller bomb which had exploded.

With this fact in mind it was decided that 23 Hawthorn Avenue was worthy of further investigation. Sure enough, there it was, nestling deep in the ground, a massive one ton bomb (1000kg). For close on two years, the occupants on No. 23, had slept, eaten, and gone about their daily lives, whilst sitting on an unexploded bomb. Now that its true status was known, there was no alternative but to dig the monster out and attempt to defuse it. To this end a Rest Centre was duly opened to accommodate those evacuated from their homes for the duration of the defusal procedure.

The task of tackling the bomb fell to the 22nd Bomb Disposal Group of the Royal Engineers (5 Batt Artillery). Once sufficient excavation had revealed the bomb, the B.D.S. set about the sensitive task of steaming out the explosive from the case of the bomb. The squad sensibly withdrew a safe distance whilst this operation was being carried out.

At a little after 5:00 p.m. on the 4th September a dispatch rider, Sapper Davies, arrived on the scene with a message. Out of curiosity, he along with the sergeant in charge, Sgt. Hammond, approached the rim of the excavation. The events which followed will forever remain a mystery, maybe they interfered with the bomb in some way, or maybe they were just extraordinarily unlucky to have gone to inspect it at the wrong moment. We shall never know. The only two people who could have told, died instantaneously when the bomb exploded.

Despite the long lull in air raids, there was one Rescue Squad, one First Aid Party and an Ambulance on the scene within five minutes. In addition to the two military casualties, there was only one other serious casualty, a small boy aged four, who although some distance away from the explosion, had the misfortune to be hit by falling masonry (part of No. 23 ?). As the dust settled, it was plain to see that for four families all that remained of their homes was a giant crater and pile of rubble.

I have no wish to be a scaremonger, but it is fair to surmise that not withstanding the best efforts of the B.D.S., many more such unexploded bombs lie undisturbed and forgotten. The likelihood of their being located in residential areas is small, but in the more remote and rural parts of the Borough they undoubtedly exist. (At the time of writing, the Thurrock-Dartford Bridge is under construction and in the course of excavations several such bombs have been discovered). Hopefully these bombs will languish in peaceful oblivion for another fifty years.

Holidays-at-Home

To compensate for seaside delights denied by the mining of beaches and associated anti-invasion measures, people were encouraged to 'holiday-at-home'. There was really no alternative, continental travel a rarity before the war, was now out of the question with the Nazi domination of mainland Europe, and even tourism in Britain was severely constrained by travel restrictions. The local councils therefore laid on entertainment in the local parks to relieve some of the monotony. One such entertainment- a beauty contest of local girls!

Romford's five most beautiful girls of 1942 attracted a record crowd of 9000 at Raphael Park for the finals of Romford's Home Holiday Beauty Contest. The winner was No.5, Miss Georgina Bowers, a waitress, aged 19, of Rainham Road, Romford. Second was No.4, Miss Vera Bradshaw of Rush Green. The other contestants were: No. 1 , Miss O. Hopgood, aged 17, a Romford shop assistant; No. 2, Miss S. Heath, aged 19, of Hornchurch, an inspectress of production at a factory ; and No. 3, Miss F. Goss, aged 22, a typist from Dagenham. I bet they all imagined their youthful exuberance had long been forgotten.

O on the 27th November 1943, Goering faithfully promised Hitler, that the Luftwaffe would mount a series of heavy attacks on London within two weeks, in revenge for heavy allied raids on Berlin. These raids were to be known to the Germans as 'Operation Steinbock', although to the British they became the 'Baby Blitz'.

Only a small German bomber force had operated over Britain during 1943 and many of these had fallen prey to the greatly improved defences. Goering insisted that at least 300 aircraft should take part in the raids and that each aircraft perform an arduous two sorties during one night. To achieve a strike force of this magnitude, inevitably meant robbing aircraft from equally hard pressed fronts elsewhere, but to carry out the Fuhrer's wishes this was duly done.

Since the last heavy raids of the Blitz back in the Spring of 1941 German scientist and designers had not been idle and as a result the Luftwaffe now had access to an array of new weapon systems. These included the Heinkel 177 four engined bomber, the only German aircraft capable of carrying two 2500kg 'MAX' bombs, the largest in the Luftwaffe's arsenal. The orders were that these exceptionally heavy bombs be used until stockpiles became exhausted, when slightly lighter weapons be used. Goering further ordered that 70% of the payload for the attacks should be made up of firebombs, as it had been clearly displayed by the R.A.F.'s bombing of German cities that whereas conventional bombs destroyed approximately 1¾ acres for every ton dropped, each ton of incendiaries could destroy over 3¼ acres. To deliver these incendiaries a new type of container was used, the AB 1000, capable of holding over 600 1kg incendiary bombs. Even a new type of incendiary entered the fray, the IBSEN (incendiary bomb with separating exploding nose). As the name suggests, it possessed a separating steel explosive nose that blew apart from the incendiary section on impact and after a short delay exploded, a deterrent to tackling the bomb once alight. Another weapon newcomer was the SB 1000 Parachute Mine, especially designed for use against built up areas. Yet another unfamiliar ingredient of the raids was the use of 'Dueppel' (window to the British), strips of aluminium foil dropped by the German aircraft, to disrupt and confuse the radar. By the end of the raids Havering was to have received a taste of each and everyone of these new aspects of warfare.

Operation Steinbock was planned to commence during a period of full moon in December 1943, but it was not until the third week of January that men and machines were ready. Finally at half past ten in the evening of Friday 21st January 1944, the first of the 220 raiders taking part appeared on the British radar screens. It was soon apparent to the radar operators that they were witnessing the start of a raid, the magnitude of which had not been seen since 1941. As they approached the coast each crew dropped radar confusing 'Dueppel' every thirty seconds. They crossed the coast around Folkestone and headed straight for their target which was set as the area surrounding Waterloo Station. Once having dropped their bomb load, though not all, they turned eastwards and headed out towards the Thames Estuary.

At 21:07 hostile aircraft were heard over Havering at an estimated height of 10,000 ft and a number of flares were seen to be dropped. At 21:12 numerous incendiaries fell on Rainham and then at 21:16 a bomber was seen to release a single bomb which descended by parachute before exploding in the back gardens of houses bounded by Harlow, Blacksmith Lane & Oliver Road, South Hornchurch. The attacking aircraft was described as a very fast twin engined bomber.

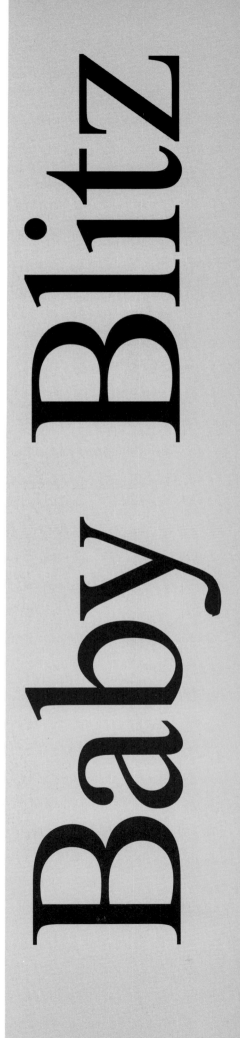

A report made at the time by an officer for the Ministry of Home Security reads as follows:-

"Observers stated the missile fell with a noise not unlike escaping steam under pressure, faster than an ordinary parachute mine and slower than an ordinary bomb, and that it burst with a colour best described as bright purplish shot with yellow streaks. A cloud of black smoke (or dust) was seen in the light of the flares of the explosion which the local post warden who was on duty in Blacksmith's Lane described as a dull thud! Mr. & Mrs. Thomas of 23 Oliver Road state that they saw the missile fall. They appear to be reliable and made no attempt to embellish their story, which is not particularly illuminating. Mr. Thomas exclaimed, "It's as big as a door, LOOK OUT!" and turned to rush inside. The missile exploded with the effects described above and both observers were promptly knocked out. They were approximately 145 ft from the point of impact and except for superficial cuts and bruises were none the worse for the experience."

As a result of the explosion twenty people were injured, the most serious being Mrs. Till who sustained head and leg injuries and a broken arm. Tragically it was the third time she had lost everything in air raids. There were fatalities however,

twelve chickens were killed where they roosted. Ironically, one five year old girl was saying her prayers for all injured people everywhere when the bomb fell in the back garden. She was cut by flying glass.

In terms of material damage, 32 homes were seriously damaged, although of major significance to those it directly affected, this explosion would not have been of great interest to the Ministry of Home Security by itself. The importance of this particular bomb was that it was thought to be an example of a new type of weapon. Every piece of available evidence was assessed in an attempt to correctly identify it. By collecting bomb fragments, measuring the bomb crater and studying the damage to surrounding buildings, the bomb was ultimately identified as the SB 1000 Parachute Bomb. It measured 4ft long by 2ft 7in. wide with an oval cross section and so Mr. Thomas' description of it being "as big as a door" was quite apt allowing for the alarming nature of his sighting, and undoubtedly had he stood to gaze at it a second longer he might not have escaped so lightly. This 1000 kg bomb was designed to fit in the bomb bay of the Messerschmitt Me. 410 and so we can safely assume that this was the offending aircraft that night.

21/1/44. The return of the parachute mine creates a scene more reminiscent of the 1940/41 Blitz. All the work of the new and deadly SB1000. The crater is in the foreground, with No's 17 - 23 Oliver Road in the background.

Nos. 8 - 12 Harlow Road suffered at the hands of the same mine. Bedrooms and bathrooms exposed to the world.

The Culprit? The Messerschmitt Me. 410a fighter bomber. It was this type of aircraft which was responsible for dropping the SB1000 parachute mine on Harlow Road/ Oliver Road, at 10:30 p.m. on 21st January 1944.

Once the bombers returned to their bases they were hurriedly re-armed and re-fuelled, and before long the sirens were signalling their return over England. At just after five in the morning the first bombs of the second sortie began falling. A Heinkel 177 released two massive 'MAX' bombs shortly there after. They fell twenty yards apart, just east of Church Lane, North Ockendon, adjacent to North Ockendon Hall. Fortunately two straw stacks took the brunt of the blast, although North Ockendon Hall was still left extremely battered by the experience. Had these monster bombs fallen on a residential area the result would have been calamitous Fortunately Havering was spared on this occasion. This second sortie once again released a quantity of incendiary bombs over the area in the new AB 1000 containers. These containers, often incorrectly referred to as 'Molotov Bread Baskets' were designed to be dropped from aircraft and then open at a predetermined height to give a concentrated pattern of fires. Worst affected was the Albert Road and Victoria Road area where numerous houses were set ablaze. A number of incendiaries also penetrated the roof of the hop store and bottling departments at Romford Brewery. For hours on that Saturday morning the main streets surrounding the brewery were lined with hoses and pumps employed in combating the huge fire that developed.

Killed by an incendiary

An incendiary bomb weighing just over 2lbs had surprising penetrating power, so much so that sometimes even a house was not adequate protection. Mrs. Fulcher describes what befell her 68 year old husband, Harold, that same night. ''My husband was sitting at the table playing patience. He always used to do this during a raid as he said it steadied his nerves. Suddenly I heard a whistle. I shouted 'DUCK!' to him. He move aside and the bomb hit him on the neck. He slipped off the chair and lay on the floor. I called out 'Harry, speak to me.' He tried to speak, his lips moved and nothing came out and then he was gone. If he hadn't moved he would have probably survived.''

Not all injuries that night were caused by enemy action. The very last anti-aircraft shell to be fired at the Luftwaffe failed to explode and returned to earth still live. It demolished chimneys of No. 30 Howard Road, Upminster, and then crashed through the roof of No.28 where it exploded, injuring three people. Mr. Walter Farnes was taken to hospital with severe shrapnel wounds to the arm.

The heaviest bomb dropped on Britain during the Second World War was the 'MAX', over twelve feet long and 2½ tons in weight. In the early morning of 22nd January 1944, Church Lane, North Ockendon, was the recipient of two of these monsters. They fell just 20 yards apart, opposite North Ockendon Hall and produced two craters 40 feet across and ten feet deep. Although showing the obvious signs of blast North Ockendon Hall was left standing, why? The reason was that in between the craters and the Hall were two straw stacks and these helped absorb the blast. Their remnants can be seen in the foreground. Sadly the Hall is no longer in existence, for it was demolished in post war years.

Death From Our Own Guns

A week later another rogue anti-aircraft shell was to strike again. A 34-year-old woman, Miss Alice Sharp, was killed when a shell exploded outside 14 Ascension Road, Collier Row. Miss Sharp was a Fire-Watcher and although it was not her night on duty she was ready to go out in an emergency. She was standing by the front door when to the accompaniment of a whistle and a crash she was struck on the head by a piece of shrapnel from the shell. Alice was rushed to hospital, but it was to no avail, she was found to be dead on arrival.

At times it seemed that the anti-aircraft shells were more hazardous to British civilians than they were to the enemy, but as if to redress the balance a terrific success was scored only ten days later. A shell achieved a direct hit on a German bomber, a Junkers 88S-1 on a pathfinding mission and caused it to break up in mid air. It then tumbled from the sky and crashed at Havering-atte-Bower.(For the full story of the crash see appendix on air crashes)

Warden At His Post Meets With Tragedy

The scale of these 'Baby Blitz' raids bore no comparison with the devastating raids that had taken place three years previously and yet there was still real danger for those unlucky enough and indeed brave enough to be on duty as an air raid warden throughout a raid. On the 3rd February, Frank Garwood was on duty outside his warden's post in the grounds of Branfil School, Cedar Avenue, Upminster. His wife, also a warden, was on duty inside. Mr. Garwood would have been on the look out for any falling bomb or incendiary, so that he could immediately report its fall and then go to the

aid of its victim. At quarter to six in the morning he may have detected the first sound of a falling bomb. It would have grown louder and louder, until suddenly he must have realized just how close it was going to fall. By this time he had left it too late and was caught in the full force of the blast, for it fell only a few yards away in the middle of the road. His wife rushed from the warden's post, only to find her dying husband lying outside. Several bungalows were partially destroyed although apart from Mr. Garwood, casualties were light.

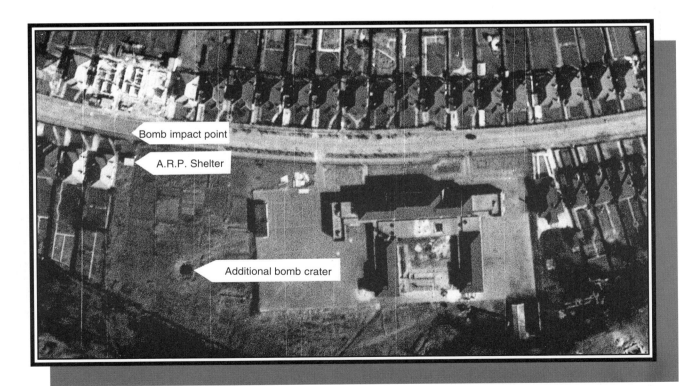

Bomb impact point

A.R.P. Shelter

Additional bomb crater

An aerial view of the damage caused in Cedar Avenue on 4th February 1944.

A fire-watcher who had been on duty close to where the bomb fell, went indoors moments before the explosion to fetch a cup of tea. He escaped all injury, but on rushing from his house to help those in the demolished bungalows, he tripped and badly injured his wrist and needed medical attention. Great gallantry was shown by one resident, Mr. George Moore, of Westway, Cedar Avenue, who successfully extinguished a gas main left blazing in the bomb crater. He modestly describes his actions of that night. "The fire was lighting up the place so much that my one thought was to get it out so that we shouldn't get any more trouble. I was the first on the scene and saw the end of the gas main alight in the crater. Two pipes were sticking out side by side, and I walked along these, then filled my steel helmet with mud and clamped it over the end of the pipe. This was quite successful, but unfortunately the pressure of the gas blew the tin hat off, and it fell into the mud and water at the bottom of the crater and was lost. I then scraped up more mud and blocked up the gas main with it." (Is that steel helmet still down there to this day? Will workmen digging up the road at sometime in the future come across a curious legacy of a forgotten act of courage?)

Bungalows in Cedar Avenue, Upminster, damaged by the bomb which fell in the middle of the road in the early morning of 4th February 1944. On the left of the picture is the Warden's Post, outside which Mr. Frank Garwood, aged 56, was mortally wounded by a bomb splinter. His wife Miriam just a few feet away inside the shelter, was spared.

The chipped concrete wall of the Warden's Post shows where the bomb splinters impacted.

The bungalows have been swathed in tarpaulins to keep the worst of the weather from the tileless roofs.

In 1994, the Warden's Post has vanished, but the railings of Branfil School remain. These are some of the few railings to have survived the various scrap metal drives of the war years. They presumably only escaped owing to the fact they were surrounding a School. An acacia tree flourishes where a life was lost.

Spared By Sabotage?

As already stated Goering had ordered that 70% of the payload for the 'Baby Blitz' should be made up of incendiary bombs and on the next raid of 13th February this is just what Havering received. The heaviest concentrations were around the southern parts of rural Upminster. A farmer and his son who farmed in the area saw a few incendiaries fall in the vicinity of the farmhouse. Seeking to avoid any further attention of the Luftwaffe they hurriedly put them out by smothering them with soil. One had fallen in a pond where it ignited and merrily burnt away under water (Yes they could do this). When daylight came they were somewhat surprised to find an undetonated incendiary bomb lying in a field. Upon looking further they discovered one or two more, then ten, then twenty, then one hundred and then finally somewhere in the region of 700. Being of a curious nature they decided to investigate exactly why so many should have failed to go off. They gingerly set about dismantling a specimen, for it was widely known at the time that a proportion of German incendiaries contained an explosive component. Fortunately no explosive charge was present and hence they were able to solve the riddle. The solution was simple, each and every incendiary had its striker pin installed upside down. How could this be? It may have been a production line oversight, but more probably it was the deliberate handiwork of one of the millions of forced labourers on mainland occupied Europe. Is it being too romantic to think that somewhere on a Nazi oppressed continent, an unknown foreign worker risked all, with his or her act of defiance, to spare this country in order that their longed for day of liberation might   be brought one tiny step closer?

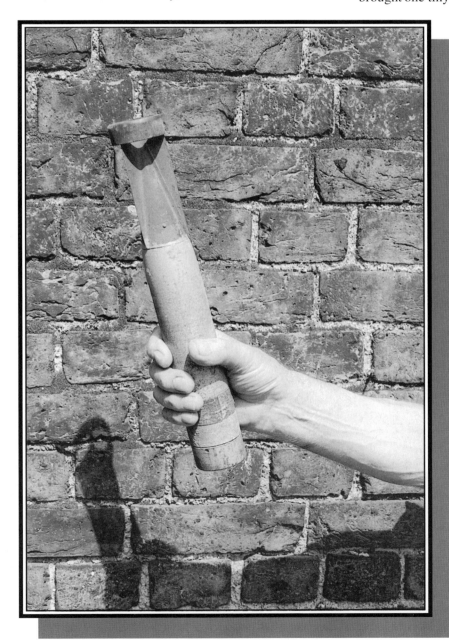

Once all the incendiaries had been collected, the farmer, who was then an air raid warden (albeit with a sense of humour), proceeded to follow the proper procedure and thus telephoned Upminster Police Station to inform them that he had been the recipient of 'some' undetonated incendiary bombs. Being quite unaware of the numbers involved the Policeman instructed him to bring them in. The bombs were therefore loaded on to a Ford Model B and as the good constable had instructed duly delivered to the Police Station. Needless to say they were somewhat taken aback at the prospect of dealing with a complete lorry load!

One of the 700 incendiary bombs was held back as a souvenir.

← DEMOLISHED

Once again Upminster was to suffer on the 23rd February 1944 when a bomb demolished a chemist's, a book shop and the four flats above, on the corner of Byron Mansions, Corbets Tey Road. Fortunately most of the residents had taken shelter elsewhere. One occupant, Mr. Cranston, decided to remain in the comfort of his home and was seriously injured as a result. Most of the shops in the parade lost their windows, but despite the broken glass and damaged stock, many were open for trade the next day. 'More open than usual' as the wartime pun goes. A subtle change of colour in the present day block work betrays the location of the Nazi aggression.

The Last German Raid

Throughout March 1944 it appeared that the 'Baby Blitz had all but finished and the first two weeks of April came and went without a single raid. Then on the 19th April the Luftwaffe mustered their forces for one last great effort. It was to be Romford's worst fire raid of the war and yet it was possibly all the work of just one or two aircraft. Four AB 1000 incendiary containers were dropped shortly after 1 o'clock in the morning. In amongst the standard incendiaries lurked those with separating exploding noses (I.B.S.E.N.) described previously. As the containers burst open at the designated height, four shoals of incendiaries, nearly 2,200 in total, were distributed over long suffering Romford below. The main concentrations were in an area from the Market Place to Cottons Recreation Ground and also from Pettits Lane to Havering Road School. Despite the valiant efforts of the fire watchers and members of the public, especially as so many were I.B.S.E.N's, the number of incendiaries was overwhelming and so a number of embryo fires took hold. These fires developed into major blazes and threatened to develop into a serious conflagration at one point.

Amongst those buildings destroyed were C.H. Allen's Garage in London Road along with the vehicles therein and Romford Brewery which was damaged for the third time. Also burnt out was Havering Road School Hall, forcing the School's closure for several days to the undoubted delight of the pupils. It was a stark demonstration of the effectiveness of this type of raid and it was all too easy to see how the fire-storms that had engulfed German cities could take hold, when so few planes could wreak such havoc here. Hundreds of people flocked to the scene as soon as the 'raiders past' siren had sounded. The whole centre of the town was so lit up that it was quite possible to read a newspaper in the orange glow. Even though there was a large amount of damage casualties were thankfully light. The only person to be killed was Mrs. Queenie Wallace, aged 27, of 5 James Square, St Andrew's Road, Romford, who fell prey to an exploding incendiary. She had been sheltering in the front room with her three children when hearing the incendiary fall in her kitchen she rushed in to deal with the menace. It exploded, a piece hitting her in the chest, killing her instantly.

It could not be appreciated or celebrated, but this was to be the last raid, by piloted aircraft, of the war.

Havering Road School, Romford, following the incendiary raid of 19th April 1944. What has the appearance of being the work of an over industrious mole is in fact the action of Incendiary Bombs with Separating Exploding Noses (I.B.S.E.N). The 2oz. charge in the separating nose was capable of forming these mini craters, nine of which can be seen in this photograph.

The Germans attempted to demolish Havering Road School from the air, whereas the educational authorities eliminated it with one stroke of the pen, by renaming it Parklands Junior & Infants. The school Keeper, Mr. Pedder, and his son help recreate the tableau of those earlier years

In the same raid of 19th April 1944 a Steel Nosed Incendiary Bomb (S.N.I.B.) landed on a Canadian Ram Tank. The tank was being stored along with others opposite Gidea Park Garage, pending D-Day. The steel nose of the incendiary increased its weight and its penetrative power, so much so, that it was able to pierce the tank's tool box, which was made of hardened bullet proof steel.

"**A**fter months of waiting, the hour has come for us to open fire! Today your wait and your work will have their reward. The order to open fire has been issued. Now that our enemy is trying to secure at all costs his foothold on the Continent, we approach our task supremely confident in our weapons; as we launch them, today and in the future, let us always bear in mind the destruction and suffering wrought by the the enemy's terror bombing. Soldiers! Fuhrer and Fatherland look to us, they expect our crusade to be an overwhelming success. As our attack begins, our thoughts linger fondly and faithfully upon native German soil.

Long live our Fatherland

Long live our Fuhrer! "

Max Wachtel 12th June 1944. (Colonel of V-1 Firing Regiment)

June 1944 saw the opening of the long awaited 'Second Front', when the Allies at last regained a foothold on mainland Europe, at Normandy.. With the Nazi war machine now being driven back on all fronts there seemed a real possibility that the war might be over by Christmas. All the suffering, saving and shortages appeared worthwhile now that there was a light at the end of the tunnel. The Luftwaffe as an offensive force was broken and so it was thought by many that the civilian was no longer to be in the front line. Unfortunately this was not to be the case. In the months that were to follow the presence of a new secret German weapon was to lay over the area like a pall. The arrival of the V-1 Flying Bomb heralded the entrance of human conflict into the robot age.

Just why did the V-1 come into being in the first place? Surprisingly the concept of an unpiloted flying bomb was not original, for both Britain and the U.S.A. had developed prototype designs by the closing stages of the First World War. The Armistice of 1918 removed the immediacy for such a weapon but its development continued, albeit at a slower pace, throughout the inter war years. With the rise to power of the Nazi Party, German military minds also considered the possibilities of such a weapon. Proposals for mass production were discarded however, as there seemed no need for the weapon after the crushing German military victories in, Poland in 1939, and in France and the Low countries in 1940.

By 1942 the supreme might of the Luftwaffe was no longer assured, and starting with Lubeck on 28th March 1942, Bomber Command initiated the systematic destruction of German towns and cities. Hitler raged and demanded retaliatory attacks against Britain. As Germany now commanded the French coast, the whole of the South East of England was now feasibly within range of a flying bomb. Inter service rivalry also gave an added boost to the flying bomb concept, for the German Army had already begun work on a rocket capable of bombarding London and thus it appeared to the Luftwaffe that they were losing their traditional role as the only means of long range bombardment. The Air Ministry in Berlin therefore gave the Fiesler Aircraft Company the formal specification of a flying bomb. It had to be an expendable weapon, inexpensive and simple to construct, but capable of reaching London. The ideal power unit for the job was the Argus Pulse Jet. It could deliver 770lb thrust, allowing a top speed of 400 mph, considerably faster than most fighters of the day, whilst still conforming to the need for simplicity.

Doodlebugs

The development of a German flying bomb had long been suspected by Allied Intelligence, as ground sources in Europe had long been reporting the existence of a sinister secret weapon with which Hitler intended to 'eliminate' London. During the summer of 1943, air reconnaissance sorties discovered the existence of strange looking ramps all aligned on England. What were they? The answer was simple. Until the Pulse Jet reached a high speed it did not develop enough thrust to keep the flying bomb airborne and so to achieve the threshold speed required, its take off had to be aided by a catapult. This consisted of an inclined track 150 ft long aligned on the intended target. At the end of the catapult the bomb reached a velocity of 150 mph and was then capable of flying under its own power. In excess of one hundred ramps were constructed along the French coast, aligned on London, Plymouth, Southampton and Bristol. Unfortunately the bombing of these sites, which were very costly in terms of lost aircraft and crew, did not have the desired result, for the Germans were one step ahead. They merely changed their method of construction, the new ramps being prefabricated and thus easily assembled within hours and hence need not be erected before they were ready to go into action.

The Germans were not having it all their own way however. They had planned to use their new wonder weapon to disrupt the Allies build up to 'D-Day', the invasion of mainland Europe, but this time schedule proved to be too optimistic and before a single V-1 had been launched, many ramp sites in Normandy and the Cherbourg Peninsula had been overrun.

By the 13th June 1944 they were finally ready. The order was given to open fire. This first attempt at a mass bombardment of London turned out to be a fiasco. The men who manned the sites were still not fully conversant with their weapon and much essential equipment had yet to be supplied. The plan had been to launch 500 that day, in fact only ten were launched, of which five crashed almost immediately and one shortly thereafter. Of the four that made it across the Channel, the first to fall on British soil was at Swanscombe in Kent. None reached Havering.

By the 15th June a lot of the earlier problems had been resolved and so in a twenty-four hour period, starting from 11:18 pm, over 150 were successfully launched. The description of this new 'pilotless aircraft' had been widely circulated to those involved in Civil Defence, but to those not privileged with this information, events that night were very strange indeed. Although the anti-aircraft guns were firing at the flying bombs, the majority had already reached the end of their prescribed journey and so crashed, as intended, without having been hit. It appeared to the layman however, that enemy bombers, with bombs on board, were being shot down in quick succession. This delusion faded, as not even the greatest optimist could believe so many bombers were suddenly falling prey to the guns. It became apparent that what one was witnessing was a new form of warfare altogether.

Men of the National Fire Service stand behind an unexploded V-1 Flying bomb being exhibited in Romford Market in aid of the N.F.S Benevolent Fund. It proved popular, over 5000 people paid a total of £97 to inspect it whilst at this location. The spherical object which can be seen beside it is one of two wire-bound compressed air spheres, which provided the power to operate the control surfaces and also inject the fuel.

❑ Rainham. The First

The dubious honour of the first to fall within the confines of Havering, seems to be shared by two flying bombs, both of which fell at 2:10 am. on the 16th June. One fell in Eastwood Drive, Rainham, where it claimed its first victim, 35 year-old, Alfred Howes. The other fell on farmland right on the boundary of Havering, North East of Moor Hall, Rainham. Later that morning a young local farmer went to investigate this strange new arrival. Whilst inspecting the shallow crater he heard the distant throbbing of yet another flying bomb. The noise grew louder and louder and then alarmingly cut out. He dropped to the floor as the flying bomb went into a dive. The blast from the resultant explosion shook the ground all around, for amazingly it fell within 50 yards of the first. After having flown so many miles it was impressive grouping. Upon investigation of the wreckage it was soon discovered that this was no ordinary example, for it was of a different and smaller design. Could it have been a prototype? As far as I am aware this was the only such specimen to fall in this country.

(ABOVE)

A V-1 that fell behind bungalows in Eastwood Drive, Rainham, in the early hours of 16th June 1944 resulted in Havering's first death by an unmanned weapon. The unlucky victim was Alfred Howes (aged 35) of 27 Eastwood Drive. It being . the first, he quite literally would not have known what hit him.

(RIGHT)

Fifty years on and Eastwood Drive is tranquil once more. Pedal power being replaced by a modest automobile.

❑ Romford

In total seven flying bombs fell in Havering that night, the most serious being that which fell in Barton Avenue, Romford at 3:30 am. A contemporary report stated, ''this missile flew over Romford from a South East direction, losing height rapidly, and when the engine cut, it fell like a stone into the rear gardens of No. 13 to 19 Barton Avenue.'' In the six houses that were destroyed seven people were left dead or dying, including an eleven month old baby.

More V-1's fell in the area that first night of mass bombardment than on any other occasion. The enemy had misjudged the range and vector of its true target, London, and this translated into Havering receiving more than its 'fair share'. A bewildered population found it impossible to sleep that night because for every V-1 that crashed at least a dozen flew on overhead, accompanied by the irregular throbbing of its engine and the thunder of the anti-aircraft guns.

A dramatic panoramic shot of the devastation caused by a flying bomb which fell in the rear gardens of No.13 to 19, Barton Avenue, Romford at 3:30 a.m. on 16th June 1944. Amongst those piles of masonry and timber, seven people lost their lives. This photograph was clearly taken at some interval after the explosion as the road has been cleared and swept of all debris. In the background a double-decker bus on Rush Green Road, heads into Romford

The same scene viewed from the other direction (looking south). An Anderson shelter, on the left of the picture, protrudes from the desolate ground, which moments before the blast would have been someone's pretty garden, in full June glory. Fences, trees and shrubs have all been lost and replaced by an alien lunar landscape.

Houses opposite those demolished in Barton Avenue also took a severe beating. Curious onlookers stare at the photographer. Are you perhaps one of the schoolboys in the foreground? By my calculation you must now (1994) be nearing your sixties.

The year is now 1994 and the houses are in a considerably more habitable condition. In many cases the replacement windows have themselves been replaced by modern double glazing. Other features that distinguish it from the earlier image are the presence of television aerials and burglar alarms.

The next day the radio and press gave detailed official information on this new arrival and so wisely helped dispel much of its sinister mystique. The name given to this new arrival depended upon what your relationship with it was. To the German propagandists it was the V-1 (Vengeance weapon No.1), which hinted at worse to follow. To members of the Civil Defence it was the 'Fly'. Initially the papers referred to it as a 'Pilotless Plane' or the more eerie sounding 'Robot Plane', and then latterly as the flying bomb. To the man in the street it was always the 'Doodlebug'.

A common misconception was that its point of impact was determined by its fuel supply, and although this could be the case if it suffered a fuel leak, its range was intended to be governed by a more sophisticated means. On the nose of the flying bomb was a small propeller which rotated with its passage through the air. A counter inside the nose cone recorded the number of revolutions and when it reached its predetermined number, two explosive charges were detonated, which brought down the flaps on the tail plane and sent the flying bomb into a dive. At this point the small amount of fuel remaining would run to the the front of the tank and hence the fuel starved engine would consequently stop. This is the technical explanation behind the Doodlebug's most memorable and terrifying feature, the few seconds of eerie silence between the engine cutting out and the inevitable explosion at the end of the short glide. It has been evocatively described as a period of 'deafening silence', for though the throb, throb, throb of the engine as it passed overhead was frightening, as long as it continued one was safe. If it did go on to bring death and destruction ultimately, this was death in the abstract, to person or persons unknown and far away, but when the engine cut out overhead it was quite a different feeling, suddenly the war was entirely personal, this was possibly the 'one with your name on it'. It is heavily cliched, but these few seconds did indeed turn to hours. People held their breath and waited, teeth clenched, hearts pounding, ears strained, with thoughts racing through the brain.............."Why have I chosen this time not to take shelter?"............"Where is little Robert?"..............."Please God not here, not me"......... and then came the violent explosion.........relief for many, tragedy for the few.

In some ways this sudden silence was a blessing in disguise for without the short warning it gave many more would have been injured or killed. It was just enough time to dive beneath a table, turn away from a window or take whatever protection was available.

One resident of Romford recollects the tension of the time. " In common, I imagine, with all other civilians in the danger zone, I maintained a continuous subconscious alertness for impending danger. I suppose one's pride and public image prevented too much overt reaction, as, during the flying bomb period I was in Romford Market Place one foggy market day. There was the usual crowd going quietly about its business, when suddenly the roar of an approaching but invisible flying bomb was heard. It was like a scene from Sleeping Beauty as everyone froze, waiting to see if the engine would cut out, indicating that it had started to dive. If just one person had dropped flat or panicked for shelter, I am sure everyone was ready to do likewise (myself included). Fortunately, the roar passed overhead in the direction of Collier Row, and, again like the Sleeping Beauty, now awakened, everyone started to move again as if nothing had happened."

In the normal course of events all the flying bombs should have behaved in the same fashion and obeyed these rules but there were many that were determined to behave unconventionally. Many of these were damaged by gun or shell fire and so sometimes dived to earth with engines still throbbing, or cut out only to start up again, or even more erratically turned round and headed back in the direction of France!

❑ Collier Row

The next serious incident to happen in the district was that which occurred on 18th June 1944, at Lodge Lane, Collier Row. At half-past five in the morning. After having been hit by anti-aircraft fire it fell in the middle of the road. The V-1 campaign was two days old and so most, but not all, of the residents of Lodge Lane had taken to sleeping the night in their shelters once more. One of those who had chosen not to do so was 70 year-old Annie

Sellen. It was a fatal mistake. Experiencing a terrible feeling of foreboding, one man insisted that he and his wife should take cover in their shelter shortly before the V-1 fell. In another home a boy was blown out of his bed by the blast and came to rest half way out of the window.

People were beginning to learn just what 1,870 lbs of 'Amatol' high explosive could do.

Roadside work proceeds in front of ravaged bungalows in Lodge Lane, Collier Row, after the fall of a doodlebug in the early morning of 18th June 1944.

Once again out of destruction came forth order.

Collier Row Once More.

Two days later and it was time for Collier Row to suffer again. This time a V-1 fell in the rear of gardens of houses between Rosedale Road and Hainault Road. Husband and wife, Arthur and Susannah Little, were two of the three destined to die that day, though there were also numerous serious casualties requiring hospitalization.

It seems inappropriate to say that someone was lucky to be buried in the rubble of their home, though in this case it was preferable to the alternative. The Doodlebug fell at five in the morning when usually the local residents would have been in the shelter in the foreground, where undoubtedly they should have perished. That morning they were instead in their homes seen demolished in the background. Nine of them were extracted alive.

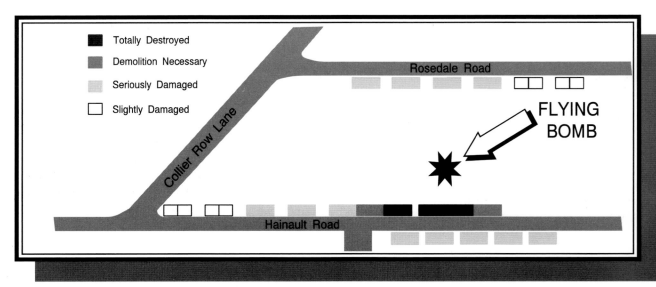

Romford & Hornchurch

Three more days, six more flying bombs. These fell across Hornchurch and Romford causing widespread damage to property and many casualties, although fortunately none proved fatal.

Rainham

On the 24th June a V-1 resulted in considerable strategic damage when it chose as its target an industrial area down Ferry Lane in Rainham. Briggs Bodies Factory and Rainham Starch Works were partially destroyed in the explosion and the fire that ensued. Thankfully, the time being 6:30 am., most employees were yet to arrive and so were spared. Not so lucky was 83 year-old Eva Starkey of the Half Way House, Ferry Lane, who died the same day from the injuries she sustained.

Collier Row Again

The very next day yet another V-1 fell in Collier Row. This particular example fell opposite the school in Clockhouse Lane. The school was intended to function as a rest centre in the event of people being made homeless, but regrettably it too was badly damaged. Two people lost their lives, one of whom Kenneth Harburn, a fireman, was killed as he ran to his shelter.

Steel framed windows at the Rainham Starch works exhibit the strange effect of blast.

Romford

In the closing days of June 1944, the only V-1 that was to cause damage to central Romford, fell on the railway embankment at the side of Victoria Road. The flying bomb, having been badly damaged by anti-aircraft fire, narrowly missed a bus, which was then violently shaken in the subsequent blast. Most of the casualties were light, the most serious of which was a man who had his leg badly lacerated by flying glass whilst waiting to be served at a pub close by. After the explosion people were eager to wash away the dust from their throats and quell their nerves, and so trade at the pub became quite brisk. In the rush, one man accidentally trod upon the cellar flap and plummeted from view, the bolt of which had been dislodged by the blast!

❏ Upminster

The first day of July and the first taste of the V-1 for Upminster. It fell on allotments, on the then unbuilt corner of The Grove and Tawny Avenue, at half past ten in the morning. One man who was painting his bedroom window at the time, heard the loud buzzing of it approaching, but mistook it for the sound of a Spitfire and so continued his work. Only on seeing his son dive to the ground in the front garden did he suddenly realise his mistake and turn his face away from the window, just in time to spare his eyes and face from the flying glass.

(Above) View of damaged houses in The Grove, Upminster, following a V-1 that crashed at 10:35 a.m. on 1st July 1944. The crater can be seen in the foreground, on allotments 25 yards from the houses. Two residents in the upstairs rooms escaped unhurt.

(Right) It is no longer possible to match the two photographs exactly, as the crater and the photographers vantage point are now buried beneath post-war houses in Tawny Avenue. I wonder if their residents know they sit astride a flying bomb crater?

❑ Evacuation

As there seemed no respite in the number of V-1 flying bombs falling on the area, Romford and Hornchurch were both designated evacuation zones for children. By mid July a third of the children had left for safer areas that included Lowestoft, Thaxted, Bungay and Eccles and further afield Barnsley and Stockton-on-Tees. It was a traumatic time for the children, though most received a warm welcome at their billets, nevertheless, some children had decided they were not going to like it even before they left. Five such evacuees arrived at Lowestoft, their destination, and caught the next train back. Travelling only on platform tickets they arrived back at Romford at 1 o'clock in the morning. On the whole the huge logistical operation went according to plan. It may have been mayhem, but it was organised mayhem. Heart rending though it was, it was still the correct decision for their parents to have made, when it is borne in mind that at the end of the the flying bomb campaign, a quarter of the fatalities in Havering consisted of children.

A group of mothers and Children from Mawney Road School, Romford pose for a photograph prior to their evacuation. The tiny uncertain children, parcelled up, labelled and awaiting delivery to some strange new land......the north! (Below) What they were avoiding, a V-1 'Doodlebug' in flight shortly after launching.

❏ Romford & Hornchurch

A steady stream of flying bombs continued to fall in the area, with two notable incidents occurring on the night of 7/8th July. The first demolished six houses, when it fell shortly before midnight in the rear gardens of Rainham Road, Hornchurch, close to Roneo Corner. The second that night fell at the corner of Mawney Road and Percy Road., Romford, demolishing 11 homes and in doing so took the life of Edith Wembridge.

❏ If only......

Then an event occurred that came so very close to terminating the entire V-1 campaign. Poor Edith might well have been the last person in Havering to have to die at the hand of the V-1. Shortly after midday on 20th July 1944 a bomb exploded in the conference room at Hitler's Headquarters at Rastenburg in East Prussia. The bomb had been planted by Colonel Count von Stauffenberg who represented a wide ranging conspiracy of senior officers and politicians. On hearing of the assassination attempt, Field Marshal Kluge, Commander in Chief West, realized that if Hitler was dead the Germans ought to begin negotiations with the Allies at once, "I would like to order a cessation of the flying bombs immediately". There was one problem.....Hitler was not dead. By accident another officer had moved the briefcase in which the bomb was hidden, and Hitler, shielded from the blast by the heavy leg of the map table, survived. The conspirators were arrested and executed, von Kluge choosing to swallow poison on his way back to Berlin. The killing would go on.

In the early part of the campaign many V-1's were brought down by anti-aircraft fire, until finally it became clear they were doing more harm than good. It was apparent that many of those being shot down onto residential areas might well have passed over harmlessly and landed on open land. In mid July it was decided that the best location for the guns would be firing out to sea from the coast, and so in the space of a few days the huge military operation of moving 1,500 guns, 23,000 men and woman and 60,000 tons of stores and ammunition to the south coast was undertaken. This redeployment of the defences proved to be a vast improvement on the old defence plan.

❏ River Thames

Included within the boundary of Havering is half the width of the River Thames, along the bank of Rainham and Wennington Marshes. When on the morning of 21st July a V-1 fell here, in the river, it still contrived to cause damage to the sea wall and the Murex Factory on the bank.

View of the Rainham Road, Hornchurch, flying bomb incident of 7th July 1944. A shattered tree, divested of its foliage, mirrors the shattered homes in the background.

Two Brothers Die in the Mouth of Their Shelter.

On the evening of 21st July 1944, the Smith family of Jersey Road, South Hornchurch, caught the sound of an approaching V-1 and quickly headed for the safety of their Anderson shelter in the garden. The two fit young boys, Gordon, aged 7, and Norman, aged 16, were first out of the house, racing each other to the shelter. The flying bomb fell 30ft away, just as they were entering their Anderson shelter, both brothers were killed.

(Seen above is their blasted shelter, riddled with shrapnel holes)

❑ Upminster

It was Upminster's turn again the same night. It fell in the rear garden of No. 51 Springfield Gardens where it scored a direct hit on a brick and concrete surface shelter. This was occupied by Lilian Welch and her 22 year old daughter, who had only just returned from evacuation. The shelter was expunged and their lives lost. Mr. Welch, who had only recently been discharged from hospital after a serious operation, was too unwell to sleep in the shelter with the rest of his family, and so spent the night indoors, where he survived, though badly injured by the blast.

All the work of a V-1 Flying Bomb which fell on to a shelter in the rear gardens of No. 49 & 51 Springfield Gardens, Upminster, at 1:42 a.m. on 22nd July 1944. Despite the proximity of the explosion, the houses nearest the crater remained standing, if a little battered.

❑ And Horses Too

Perhaps a thought ought to be spared for the other victims of the V-1. Man's inhumanity to man was not confined to his own species, but extended to members of the animal kingdom. Whilst it was possible for the human population to seek out some form of shelter, livestock, innocently grazing in an open field, was left especially vulnerable. Two such horses were killed in the small hours of 23rd July when a flying bomb fell in a field to the north of Gallows Corner.

❑ Rush Green

As on many other occasions, surface shelters proved to be very susceptible to blast damage. When a flying bomb fell in the rear gardens of houses between Gorseway and Rush Green Road, Romford, at breakfast time on the 5th August, the bomb landed between two shelters, completely demolishing them both. In all five people lost their lives. They were Mrs. Clara Kinch, aged 74, May Elliott and her twelve year old son, Antony, Mrs. Barnes and her seven year old son, Alan. Alan's brother was blown out of the shelter by the blast and was taken to hospital with serious injuries. Mr. Elliott was on his way to work when the bomb fell. Thinking it sounded near to his home he returned to discover his house destroyed and his wife and child killed. Mrs. Kinch's son was on night-work that particular week, but because he missed his usual bus he was only just approaching home when the bomb fell. His tardiness saved him, although it was impossible to be thankful, when his mother lay dead in the wreckage of her shelter.

❑ Elm Park & Collier Row

Elm Park lost two of its inhabitants early next day when a V-1 fell on 49 St. Andrew's Avenue, at three thirty in the morning. Husband and wife, Edith and Frederick Newham were the two selected to perish on this occasion. Before the day was out Charles Tubby would have joined them, as a result of a second V-1 which caused extensive damage on the corner of Hillfoot Road and Collier row Lane, Collier Row.

❑ Upminster

The flying bomb could not differentiate or indeed respect religious buildings and so it comes as no surprise that on the 7th August a tiny chapel was destroyed along with three cottages in Hall Lane, Upminster. Firemen managed to save the organ of the chapel by extracting it through a window. One of the casualties, Mrs. Holman, aged 75, of Tyes Cottage was rushed to Harold Wood Emergency Hospital, where she died from her injuries two days later.

❑ Marrows & Rhubarb

Over the next three week period from the 7th to the 27th August most of the flying bombs fell in open country and thankfully caused few casualties. Though even when a V-1 fell in a field it could still mean a financial loss for somebody. Such as the one which fell in a field alongside the A13 where it destroyed 3/4 acre of rhubarb and 1/2 acre of marrows.

❑ The Last?

The success of the British defences, a combination of Fighters, Balloon Barrage and Anti-Aircraft Guns, culminated on 28th August with the shooting down of all but four of ninety-seven bombs which approached the coast. This was an amazing achievement, although local residents might have been more ecstatic had not two of these four fallen in Havering. The second of these came down in Gainsborough Road, South Hornchurch, causing still more damage and suffering.

By now the Allied advance in Northern France had overrun virtually all the launching sites, and for the civilian population at least, it seemed the war was over. There was widespread feeling that Germany was close to capitulation. Duncan Sandys, Parliamentary Secretary, rashly announced that "except possibly for a few last shots, the Battle of London is over". The very next day the first of the V-2 Rockets fell on England. Havering had not seen the last of the V-1 however. With the loss of their launch sites the Germans instead switched to using aircraft to launch their flying bombs. They were suspended below the inner wing of ageing Heinkel 111's stationed at bases in Holland and Northern Germany. The crew of these aircraft had the unenviable task of taking off with a ton of high explosive and petrol slung precariously below their wing and then flying along barely 300ft above the sea to avoid radar detection. At the last moment, when forty miles off shore, they had to climb to 1500 ft, so as to release their deadly weapon. The pulse jet on the V-1 was then ignited and the whole contraption released to fly on to the target under its own power. Apart from making a sitting target for fighters the crew of the mother plane were often presented with other problems. Sometimes the flying bomb would refuse to detach itself or more frequently with the sudden extra thrust both aircraft and bomb were sent spiralling into the unforgiving North Sea. Even when released successfully the accuracy of such a launch proved very poor. If you were on the receiving end however, it mattered little if you were the intended target or not. Instead of approaching from the South East, in line with the ramps of Northern France, these new waves of flying bombs came in from the East, over the Thames Estuary. The anti-aircraft guns and aircraft were moved to intercept them as they flew in from the new direction, but inevitably some made it through.

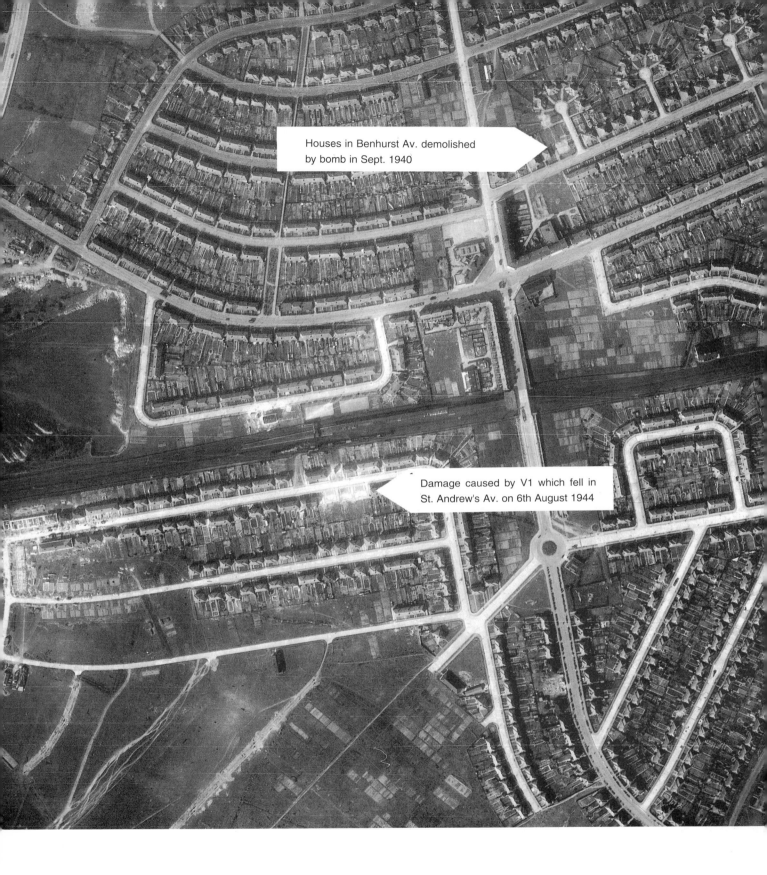

Houses in Benhurst Av. demolished by bomb in Sept. 1940

Damage caused by V1 which fell in St. Andrew's Av. on 6th August 1944

An aerial view of Elm Park taken some months after the end of the war, but still displaying the scars of war.

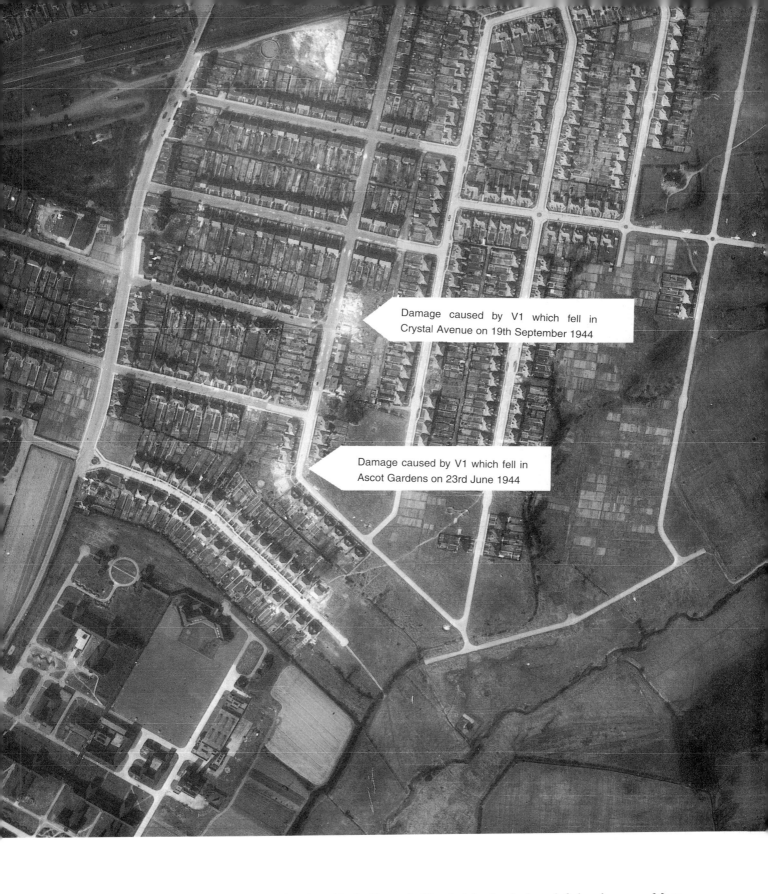

Damage caused by V1 which fell in Crystal Avenue on 19th September 1944

Damage caused by V1 which fell in Ascot Gardens on 23rd June 1944

Another aerial view, this time of Hornchurch, with St George's Hospital in the bottom left hand corner. More bomb sites and an unfinished housing estate.

Same weapon, different means of delivery. An air-launched flying bomb fell in the rear garden of No.35 Crystal Avenue, Hornchurch, at 4:20 a.m. on 19th September 1944.

A seemingly uniform row of houses conceals the fate of a number of homes and their residents many years before.

❏ Hornchurch
Two in Nine Minutes.

The first air-launched V-1 to fall in this area occurred on 19th September 1944 at 4:20 am. in Crystal Avenue, Hornchurch. In the demolition of six houses that ensued six people were killed. Amongst the dead was Ivy Edmunds and her 3 year old son Raymond and Daisy Northover and her 5 year old daughter Valerie. Barely had the emergency services arrived at this first scene of devastation when another air-launched flying bomb fell in Hornchurch, upon an unoccupied shelter in Great Gardens Road. It was the last V-1 incident to result in fatal casualties, although tragically it was the worst of the entire campaign, with a total of eleven people losing their lives. In fact, one third of all those killed in the V-1 offensive lost their lives in the nine minutes separating these two V-1's.

As with all the preceding incidents there was no guarantee of survival even for those wise enough to take cover. Two occupants in an Anderson shelter adjacent to the one where the missile fell were killed in the blast, partly due to the fact their shelter was inadequately covered. Even the indoor Morrison shelter was not entirely secure. A nine month old baby girl sustained concussion, but was lucky to survive, when she was blown out of hers and into the garden. Tragedy touched many households that morning, perhaps the most poignant being that of the Chumley family. Husband and wife, Alfred and Gwendoline, were both killed along with their four young children. The youngest of whom, John, Gwendoline had endured the rigours of childbirth to bring into the world just six weeks previously. One of her other children, six year old Margaret, was rescued from the wreckage alive, pathetically asking for her dolly. She was to die in Oldchurch Hospital the same day. All the children had only returned from evacuation the previous night.

A total of eleven people were to lose their lives in this final blaze of tragedy at Great Gardens Road, Hornchurch, on 19th September 1944. Two people were killed by blast in the inadequately covered Anderson Shelter in the centre of the picture.

The Culprit. A Flying Bomb precariously slung under the wing of a Heinkel He 111 bomber, in preparation for an air-launch.

❏ And then they ceased

Three more air-launched V-1's fell in the Havering area, the last being that which collided with trees just south of Berwick Pond Farm, Rainham, at 11:15 pm. on the 11th November 1944 (symbolically Armistice Day). Exploding in the air as it did, it caused no crater, though it destroyed numerous farm buildings and set two trees ablaze.

Nationally the air-launched flying bomb campaign ground to a halt in January 1945 as the German air bases and supply routes became untenable. In a last ditch attempt to continue the offensive three ramps at Ypenburg, Vlaardingen and Delft in Holland were constructed for launches against London. The range having been thus increased the fuel capacity was increased at the expense of the warhead's size, which was reduced to 1,000lbs. Of the 275 that were launched against this country from these ramps, only 125 reached the coast and only 13 made it to London. Some of these examples were seen and heard in the Havering area, though fortunately none chose to fall here. The last V-1 fell prey to anti-aircraft gunners on 29th March 1945. Thus ended the relatively brief , but extremely memorable flying bomb campaign against the British people.

❏ Counting The Cost

The final tally of V-1's for Havering was:

Hornchurch Urban District 41

Borough of Romford 21

Over one third of the houses in the area sustained some degree of damage. Out of the 26,000 houses in Hornchurch, 29,000 were damaged. These seemingly irreconcilable statistics are accounted for by the fact that some houses were damaged on up to seven different occasions!

Buildings are replaceable, not the forty six lives lost to Vengeance Weapon No.1.

The Date	: 16th September 1944
The Time	: 10:37 p.m.
The Place	: The Hague in the Netherlands.
The Command	: Funf.........!
	: Vier.........!
	: Drei........!
	: Zwei.......!
	: Ein..........!

The German soldiers of Mobile Artillery Attachment No. 485 watched intently, from the safety of their slit trenches, as their new wonder weapon roared into life, very slowly inching off the launch pad until above the tree line. Gaining speed all the while, it began to lean to the west until at an angle of 43 degrees to the horizontal. Gradually the glow from its engine in the night sky grew fainter and fainter until it disappeared from German eyes altogether. Their task completed, the soldiers set about dismantling their equipment.

Five minutes later and over two hundred miles away, on the other side of the North Sea, a recently harvested field of corn at Hill Farm, Noak Hill, was gathering dew. Without warning and to the accompaniment of two ear splitting bangs a crater mysteriously appeared in the midst of the corn stubble. This was the first of Hitler's much vaunted V2's to fall within the confines of Havering. With all the farm labourers safely at home, it harmed no one, but red hot fragments set fire to an unthreshed corn rick. To add to the enigma surrounding this incident, other fragments were found covered in ice

Mystery Crater No. 1   16th September 1944 Hill Farm, Noak Hill

Let us study the evidence; no air-raid warning was in force at the time, there was the sound of two explosions, and both red hot and ice cold fragments of metal were found surrounding the crater. A puzzling case indeed, but definitely no gas main!

V2 Rockets

The Germans had set as their aiming point an area 1,000 yards east of Waterloo Station. They had no way of knowing if they had succeeded in reaching their target or indeed how many people it might have killed. As it turned out they were a little over fifteen miles wide.

Allied Intelligence had long known about the development of the V2 Rocket by the Nazis, but it was mistakenly believed that the invasion of mainland Europe by the Allies in June 1944, had greatly reduced their likely use. With virtual elimination of the V1 Flying Bomb menace, the Government had prematurely announced on 7th September that ''the Battle of London is over''. Thus the local population, apart from those officials 'in the know', had no inkling as to the culprit of this strange occurrence. The whole subject of Rockets was shrouded with a cloak of secrecy. A total press blackout remained in force for two months. As there had been no air raid warning in operation at the time of the explosion, and as no aircraft had been seen or heard overhead, the whole affair was most puzzling for the man in the street. To confuse matters further, the authorities were instructed to imply that this mysterious explosion was the work of a delayed action bomb or possibly a gas main explosion.

Two contemporary accounts of the incident were given in a report to the Ministry of Home Security. The first by R.E. Thallon, an Intelligence Officer, reported the following. "P.C. Monnington was at Gallows Corner at the time of the above incident and was looking skywards in an easterly direction. He states, 'I saw what I took to be a shooting star travelling at the speed one usually associates with such a phenomenon. The colour was at first white hot, then the trail widened and turned a dull reddish white. It went out of sight behind landmarks in the direction of Noak Hill and in a matter of seconds there were two explosions from that direction.' P.C. Monnington is a reliable witness."

The second report was made by R.J. Robins:-"On the night of 16/17th September I was staying at the White Hart Hotel, Brentwood, my bedroom window facing approximately south-west. I had gone to bed at 10:30 p.m.. Shortly afterwards I was startled by a very loud explosion in the air, apparently slightly to the north. The bedroom was shaken and curtains at the window disturbed. A few days previous to this I had been investigating 'Rocket Projectile' incidents where two explosions were reported. I was therefore at once on the alert to note any further explosion. At approximately five seconds afterwards there was a second explosion in the direction of Noak Hill and I was instructed to investigate. I found that heavy fragments were scattered on the east side of the crater for approximately 300 yards and lighter fragments up to one mile further east. The nearest fragment to the White Hart Hotel being approximately 1½ miles.''

One of the larger fragments recovered from Hill Farm, Noak Hill, was this turbine. It was driven from steam derived from the chemical reaction between hydrogen peroxide and calcium permanganate. It powered two pumps, one for each of the two fuels, alcohol and liquid oxygen. The turbine developed 600 horsepower, which enabled it to inject 8½ tons of fuel into the combustion chamber within the space of just 60 seconds.

A V-2 Rocket, steadied by its Meillerwagen, is made ready for launching. The Meillerwagen was an ingenious dual-purpose piece of equipment, serving as both rocket transporter, and launch frame. The rocket was placed upon the Meillerwagen, in a horizontal position, at the storage depot and then towed to the launch site behind a lorry. The Meillerwagen's integral hydraulic rams lifted the rocket into a vertical position in preparation for launching. It then acted as an inspection gantry for prelaunch servicing.

This was not the first rocket to have fallen on Britain. That dubious honour goes to Chiswick, where a rocket had fallen eight days previously. A second fell sixteen seconds later at Pardon Wood, Epping. The arrival of these weapons marked the climax of years of development which had been fraught with setbacks and disasters. The German liquid fuel rocket programme had started in the the early 1930's, but it was not until 1942 that the first V2 was nearing completion.

What of the curious phenomena that were observed at Noak Hill, with Havering's first rocket? Why the double explosion and why was some of the debris found to be red hot whilst other parts were covered with ice? The answer to the first question is relatively straight forward. The first explosion was the sound of the warhead exploding on contact with the ground, whilst the second, which tended to continue as a rumble, was a sonic boom caused by the rocket's supersonic flight through the atmosphere. It must be remembered that this was in the days before aircraft could break the sound barrier and so such bizarre noises were entirely unfamiliar. The solution to the second problem is equally scientific. On passing through the atmosphere faster than the speed of sound, the outer casing of the rocket became extremely hot. The combustion chamber was also at a very high temperature and the explosion itself released further heat. This explains the red hot fragments but not why some parts were covered in ice. This was due to one of the rockets sources of power, liquid oxygen. If there happened to be any remaining at the moment of impact this would be released and immediately evaporate. Any fragment in contact with this liquid would be thus cooled to freezing point Q.E.D.

Havering might just have received this one rocket had events on the continent gone more favourably. On 17th September 1944 Operation Market Garden was launched by the Allies. Its objective was to secure a bridgehead over the Rhine at Arnhem and so facilitate a rapid drive right into the heart of Germany and hopefully end the war in 1944. With the airborne landings the German Rocket Batteries around The Hague were forced to retreat for fear of being cut off. This took them out off the reach of London and they took aim at Norwich and Ipswich instead, without much success. Unfortunately Arnhem proved to be 'a bridge too far' and enabled the Rocket Batteries to re-group and reinstate London as their target. Thus another rocket fell in this area on the 11th October 1944 at a quarter past five in the morning. It exploded in a field of potatoes at Whitepost Farm, North Ockendon and produced a crater over forty feet in diameter and thirteen feet in depth. Once again a hay stack and two straw stacks were set ablaze.

A difficult decision for the authorities to make was concerning the use of air raid warnings when under attack by the Rocket menace. Radar tracking stations on the coast were able to pick up the skyward rockets over Holland and in theory give a four minute warning of their arrival. This is where a painful quandary arose, to warn or not to warn? It was not an easy choice. By the time the warning had been passed to the local area and the siren sounded it was calculated there would be little over a minute to take cover. This it was reasoned might induce panic in the population. Also despite being able to watch the rocket being launched there was no way of knowing where it was going to land. Unlike raids by aircraft or even flying bombs, there was no possibility of giving localized alerts in the perceived area of danger and so a blanket alert would have to be given for the whole of South East England. It was felt that either people would soon disregard warnings when they so infrequently pertained to themselves, or that if they did keep running for shelter they might paralyse the whole of the war effort in the South East. The decision was therefore taken not to warn, and so it was that the population came to believe that none was possible. There was however, one notable exception when it came to warning signals. Where the London Underground passes under the Thames was a highly vulnerable point. Should a rocket have breached a tunnel there, it could have flooded the whole of the network and so they were privileged with advanced notice, which provided just enough time to close the flood doors on either side of the Thames.

This was not the only information kept from the public, for as already stated, no mention was made of the Rockets in the press for two months. Newspaper editors were obliged to fill their paper with trivialities whilst all around V2 Rockets were raining down. The press blackout may have been damaging to morale, but it was essential that the enemy be given no information as to where their missiles were falling and so possibly improve their aim. The South East of England had to suffer in silence. Rumours of course spread, but the majority of people in the rest of the country were blissfully ignorant that the suffering had not stopped with the Flying Bombs, but continued unabated. Regrettably this led to a drift home of evacuated mothers and children, who on returning were alarmed to find the area as perilous as ever. In reference to the earlier assertions that these explosions were the result of gas mains exploding, some wag dubbed them flying gas mains. Finally, impatient and frustrated with the lack of response emanating from the British media, the German News Agency broke its silence on November 8th 1944 and announced to the world the arrival of its new wonder weapon. Churchill was then obliged to make a statement in the Commons and only then was the press free to give a sketchy outline of the ordeal its readers had become all too familiar with over the preceding weeks.

AIR MINISTRY FILE No B.28812

TOP SECRET

D.C.A.S. Copy to A.C.A.S. (Ops)

Rocket Attacks
Statement by the Prime Minister

With reference to the attached minute by S.6., I attach a note in general terms on the R.A.F. countermeasures employed and the results achieved.

2. I have assumed - I hope correctly - that you would not wish to refer to radio countermeasures; and I have not mentioned the warning system which was operated for closing the floodgates of the tubes under the Thames, as this would give a hint as to the possibility of radar detection of rocket flight and might lead to questions why air raid warnings of their approach were not given.

3. The note is probably in more detail than you will wish to put in, but I have completed the story as I see it and you will be better able to decide what can be deleted.

25th April, 1945

D. of Ops.(AD)

Cynical Betrayal or Pragmatic Decision?

The fact that it was possible to give air-raid warnings of the approach of rockets and that it was decided not to do so, was of potentially great embarrassment to the Government, and could well have resulted in a public outcry. This Air Ministry document relates to a further statement on rockets, Winston Churchill was due to make to the House of Commons after the attack had ended. It shows just how carefully it had to be worded so as not to give the game away.

In the days prior to his first announcement four rockets fell in the Havering area, three of these on November 5th, Guy Fawkes Night. These were pyrotechnics on a scale far removed from those usually associated with this festival.

So far damage had been light but this run of luck ended at twelve minutes past five on the morning of 15th November when rocket No. 9 fell in Ainsley Avenue, Romford. Two houses were completely destroyed by the blast and a further three were damaged beyond repair. Mr. & Mrs. Connelly together with their teenage son and daughter were all buried under the rubble that had once been their home. They were dug out of the mound of masonry and timber and rushed to hospital with serious injuries. Their neighbours Mr. & Mr. Brown heard nothing of the explosion! The Pearce family, who were sleeping in their shelter, also knew nothing of the explosion, although only fifteen yards from where the rocket fell. The first they heard was the sound of masonry falling on the roof of their shelter. This curious occurrence was a common feature of the rocket for anybody within a range of 300 yards of the impact. This 'zone of silence' was thought to be caused by the out-rush of air from the explosion, creating a partial vacuum in which no sound could travel.

Destruction to homes as a result of a rocket which fell in Ainsley Avenue, Romford, on November 15th, 1944. It is hard to imagine that the people in the neighbouring houses heard nothing of the explosion.

Catastrophe in Collier Row

This last explosion, bad as it seemed, only hinted at the carnage a rocket was capable of causing. If a demonstration was needed of its awesome power one was not long in coming.

Early next morning at 7:40 am. Romford suffered its worst rocket incident of the war. It fell in the rear gardens of houses at the junction of Collier Row Lane and Rosedale Road. If Hitler could have seen the scene that morning no doubt he would have rubbed his hands with glee. The destruction was appalling. Eighteen homes demolished and what of their occupants? The rocket had fallen just as people were leaving to go to work and so the exact number of victims was uncertain for some time. Eventually thirteen bodies were recovered, all but one were women or children. Among the lives lost that November morning were Florence Copsey and her eight year old son Leonard, Minnie Earl and her two sons John (13 years) and Ronald (11 years). A bus happened to be passing 100 yards away from the point of impact. The passengers witnessed a vivid flash of light followed by the blast which gave the bus a severe shaking. Another bus was commandeered to help with the wounded. In addition to those who died, 32 people were miraculously extricated from the debris alive, although seriously wounded, and taken to hospital. A schoolboy who was soon on the scene remembers being amazed how the skyline had changed so dramatically since he saw it last. Gone were the row of semi-detached houses in Collier Row Lane, gone were a row in Rosedale Row beyond, and then this damage merged with that produced previously by a flying bomb in Hainault Road and so now from where he stood in Collier Row Lane he could see through to Mawney Road and beyond. Even many of the houses left standing were so damaged that they would have to be demolished. In all, 800 homes received some damage as the result of this one blast. Once again people in the immediate vicinity heard nothing of the explosion but experienced the full force of the blast, this included the policemen of Collier Row Police Station directly opposite. The rescue work continued late into the night with Alsatian tracker dogs being used to locate the victims. A council employee has a vivid recollection of visiting the site, "I well remember cycling to this 'incident' to check the damage to food shops, and slipping in a pool of blood as I got off my bike."

This shot was taken from Rosedale Road, looking out to Collier Row Lane.

Rosedale Road following the fall of V-2 Rocket on the morning of Nov 16th 1944

More Scenes of the Collier Row Lane Rocket of 16th Nov. 1944

(Left) Romford's worst Rocket incident occurred at 7:40 am on the 16th November 1944. It fell in the rear gardens of houses on the junction of Collier Row Lane and Rosedale Road. What had been a neat row of suburban homes was left a pile of masonry and sorrow. Thirteen people lost their lives here, twelve of them mothers and children. (The Mobile Civil Defence Canteen in the foreground has signwritten on the door, "Donated by the traders of Romford".)

(Above Right) Destroyed maisonettes in Rosedale Road

(Below Right) Without photographic evidence it would be hard to believe that such a fate had befallen dwellings in this road. To own a car in 1944 was quite exceptional. Come 1994 the situation has reversed.

(Left) The year is now 1994 and not a hint of devastation remains. Post war 'Semies' replace those lost. The tree on the right of the picture apparently survived the blast and now exhibits 50 years of further growth.

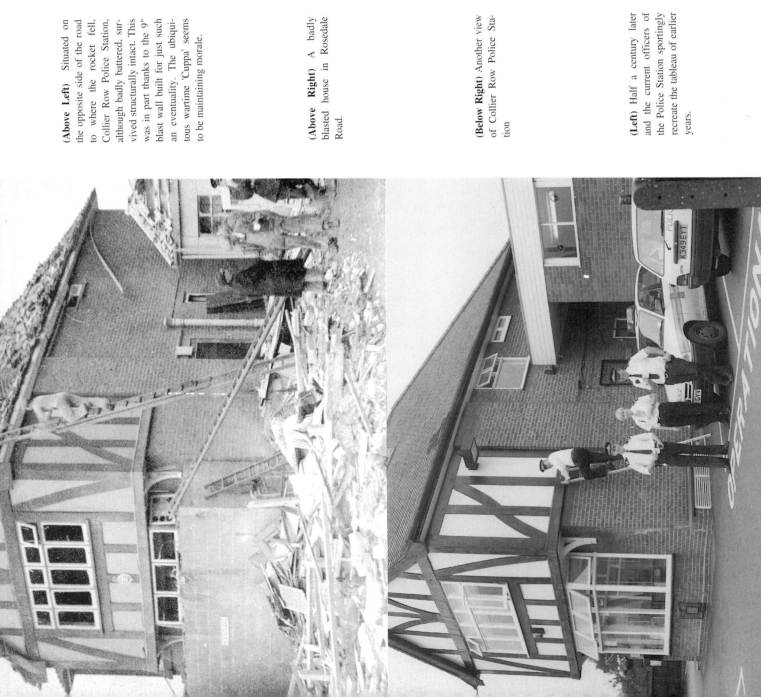

(Above Left) Situated on the opposite side of the road to where the rocket fell, Collier Row Police Station, although badly battered, survived structurally intact. This was in part thanks to the 9" blast wall built for just such an eventuality. The ubiquitous wartime 'Cuppa' seems to be maintaining morale.

(Above Right) A badly blasted house in Rosedale Road.

(Below Right) Another view of Collier Row Police Station

(Left) Half a century later and the current officers of the Police Station sportingly recreate the tableau of earlier years.

On the 21st November 1944 a rocket exploded in the air over Wennington Marshes scattering debris over a wide area but causing little damage. An air burst provided masses of material for the schoolboy souvenir hunters, and yet even their voracious appetite could be met when confronted with the size of some fragments. The Rocket Motor (Venturi) being fairly robust, often survived intact but owing to its weight many languished unwanted in the more remote parts of the Borough for many years. Many fragments must still remain on the marshes and in wooded areas to this day. I wonder how many more are kept as prized trophies in the bottom drawer of the older residents of Havering.

The next serious incident occurred just after 11 am. on the 26th November. The rocket actually fell on waste ground, but caused substantial damage to houses in Victory Road, South Hornchurch. Being a fine morning, people had been working in their gardens and were caught by the blast. Working away industriously that particular morning was Mr. F.W. Revell trimming the hedge at the side of his cottage, while next door his neighbour was chopping wood in

his back garden, both were killed instantly. Those indoors fared little better, Mr. Bull's five year old son Brian, who was possibly watching his father work, was also to die from his injuries. Many were trapped in the wreckage of their homes. In one house, where Mrs. Merry and her four year old daughter were trapped, the radio set continued to play amongst the rubble and to accompany it a grandfather clock that had not worked for years started to chime continuously. Outside in the street a mother and baby lay seriously injured in the gutter, surrounded by broken slates and splinters of glass, tended and comforted by another resident although injured himself.

A further ten rockets fell through December and early January 1945, without causing any serious damage or loss of life, although some came very close. One of these fell on allotments to the west side of Elmhurst Drive, Hornchurch and although 33 people were slightly injured by flying glass and hundreds of homes sustained some damage it was still a far cry from the devastation that would have resulted had the rocket fallen slightly to the east.

A rocket motor or Venturi from a V-2 Rocket. In order to prevent the hot exhaust gases from melting the mild steel combustion chamber, the liquid oxygen fuel was first pumped round the outside of the walls, before entering the chamber to provide the thrust.

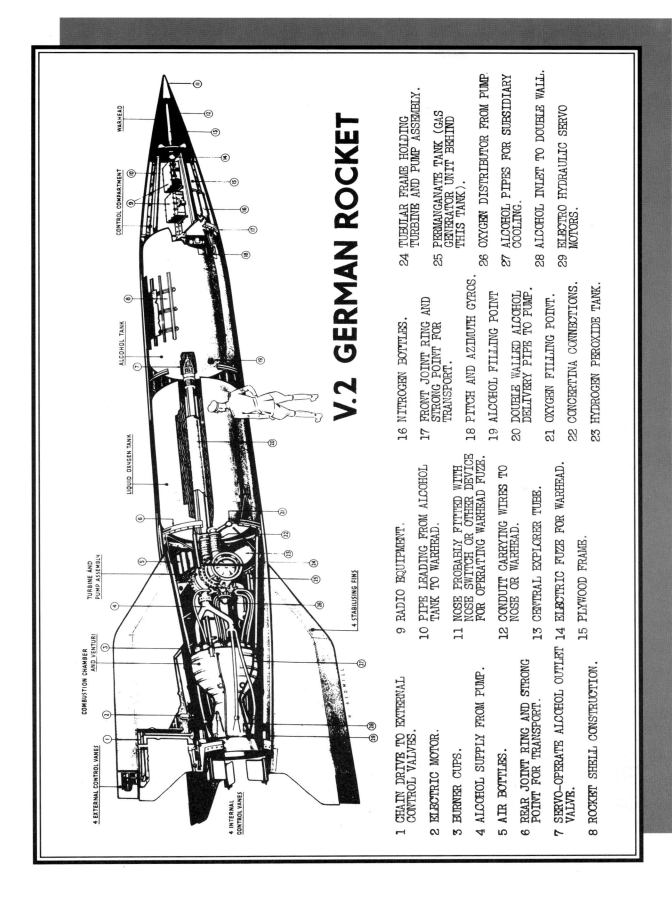

V.2 GERMAN ROCKET

1 CHAIN DRIVE TO EXTERNAL CONTROL VALVES.

2 ELECTRIC MOTOR.

3 BURNER CUPS.

4 ALCOHOL SUPPLY FROM PUMP.

5 AIR BOTTLES.

6 REAR JOINT RING AND STRONG POINT FOR TRANSPORT.

7 SERVO-OPERATE ALCOHOL OUTLET VALVE.

8 ROCKET SHELL CONSTRUCTION.

9 RADIO EQUIPMENT.

10 PIPE LEADING FROM ALCOHOL TANK TO WARHEAD.

11 NOSE PROBABLY FITTED WITH NOSE SWITCH OR OTHER DEVICE FOR OPERATING WARHEAD FUZE.

12 CONDUIT CARRYING WIRES TO NOSE OR WARHEAD.

13 CENTRAL EXPLORER TUBE.

14 ELECTRIC FUZE FOR WARHEAD.

15 PLYWOOD FRAME.

16 NITROGEN BOTTLES.

17 FRONT JOINT RING AND STRONG POINT FOR TRANSPORT.

18 PITCH AND AZIMUTH GYROS.

19 ALCOHOL FILLING POINT

20 DOUBLE WALLED ALCOHOL DELIVERY PIPE TO PUMP.

21 OXYGEN FILLING POINT.

22 CONCERTINA CONNECTIONS.

23 HYDROGEN PEROXIDE TANK.

24 TUBULAR FRAME HOLDING TURBINE AND PUMP ASSEMBLY.

25 PERMANGANATE TANK (GAS GENERATOR UNIT BEHIND THIS TANK).

26 OXYGEN DISTRIBUTOR FROM PUMP.

27 ALCOHOL PIPES FOR SUBSIDIARY COOLING.

28 ALCOHOL INLET TO DOUBLE WALL.

29 ELECTRO HYDRAULIC SERVO MOTORS.

137

Havering's Worst Rocket Penerley Road, Rainham

*A*ll was calm in the Howells' household of 49 Penerley Road, on the night of 15th January 1945. It was a little after 11 o'clock at night, half the family had gone to bed, whilst the other half was preparing to do so shortly. The father of the family, Jehoyda Howells, and his eighteen month old son, Robert, were asleep in an upstairs bedroom. In an adjacent bedroom slept Mr. Howells' wife, Caroline, and their seven year old daughter Patricia. Downstairs in the kitchen the elder children Rita, Margaret and Howard were busy making themselves a bedtime cup of tea.

Margaret Howells, then 24 years of age, recollects the events that followed;

"I remember a huge explosion and then I must have been unconscious for a while. When I regained consciousness I could feel the pressure of people walking on the debris which was on top of my face. I then realized that I was buried alive and wondered whether anyone would find me. From somewhere in the rubble I could hear my father telling us to keep shouting so that people would hear us. I must have lost consciousness again because the next thing I remember was being lifted out and feeling an iron bar in the debris catch me across the throat.

My next memory was in hospital, where they had to cut my clothes off me. I could hear my sister Rita screaming in the background. My injuries were extremely severe and I was in considerable pain. I later learnt that I was not expected to recover and was in hospital for over a year. Over this period I was visited by friends and relatives and was told by everyone that my mother and father and all the family had survived. I thought how marvellous that everyone was alright. After six months the vicar of Rainham informed me that my mother, father and two brothers had died in the incident. The shock of this made me just want to die and I never wished to leave hospital. Rita, my sister, was still in Hospital with me and it was left to me to tell her the terrible news. I remember Rita crying that she was now an orphan. Having both been told how well our parents were, this news was absolutely devastating. After a year I was discharged from hospital and went to live with my grandparents at Orsett Heath. I got married shortly afterwards and we moved

back into 49 Penerley Road after it had been rebuilt. Although I was older than most of my brothers and sisters it was a terrifying experience that still haunts me to this day, even the writing of this has brought back unhappy memories that sadden me."

Margaret and Rita's, seven year old sister, Patricia, may have escaped the serious injuries they had sustained, but events were equally traumatic for her.

"I can remember being buried under the rubble of the house. I could hear people walking on top of all the debris. My mother told me to hold onto her nightdress and to be a good girl and stop crying. After about six hours I heard someone say, "I have found someone here." I then heard my sister Rita say, "Get my little sister out first". I was then lifted from the rubble. It was very dark, but I could see a lot of people standing in the road. Suffering no injuries other than slight cuts and bruises, I was not sent to hospital, but was taken in by one of the neighbours from the far end of the road. I was unaware of my parents and two brothers deaths until the time of their funeral. I was standing at the Rainham Clock Tower when the funeral cars turned towards the church. The people who had taken me in, informed me that my mother, father and two brothers had been killed and that this was their funeral. This has stayed with me all my life and upsets me, even now, to recall it."

Caroline, the sisters' mother, was rescued from the remnants of her home still living, though tragically she died in the ambulance on the way to the hospital. Her husband, Jehoyda, suffered a haemorrhage and died whilst a heavy piece of debris was being lifted from his body. Howard, who often stayed out late, might have been spared that night if it were not for the strict instruction of his father to be home early that particular evening. Two members of the Howells family were not at home that night however, for they were in the comparative safety of the army, from where they were subsequently sent home on leave, but not told the reason why. They only learnt the fate of their family as they rounded the end of their road.

The Howells family terrible loss was compounded by the deaths of ten of their neighbours. It was to be the highest death toll of any rocket to fall in the area.

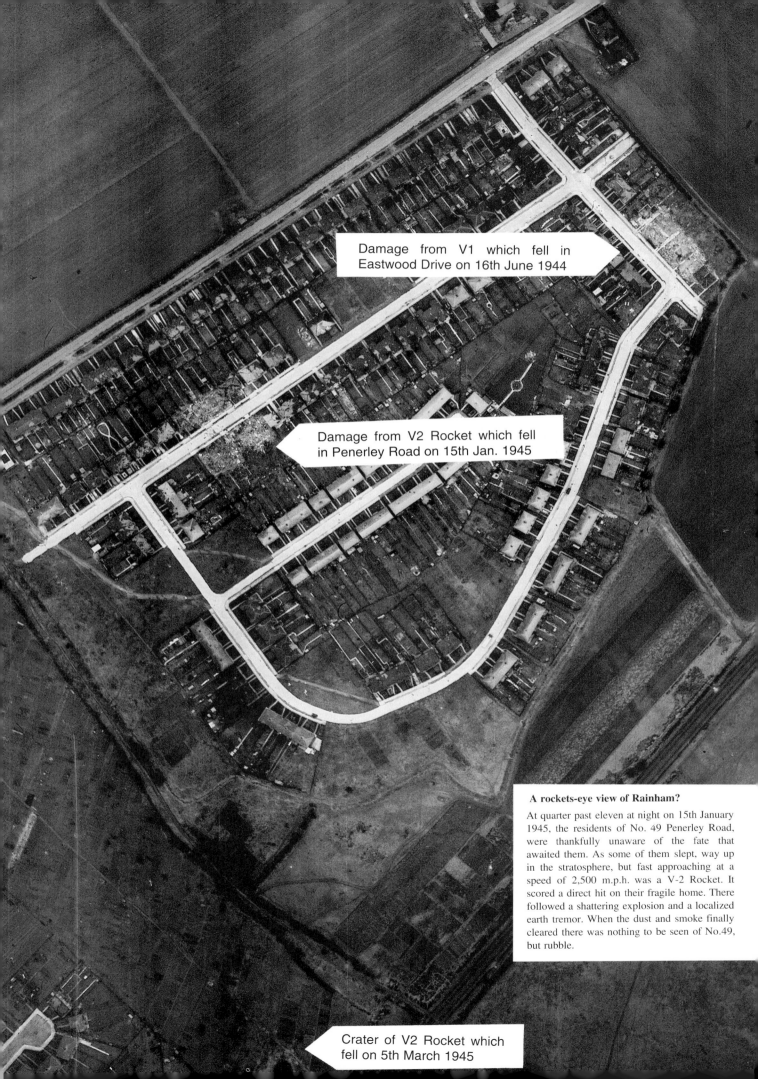

Damage from V1 which fell in Eastwood Drive on 16th June 1944

Damage from V2 Rocket which fell in Penerley Road on 15th Jan. 1945

A rockets-eye view of Rainham?

At quarter past eleven at night on 15th January 1945, the residents of No. 49 Penerley Road, were thankfully unaware of the fate that awaited them. As some of them slept, way up in the stratosphere, but fast approaching at a speed of 2,500 m.p.h. was a V-2 Rocket. It scored a direct hit on their fragile home. There followed a shattering explosion and a localized earth tremor. When the dust and smoke finally cleared there was nothing to be seen of No.49, but rubble.

Crater of V2 Rocket which fell on 5th March 1945

❏ Upminster's First

Upminster received its first rocket four days later at just after 1 o'clock in the morning. It fell in a field at the rear of houses in Argyle Gardens. Twenty four homes were made uninhabitable and at least 150 houses sustained some minor damage. Baptist minister T.W. Slemming, of Upminster Baptist Church, was one of the first to arrive on the scene and rescued Mrs. Morton and her daughter from the upstairs of their damaged home and then went on to give first aid to other casualties. In true Good Samaritan fashion he took ten of the victims, rendered homeless by the rocket, back to the sanctuary of his own home where they spent the night.

A rocket crater sits incongruously amongst a field of corn sheaves. This aerial view of Upminster shows just how close the residents of Argyle Gardens came to disaster. By the time this August scene was taken, the houses have been repaired and their roofs replaced, the rocket having fallen some months earlier.

❏ Ardleigh Green

The next two rockets fell without incident, until on the 26th January 1945 at around ten o'clock in the morning a rocket fell in the rear gardens of Staffords Avenue, Ardleigh Green. It created a massive crater 53 feet across and 25 feet deep. Over forty tons of soil had been ejected in the explosion and now lay about the crater in gigantic boulders. Adjacent to the crater was the Lacranoid Factory and the Ardleigh Green School, both of which were badly damaged. In the former two teenage girl workers lost their lives and tragically a twenty year old W.A.A.F., Miss Joyce Barrett, who had only just returned from leave was also killed. At the school the windows were blown in , the ceilings brought down and water pipes burst. Many of the pupils had escaped injury by diving under their desks for protection, and to their credit the children remained calm throughout. The teachers helped administer first aid to those in need and escorted the remaining children out of the building, picking a path between the flowing water, glass and rubble. It was so bitterly cold that January morning that when the clean up operation began it was impossible to discern what was ice and what was glass.

140

❑ Harold Wood

Rocket No. 35 was Harold Wood's worst incident. It fell in David Drive at 6:50 pm. in mid January 1945, where it succeeded in demolishing seven bungalows. Twelve people were killed and 34 seriously injured. Mrs. Daisy Hunt and her seven week old baby were buried under the remnants of their bungalow for one and a half hours before rescuers brought them both out alive, the baby still in her arms. Not so lucky was one boy named Brian Betts, who had the pure misfortune to be cycling past at the moment the rocket fell. He died shortly after being rushed to hospital.

Rocket No. 35 fell at 6:50 p.m. on 13th February 1945 in David Drive, Harold Park. A row of seven bungalows was destroyed and their residents killed or maimed. The rocket was an indiscriminate form of warfare and as such there was no quarter given to even the youngest of children. Amongst the dead was Sydney Melville, his wife and their two children, aged four and six.

The bricks and mortar may have been repaired, but how many families still retain the memories and scars of one winter's evening in 1945.

141

❑ Gidea Park

Four more rockets brought about no additional loss of life and then on the evening of 20th February a rocket broke up in the air without exploding, the warhead of which continued its journey earthwards, picking as its target the rear garden of No. 53 Fairholme Avenue, Gidea Park. A gas main was caught alight, but surprisingly it proved to be more of a help than a hindrance, for until a mobile searchlight was brought to the scene it was the only light by which the rescue workers could work. When the searchlight did arrive and illuminated the area, the full extent of the devastation became apparent and it was clear that once again the death toll would be very high, but just how high it took some time to establish. As one body after another was extricated from the ruins the number reached double figures and finally climbed to twelve, which included three children. Amongst their number was one body, that had been thrown to the opposite side of the road, and for which no identification was possible. Positive verification was only finally made possible by the fact that the body was missing two fingers from his left hand and thus it was established beyond doubt that this was the body of Mr. Arthur Norris, a dentist from Romford, who had lost these same two fingers in a shooting accident some years previously.

The scene in Fairholme Avenue, Gidea Park, on 21st February 1945, following a rocket attack the previous evening. The destruction of a row of semi-detached houses reveals an unfamiliar view over the Romford to Chelmsford railway, to the rear of houses in Carlton Road. Someone's prized car lies battered in the rubble, after the garage in which it was housed was destroyed.

Rebuilt to the same design, the new houses blend in inconspicuously with the rest of the street and belie the sorry scene that once existed.

A view of No. 54a, the bungalow immediately opposite the demolished houses in Fairholme Av.

The present owner of the bungalow, pictured left, was somewhat surprised to see the condition of his home in 1945, "Had I known I might never have bought it."

With the first week of March 1945 came the next disastrous impact. This time it was a direct hit on Ferro Road, Rainham. Six people (five of them women) were left dead or dying and at least a dozen others seriously wounded. Great heroism was shown by Dr. Stephens, who although badly injured himself, still administered first aid to those more seriously injured. Of minor importance in comparison, Rainham had lost another four houses. The rocket motor (venturi) of the culprit was to be seen lying 200' away.

142

Destination Havering?

Fortunately not, as this is one of the British controlled launches at Cuxhaven in October 1945, using captured German rockets.

Upminster Again.

With a WOOOMPF and a CRASSSSHHH!

My elder brother, Frank, and I were both sleeping downstairs in the back room of our house, no. 48, Waldegrave Gardens, with our beds against the internal walls of the house. As it was in the latter stages of the war, we no longer slept in the shelter, our parents having returned to their bedroom in the front upstairs, but deeming it safer for us to be downstairs.

We were suddenly awakened by what seemed to be a combination of a huge WOOOMPF and a CRASSSHHH. Then it was silence for what seemed a long time but was probably only a few seconds before sounds returned. Then we realised that something awful had happened. We afterwards learnt that a V2 rocket had dropped on the house opposite to ours.

We both found ourselves covered in bits of glass, debris and the heavy curtains from the window. Frank eased himself out of bed, telling me to stay put, found his slippers to put on, and shuffled his way in the dark to near the bottom of the stairs. On calling for our parents, he was very surprised to hear them answer from the direction of the garden! The whole of the front half of the house had collapsed and my parents found themselves at a crazy angle with a large lump of chimney above them. They had to ease themselves out of bed very carefully in order not to dislodge or move the wreckage any more. In spite of that they had both managed to find their slippers and dressing gowns to put on. It seemed ages before they both joined us in the back room. My father had fallen down a deep drain manhole trying to pick his way round what had been the front of the house.

After we had pronounced ourselves OK, we found that the electricity was still on and that the lights still worked. We could not see what was going on in the rest of the road, but we could hear a lot of what was going on with regard to the rescue of the occupants in the houses opposite. One of the houses was burning due to the Ideal boiler emptying its fire, and there was a distinctive smell pervading everywhere of dust, damp, and burning wood.

Someone, probably a warden or a policeman came round during the night to check that we were all OK, and that we were the occupiers of the house, what was left of it. A precaution, I was later to learn, to stop any looting that may, and did, happen.

When dawn came, we were able to see the extent of the damage. A total of 11 houses were so badly damaged that they had to be completely rebuilt. There were groups of neighbours dotted about either relating their experiences or in the main just silently watching the continuing rescue work. In the mean time my parents had systematically tried to clear the kitchen, which was in the back of the house, and what with broken crockery and provisions seemingly everywhere, it seemed impossible. However they managed to boil the kettle, the gas amazingly being still on, the pipes not being damaged our side of the road, and made a hot drink. During the next hour or so, the telephone in the next door house rang, but as my mother tried to find it in the rubble and pick it up, it stopped. How on earth it was still connected amazed us as the telephone pole carrying the lines had been blown like a battering ram into next door. Fortunately no one was badly hurt on our side of the road, but unfortunately there were at least eight serious casualties on the other side of the road, of which five, including two children, died.

Early next day quite a number of people came to offer shelter to those of us who had lost their homes. Lifelong friends of my parents, who then lived in Ashleigh Gardens, took us in for a few weeks until the local council found us accommodation, firstly in Howard Road, (furnished), and then in Courtenay Gardens which we managed to furnish with sufficient furniture salvaged from the wrecked house. It was in the second house where we celebrated VE-Day, less than two months after we had been bombed out!

I must admit there are a lot of blanks in the picture of that night and the following morning in my memory. After all it was 49 years ago. But I do remember the date 12.3.45. One cannot forget that simple sequence of numbers.

Ian Holt

(Opposite) An aerial view of Upminster taken after the end of the war. The V-2 Rocket damage in Waldegrave Gardens is still all too apparent. Notice the London bound steam train in the centre of the picture.

On mainland Europe the position of the German Forces was worsening fast. The Allies were now penetrating deep into Germany and had even successfully crossed the Rhine at Remagen and yet still the rockets came, with an average of one a day falling in Havering. The firing point for the rockets around the Hague had been bypassed by the rapidly advancing allies and so the Germans could sit there with relative impunity and still bombard England by day and by night although, so very near to defeat themselves.

A direct hit on 7 - 9 Manser Road, South Hornchurch, on the 14th March 1945, would no doubt have been ranked as their next success for once more eight civilians were killed and ten houses consumed. Sniffer dogs were brought in when it became apparent that one victim was unaccounted for and eventually the mutilated body of an eleven year old boy was discovered and identified, his mother's body already having been found.

A chance shot took place three days later when a rocket fell upon a 22 ton steam engine at Cold Harbour Jetty, Rainham Marshes. The Jetty and surrounding buildings were badly damaged, but thankfully it was half past three in the morning and so there were no casualties

Man of Courage and his Quarry.

Major Gerhold poses beside his trophy, a one ton warhead, following a successful bomb disposal operation at Hutton. Shortly after this photograph was taken he went on to defuse the unexploded rocket which fell in Northumberland Avenue, Heath Park, Hornchurch.

Unexploded Rocket

A reliable weapon the rocket was not. Apart from the many launch failures out of sight and earshot of Havering, at least four premature airbursts took place right over the heads of the population in various parts of the districts. There were also at least two airbreaks, this being where the rocket breaks up in mid air, the warhead falling to the ground and exploding independently. Unlike a conventional bomb, however, it was exceptionally rare for an intact rocket to fall to earth without exploding. The first to do so fell in a field at Paglesham in Essex on the night of 11th March 1945, six months after the start of the campaign and only two weeks before its termination. The officer in charge of defusing it was Major Gerhold of No.22 Bomb Disposal Company of the Royal Engineers. The warhead of the rocket penetrated 37 feet into the ground and so Major Gerhold's men were still digging it out when a second unexploded rocket fell at Hutton, Brentwood, a week later. Leaving the first rocket still armed, Major Gerhold left Paglesham to deal with this new arrival. This one proved to be nearer the surface and although sailing in uncharted waters, he began the long process of making it safe. The novelty value of an unexploded rocket brought brass hats by the score until it seemed to the good major that, ''All interested parties bar King Farouk were present.'' After checking for anti-handling devices with X-Rays the rocket was defused and the Amatol explosive steamed out. No sooner had this task been accomplished than a third unexploded rocket fell at No.45 Northumberland Avenue, Heath Park, Hornchurch at 5:40 am. on 20th March 1945. Once again the onerous duty of dealing with the missile fell to Major Gerhold. Being a residential area hundreds of homes had to be evacuated before work could commence. On this occasion the warhead, although buried, had been split open on impact and so once located he was able to scoop the explosive out by hand. Now that the rocket was disabled, it was dismantled, and taken away by lorry for further inspection by the Governments research 'boffins'.

The Final Day

In a final gesture of defiance three rockets dived to earth on the 26th March. The first in the early hours of the morning landed at the rear of houses on the south side of Ravenscourt Grove, Hornchurch, taking three more innocent lives in the process. It was a bleak rainy night. No sooner had countless roofs been stripped of their tiles than the rain started to pour through. Two of the dead were husband and wife, Mr. & Mrs. Turner. Her body was dug out of the ruins of their home, whilst her husband's body was found lying outside the house, having been blown there by the force of the explosion. Somewhere in the region of 1000 houses suffered some degree of damage that night.

This photograph was taken across the rocket damage towards houses on the western end of Ravenscourt Grove.

Looking across the devastation in Ravenscourt Grove towards battered bungalows in Ravenscourt Drive.

❏ Romford

The second rocket that day broke up in the air, the warhead choosing to fall in the centre of Mawney Road, Romford. This rogue warhead claimed the last two fatalities in the area and demolished 15 houses. As in any conflict, to be killed so close to the end of hostilities seems to somehow increase the tragedy. The last rocket of the day fell at 10:35 pm. at Noak Hill, where with some irony it demolished the Victory Hut. The citizens of Hornchurch and Romford waited for the next to fall.......it never came. The last rocket to fall on Britain, fell in the afternoon of the following day, at Orpington.

(**Above**) Although in its death throes, the Nazi regime was still capable of killing British civilians. The penultimate rocket to fall in Havering was that which fell in the centre of Mawney Road, Romford, at seven o'clock in the evening of the 26th March 1945. The rocket had in fact disintegrated in the air, the crater being caused by the detached warhead. The venturi fell over ½ mile away. The crater can be seen in the middle of the road, on the extreme left of the picture.

(**Right**) Motorists pass over the exact site of the crater, unaware that it was once the target of German aggression.

❑ Grotesque & Evil

By its very nature every weapon of war is grotesque, yet the rocket attained a degree of evil that was quite unique. It was like a primitive god, uncertain, inconsistent, and unjust. Almost as though Hitler had adopted the guise of Zeus himself, and could command bolts of devastating retribution at will. At any hour of the day or night, death or mutilation might come. This random, murderous power led many to hanker after 'the good old days' of the Doodlebugs, which at least gave some warning of its imminent arrival. Yet at the same time there are few who could not but admire the pinnacle of scientific achievement that the V2 represented. It was after all the same technology which would eventually take men to the stars.

Havering was fortunate that the V2 rocket never reached its full potential. The programme was dogged by problems and failures and constant modifications seriously undermined their mass production. The intention had been to fit the warheads with proximity fuses in order that they detonated a few feet above ground level. The technicalities of such a system were never fully mastered and most rockets were fitted with standard impact fuses and as a result buried themselves deep in the ground before exploding. This produced some spectacular craters but meant that most of the blast was sent up vertically where it was less likely to cause damage.

❑ The Score

Whereas the Doodlebug was launched around the Pas de Calais area, most of the rockets launched against England came from the Dutch coast. The upshot of this was that while any malfunctioning or disabled V1 Doodlebug fell on Kent, the trajectory of the rocket brought it straight over Essex. Therefore, any missile that fell short had a high probability of falling on the Havering area and this probability turned into reality. Of the 1,120 Rockets to reach our shores, a total of 61 fell within the confines of Havering, 5.5% of the total, or 1 in 20. Breaking Havering down into its separate wartime entities i.e. the Borough of Romford and the Urban District Council of Hornchurch we find that there were 22 rockets in Romford and 39 in Hornchurch. I was somewhat surprised by this latter figure as this means Hornchurch received more rockets than any other district in the country. Surprisingly, to my knowledge, this has never been acknowledged in any writing on the subject. Indeed it is sometimes claimed that Ilford was the 'top scorer' and although it is true that it gained more rockets than any other then metropolitan borough, with a grand tally of 35,

it was still some way behind Hornchurch's total. It would be foolish to look upon this numerical fact with pride when one just reflects what these figures meant in terms of human suffering. It is though, I think, eminently worthy of a footnote in history. (Ironically one of the safest places to be during the rain of rockets, was the City of London, not one fell within its borders!)

It is the humble soldier on the ground who must take the credit for the final defeat of Hitler's 'Vengeance Weapon No.2', for even though the Allies gained air superiority and achieved great leaps of technology in radar and related defence schemes, it was not until all the supply lines were cut that the campaign finally fizzled out.

❑ What Might Have Been

What if? Armchair strategists are prone to ask this question with annoying frequency, but in this instance it perhaps merits an answer. Had the rocket programme been given a higher priority earlier in the war it is quite likely that the German War Office's order for 12,000 rockets from the Central Works Factory at Nordhausen, issued on 19th October 1943, might have been met in full. Had this quantity been dispatched to England, and allowing for a 10% failure rate, Havering could have expected somewhere in the region of 500 rockets. The Allies would probably still have won the war, though Havering would have looked a very different place come V.E. Day.

❑ The Cost

The real cost was eighty-two lives. Wives, brothers, sons, daughters, new borns, husbands, mothers, sweethearts, sisters, fathers, neighbours and friends, killed by an enemy remote and unseen.

To achieve this the Nazi regime had to spend £12,000 a rocket and so for the 61 that fell here they in theory spent £ 732,000 in 1945 money. Today (1993), that translates into £ 18,300,000. Unlike the cost effective V1, the rocket swallowed valuable German resources and diverted materials (liquid oxygen, aluminium, hydrogen peroxide, alcohol) from other less spectacular but more effective war winning weapons. Thus Havering, if only by default, in consuming a large percentage of this expensive Nazi technology, played a considerable, if unintentional, part in shortening the war, but at what price?

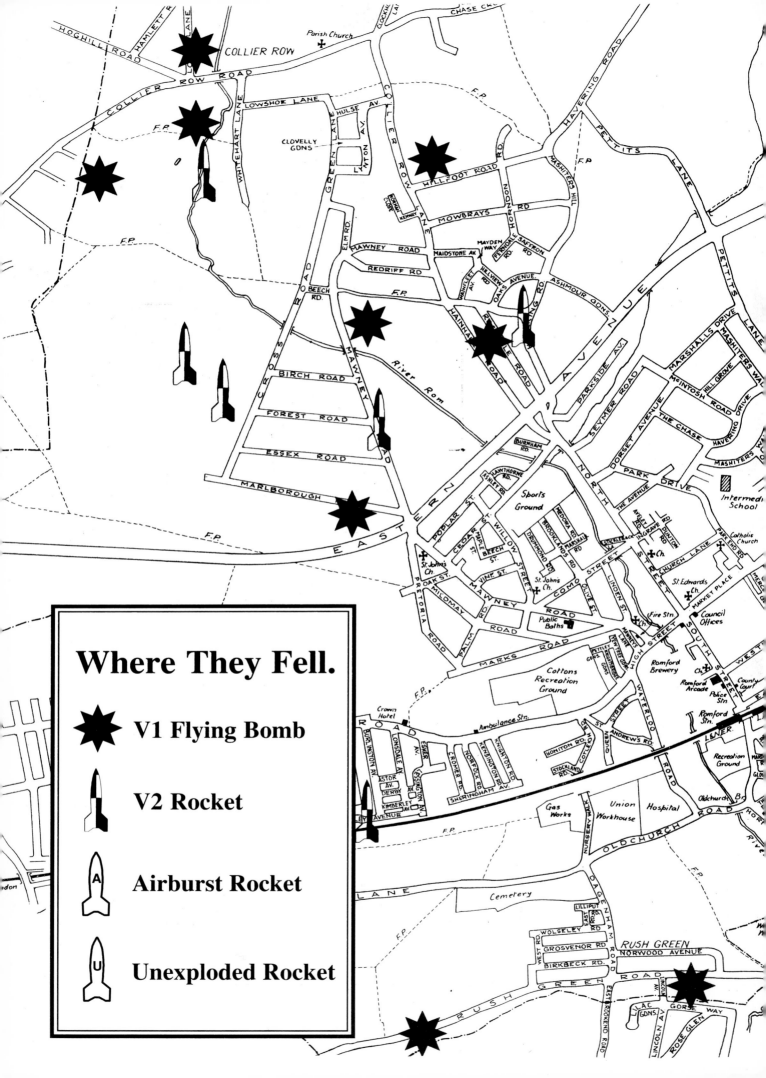

Where They Fell.

✴ **V1 Flying Bomb**

V2 Rocket

Ⓐ **Airburst Rocket**

Ⓤ **Unexploded Rocket**

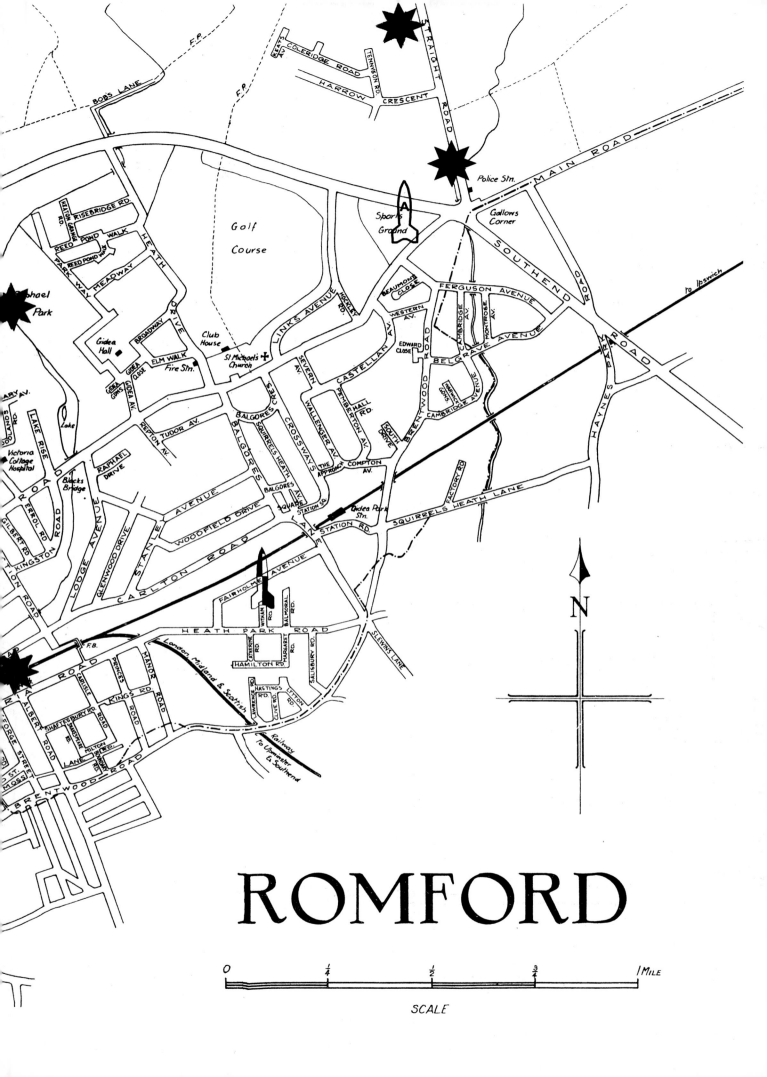

ROMFORD

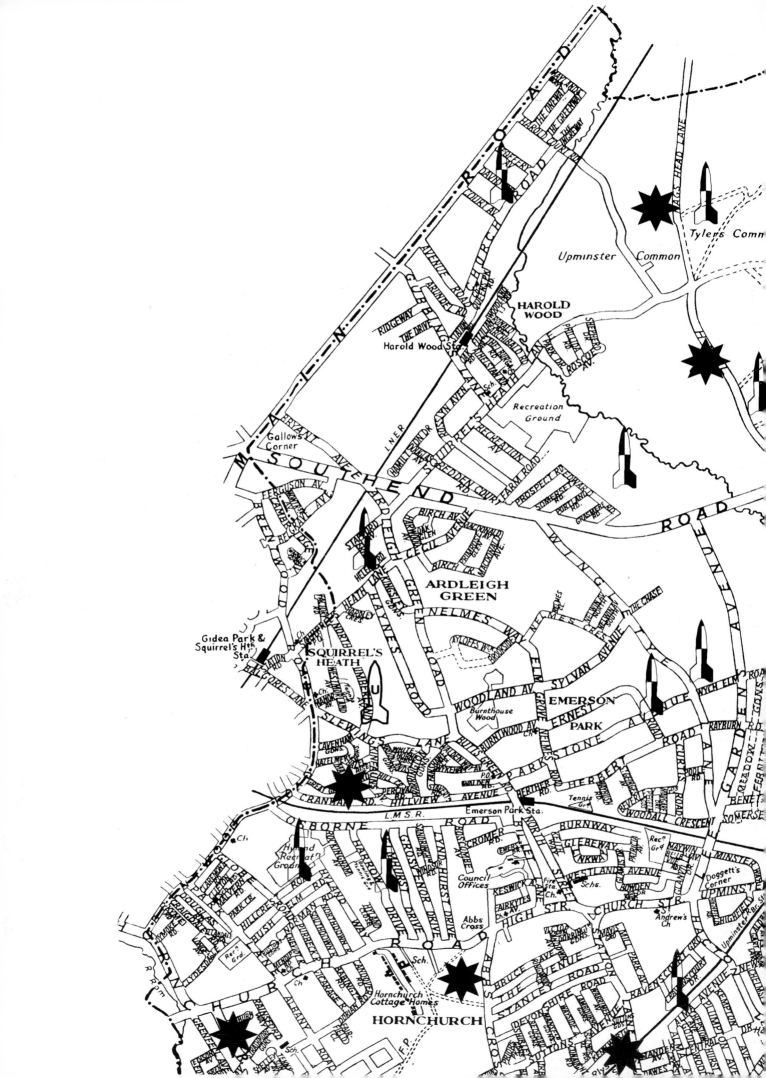

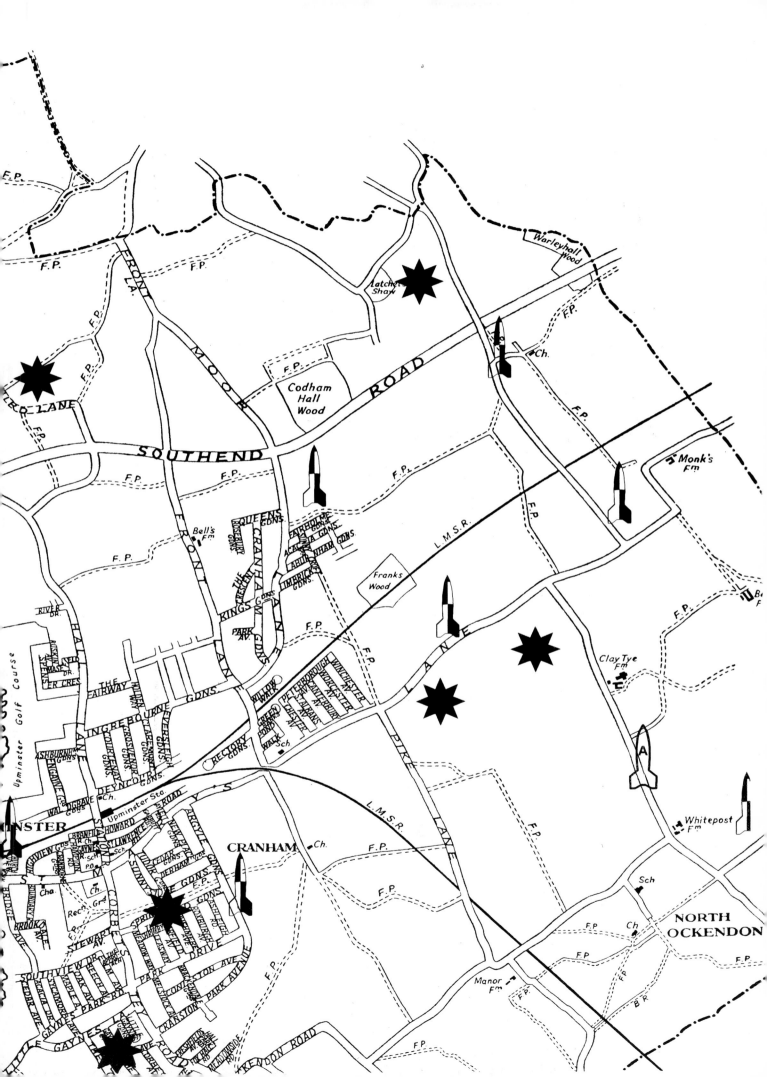

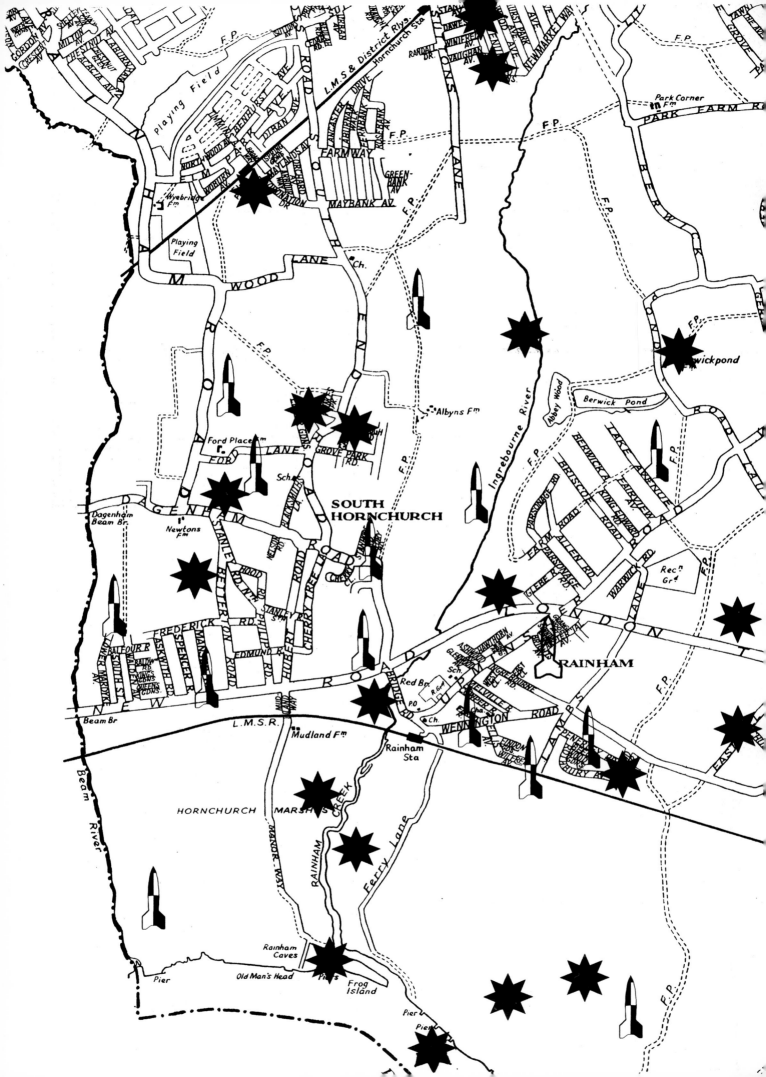

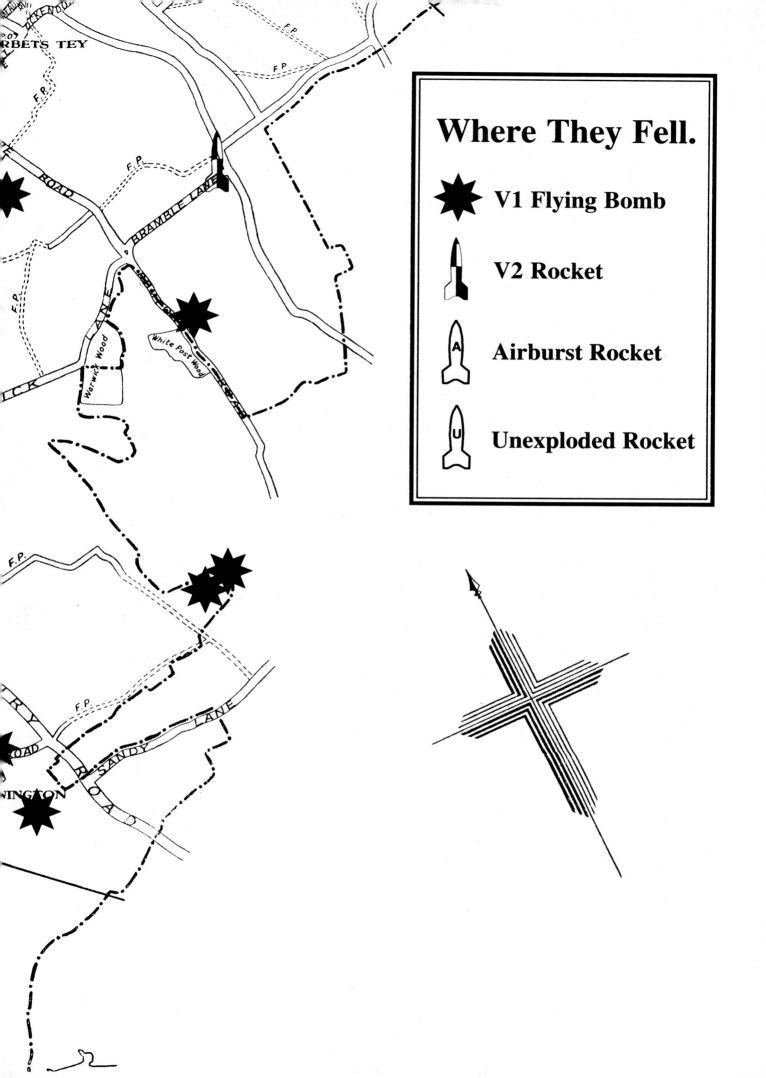

Where They Fell.

★ V1 Flying Bomb

⬛ V2 Rocket

⬛ Airburst Rocket

⬛ Unexploded Rocket

From Whence They Came

Havering To Holland 187 Miles

The British Government led the general public to believe that no warning of the V2 Rocket's arrival was possible. In fact, Allied radar engineers were presented with a ring side seat of the entire proceedings, yet they could only sit helplessly by as the blip on their screens heralded the launch of yet another V2 Rocket. In four minutes time this innocuous little blip would bring death and destruction somewhere in Southern England. Whilst not able to predict the eventual point of impact after their 60 mile high flight into the stratosphere, it was at least feasible, in conjunction with other radar stations, to pin point the launching area by triangulation. This information was top secret in 1944, but fifty years on it is at last possible to reveal the launch sites for most of the V2's that fell in Havering. (See V2 table on pages 179-182 for more precise details on each rocket.)

● Valkenburg

● Wassenaar

● THE HAGUE

● Voorburg

Looduinen ●

● DELFT

Monster ●

● Poeldijk

S' Gravenzande ●

● Naaldwijk

Hook of Holland ●

● ROTTERDAM

Conclusion

To attempt to write a conclusion on, or an explanation of, this tortuous period of Havering's history is a daunting if not impossible task. I merely hope that, depending on your age, I have refreshed your memory or introduced you to the salient points of a unique period of this century. Warfare is not one of man's most endearing activities and yet it still possesses a curious fascination. There may have been other wars before and since, but when somebody mentions simply 'the War' there is no mistaking to which one they refer. As well as being a global conflict this was a war that placed civilians in the front line, as a legitimate target, to be bombed, maimed and killed.

The War not only divides the first and latter halves of this century, but also divides the population like no other experience. If the wail of a siren gives you an empty feeling in your stomach, or the recorded throb of a Doodlebug a shiver down your spine, then like as not you were born before the war. Should these sounds mean nothing to you then you belong to the fortunate section of the community who emerged into the light of this world without the ever present threat of death from the skies   As the millennium approaches, the proportion of these two distinct groups inevitably becomes ever more one sided. It will not be many years before the war is no longer a human memory at all. It will have become merely some grainy black & white film footage on a documentary. War brings out the best and worst in mankind. There were those brought to action of great heroism, who in peacetime would have never had the opportunity to display such qualities, whilst there were the very few, who sunk to the depths of looting and black-marketeering.

What were the true risks of living through that period? Theoretically, each citizen of Havering was subjected to the mathematical risk of 1 in 500 of being killed as the result of enemy bombing. How many people felt those odds shorten dramatically at the sound of a Doodlebug cutting out overhead, or with the growing whistle of an earthbound bomb.

At the close of hostilities Havering's loss of life numbered 293 souls. How should one refer to such loss of life? A tragedy, a disaster, a calamity, a catastrophe? Before making a decision we should perhaps take a less parochial view and look at what was simultaneously befalling other parts of the globe. What hyperbole for instance should one use to describe the 4000 Russians who died each day under the siege of Leningrad, or the 60,000+ Germans who perished in the great Dresden fire-storm, or the 80,000 Japanese killed at Hiroshima. These of course dwarf our ordeal in magnitude, but one should not become numbed by these statistics. It is all to easy to let these figures blur and their significance become lost. Havering's statistics were flesh and blood, not numbers. There was 83 year-old Eva Starkey, robbed of a peaceful end to her twilight years by the monstrous force of a V1. Then there was little John Chumley, just six weeks old, denied life just at the outset. It is tempting to say that each death was mourned equally by those that knew and loved them dearly and yet the reality is that often nobody remained to mourn their passing, all having suffered the same fate. Who for instance grieves for the unidentified female in grave LL1670 at Romford Cemetery. The only reflection one can make, is that wherever possible, each individual victim, whether father, mother, sister or aunt, should be accorded due solemnity as the years pass and the conflict in which they perished inexorably slips into that of a previous century.

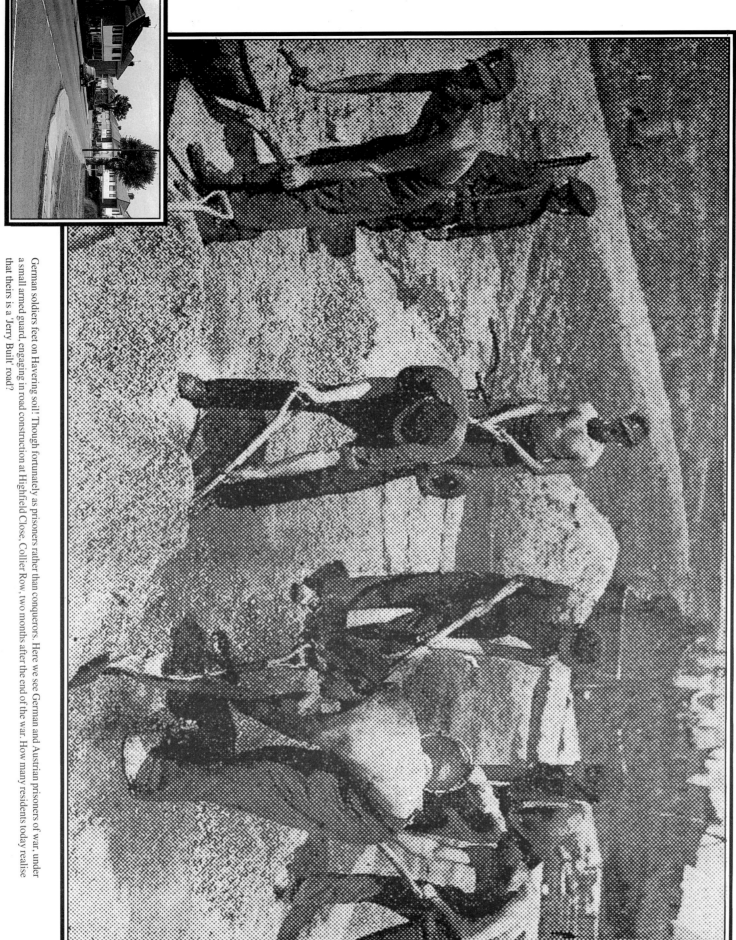

German soldiers feet on Havering soil! Though fortunately as prisoners rather than conquerors. Here we see German and Austrian prisoners of war, under a small armed guard, engaging in road construction at Highfield Close, Collier Row, two months after the end of the war. How many residents today realise that theirs is a 'Jerry Built' road?

Crashed Aircraft

■ **22/5/40   03:45   British Hampden Bomber Crashed in Rainham.**

(See pages 20-22)

■ **7/8/40   13:00   Spitfire Crashed at Hornchurch.**

Taking off from Hornchurch Aerodrome Spitfire R6617 crashed and caught fire. The aircraft was burnt out but Pilot Lieutenant C.G.C. Olive escaped unhurt.

■ **24/8/40   16:00   Defiant Shot Down Over Hornchurch.**

On the 24th August the first attack on Hornchurch Aerodrome occurred and in the attack Defiant L6965 was shot down over the aerodrome during combat with Bf 109's. Pilot Officer R.S Gaskell was injured, but his gunner Sergeant W.H. Machin died of the wounds he received. The Defiant was a two seater fighter and this particular example was from No. 264 Squadron which had arrived at Hornchurch only three days previously. The Defiant was outclassed by the enemy fighters and, as losses proved so heavy, the squadron was withdrawn to Duxford on the 29th August, to act as night fighters.

Defiant L6965 (second from left) pictured whilst fresh from the factory. In a few short months this pristine aircraft would lie a twisted wreck on Hornchurch soil, fatally wounding Sergeant Machin in the process.

■ **24/8/40   16:00   Heinkel He 111 Crashed at Clay Tye Hill, North Ockendon.**

One of the aircraft sent on the mission to bomb Hornchurch Aerodrome was Heinkel 111 (A1+KT). It was hit by anti-aircraft fire which disabled its port engine. Two aircraft of No.615 Squadron then attacked it and successfully shot it down. The two pilots were Squadron Leader J.R. Kayll and Pilot Officer S.A.P. McClintoch. Two members of the German crew were wounded (Uffz. K. Platzer & Uffz. H. Hermans) and had to be helped clear by the other members of the crew (Lt. W. Luttigen, Uffz. O. Lackner and Fw. A. Fraas. The aircraft then exploded. (See page 24)

■ 26/8/40 15:15 Hurricane Forced Landed Near Upminster.

After suffering severe damage at the hands of a Bf 109 during combat over the Thames Estuary, Sergeant E.M.C. Prchal managed a forced landing in a field adjoining Cranham Hall, near Upminster at 3:15 pm. He was slightly wounded, but his aircraft, although damaged, was thought to be repairable. Hurricane P3157 came from 310 Squadron which was based at Duxford. Any crashed plane was a potential target for souvenir hunters, but not all souvenir hunters were as brazen as one baker's roundsman from Upminster. Frederick A.D. Major, who was nineteen years old, was stopped by P.C. Osborne and in the back of his delivery van the policeman discovered a complete machine-gun from the crashed Hurricane. In court he admitted taking it as a souvenir and was fined £4.

The pilot, Edward Prchal, a Czech who had joined the R.A.F. in July 1940, was to achieve an unfortunate footnote in history. On July 4th 1943 Prchal was the pilot of a Liberator, on which General Sikorski, head of the Polish government-in-exile, was travelling. The Liberator was due to fly from Gibraltar to London, but shortly after take off the aircraft crashed into the sea. All on board were killed, except for Prchal who was pulled from the water unconscious and badly injured. The mysterious events of that day have proved fertile ground for subsequent conspiracy theories, with allegations of Russian or even British involvement in the crash.

Prchal died in California in December 1984. His ashes were taken to England, where half were sprinkled over the channel and the remainder buried in Brookwood Military Cemetery.

■ 30/8/40 12:10 Spitfire Crashed at Damyns Hall Farm, Upminster.

Sergeant I. Hutchinson of No.222 Squadron suffered damage to his Spitfire R6719 following combat with Bf 109's . He attempted to make his base at Hornchurch but was forced to land at Damyns Hall Farm, Warwick Lane. Hutchinson made a wheels up landing in a field where the aircraft was only slightly further damaged. He had sustained a 2 inch diameter hole in one of the propeller blades, which had apparently not been revolving on landing as not all the blades were bent. Apart from this there was no visible signs of damage. His aircraft was guarded by two soldiers from the local gun-site, before being removed by lorry. Hutchinson was unhurt on this occasion, though during the rest of the Battle of Britain he was shot down a further three times (Sept 14th, 18th & 30th), the last occasion on which he was wounded.

■ 30/8/40 12:45 Messerschmitt Bf 109 Crashed in Bridge Road, Rainham.

During combat over Hornchurch Flying Officer B.J.G. Carbury 9 (603 Squadron) managed to shoot down Messerschmitt Bf 109E-1 (4806). After losing a wing, Oberlt. L Hafer baled out. It was two days before he was found dead with an unopened parachute in Ingrebourne Creek. His aircraft crashed at Bridge Road, Rainham, where it burnt out.

■ 31/8/40 13:15 & 18:00 Six Spitfires Destroyed on Hornchurch Aerodrome.

In the worst raid on the aerodrome the R.A.F lost six spitfires whilst taking off.

(See page 25)

■ 31/8/40 13:30 British Hurricane Crashed on Wennington Marshes.

On the day of the large raid on Hornchurch Aerodrome a Hurricane of No. 310 Squadron from Duxford engaged a force of Dorniers Do.215's over the Thames Estuary. The Hurricane was jumped by one of the defending fighters and promptly shot down. The plane crashed to the south of Wennington Church, where it burnt out. The Czech pilot, Jaroslav Sterbacek was classified as missing. On August 13th 1978 the Essex Historical Society excavated the site and recovered six of the eight Browning .303 machine guns, as well as parts of the undercarriage.

■ 7/9/40 16:43 British Bomber Crashed at East Close Rainham.

At 3:50 p.m. a Blenheim bomber of 600 Squadron was returning to its base at Hornchurch when it suffered engine failure in the port engine and crashed inverted in East Close, Rainham. Both Sergeant A.F.C. Saunders and Sergeant J.W. Davies were killed. The plane was partially burned out.

■ 7/9/40 17:10 Messerschmitt Bf 110 Crashed at Park Corner Farm, Upminster.

On the 7th September the Germans altered their tactics of the air offensive and sent a major daytime raid against London. This gave the R.A.F. a welcome respite from the airfield attacks which were having such a damaging effect. The hope was to force the R.A.F. to commit its carefully hoarded reserves of fighters so that they could be destroyed by the numerically superior German force. These attacks marked the beginning of the 'Blitz'. One of

160

the fighters escorting the bombers to their target was a Messerschmitt Bf 110 serial A2+NH. It was attacked and shot down by three British fighters piloted by Flying Officer J.B. Holderness, Pilot Officer S. Janough and Flight Lieutenant B. Lane. Hans Mescheder, the gunner and radio operator, baled out shortly before the crash, but his parachute failed to open and he fell to his death in a field behind Frank's Cottages in St. Mary's Lane, Upminster. The pilot, Kurt Schunemann, bailed out too low and was killed. The aircraft went on to crash and disintegrate at Park Corner Farm, Hacton Lane, Upminster. The body of Mescheder (aged 20) and the remains of Schunemann (aged 22) were recovered and given a full military funeral. Simple wooden crosses mark their graves at the German Military Cemetery at Cannock Chase, Staffordshire. Forty four years on, the crash site was excavated by the Essex Historical Aircraft Society on Sunday 23rd September 1984, after weeks of careful investigation to find the exact impact point. One of the most impressive finds was one of the two Daimler-Benz V-12 engines. This can now be viewed at the Aviation Museum located in the Coal House Fort, East Tilbury.

The exhumation of a Daimler-Benz Db 601 V12 engine by members of the Essex Historical Aircraft Society. It had laid dormant at Park Corner Farm for 44 years, after the Messerschmitt it help to power crashed at that site on the first day of the Blitz.

■ 15/9/40 14:15 British Plane Crashed Near Lodge Lane, Collier Row.

British aircraft crashed at Nashs Farm, Lodge Lane. Pilot believed to be safe.

■ 27/9/40 12:00 Spitfire Crashed Near Wennington.

Just before midday on 27th September, Spitfire R6720 of No. 222 Squadron from Hornchurch, was patrolling over Maidstone when attacked by Messerschmitt Bf 109's. The Spitfire piloted by Sergeant R.H. Gretton crash landed in a field to the rear of the Noak Cafe in Wennington. He was rushed to Oldchurch Hospital, where he would spend the next five months, having sustained multiple back injuries and a lacerated lip.

■ 12/10/40 16:40 Spitfire Crashed in Hornchurch

Sergeant J. McAdam was taking off from Hornchurch Aerodrome in his Spitfire when the engine cut out and he was forced to crash at Globe Road, Hornchurch. His aircraft was a write off, but he escaped unhurt. McAdam had already had an eventful Battle of Britain. On the 7th September he had been shot down over Rayleigh. On the 23rd September he was shot down into the sea off Dover, though tragically on 20th February 1941 he was shot down by a British aircraft, again over Dover. His dead body was picked out of the sea and buried at Ballyharry Cemetery, Island Magee, Co. Antrim.

■ 18/10/40 19:00 Hurricane Crashed on Maylands Aerodrome.

Hurricane P5206 of No. 249 Squadron sustained damage to its wings when it crashed at Maylands Aerodrome. The pilot was unhurt.

■ 25/10/40 12:07 Hurricane Crashed in Woodstock Avenue, Romford.

Just after noon on 25th October 1940, Pilot Officer William B. Patullo in his Hurricane V6804 crashed into a house in Woodstock Avenue, Romford. He had been on a routine patrol and the cause of the crash was unknown. Although rescued from the wreck, still alive, he died from his wounds the next day in Oldchurch Hospital. Only 21 years of age at the time of his death, Patullo had already achieved considerable combat success, having shot down two Do 17's, an He 111, a Bf 110 and a Bf 109.

■ 1/11/40 21:45 Heinkel He 111 Crashed in Hornchurch.

After having been hit by anti-aircraft fire Heinkel He 111P-2, serial G1+JS crashed on flats in Matlock Gardens, Hornchurch. Two of the crew successfully bailed out. They were the pilot Leutnant Hans-Adalbert Tuffers and Uffz.Josef Haverstreug. The two remaining crew Unteroffizier Richard Bubel and Josef Juvan perished in the crash. Three civilians were killed when burning petrol from the plane engulfed their Anderson shelter. (See pages 47-48)

■ February 1942 British Fighter Crashed Near Upminster.

A member of No. 21 Platoon of the Home Guard, Private F. Tate witnessed a British fighter crash near his home. He rushed to give assistance and with some help dragged the unconscious pilot from his blazing machine shortly before it exploded. Tate cut away the pilot's smouldering parachute and performed first aid on his fractured leg.

■ 24/3/43 Spitfire Crashed in Hornchurch

Flying Officer R. Sanders-Draper, an American citizen, experienced engine failure at a height of 200 feet, shortly after taking off from Hornchurch. He crash landed, narrowly avoiding Suttons School, in Suttons Lane. The young American was killed in the crash, but as it was felt he had prejudiced his own life in order to save the school, it was subsequently renamed Sanders-Draper School in his honour.

■ 14/9/43 16:42 Mustang Fighter Crashed in Rainham.

A Mustang fighter crashed in a field to the west of Rainham Road and 150 yards north of the Junction with the A13. The pilot injured his leg and the plane was partially destroyed by fire.

■ 5/11/43 13:00 R.A.F. Fighter Crashed Landed in Rainham.

Shortly after taking off from Hornchurch Aerodrome, a British fighter crash landed by the A13 Arterial Road in Rainham. The pilot was only slightly injured in the accident.

■ 13/2/44 20:50 German Bomber Crashed at Havering-atte-Bower

On the night of 13th February 1944 a German Bomber, a Junkers Ju 88S-1, was on a pathfinding mission over London, its task to mark the target area with flares. Two powerful BMW 801 G-2 engines combined with its black camouflage made it an unlikely target to be shot down. Nonetheless the searchlights picked it out and with unusual accuracy the anti-aircraft guns scored a direct hit almost immediately. The aircraft broke up in mid-air at 9,000ft. The tail gunner/radio operator, Helmut Niedack, 24, attempted to scramble clear of his fragment of aircraft as it tumbled to earth, but found himself entangled with his machine-gun. Eventually he managed to extricate himself and his parachute from the shattered plane. At the end of his parachute jump a barbed wire fence lay in wait in the back garden of a house in North Road, Havering-atte-Bower. Once more entangled, this time with the barbed wire, and now with a broken arm to contend with, he cried out for help. A neighbour heard his pleas and came to his assistance. The German airman was relieved of his luger, flying helmet and life-jacket, before being taken to the village first aid post for treatment. His parachute also mysteriously disappeared, although as A.F. Kilby related in ''A Village At War'', there were a number of nice silk dresses being worn in the village some time later.

Neither of his crewmates managed to escape from the aircraft before it crashed. The pilot, Corporal Herbert Ehling, aged 23, and the observer Sergeant Josef Weikert, aged 25, are both buried at the German Military Cemetery at Cannock Chase, Staffordshire.

The remains of the plane crashed south of Bower House, Orange Tree Hill where most of it was destroyed by

A German aviator returns to Havering after an absence of 42 years. Helmut Neidack, the sole survivor of a Junkers 88S-1 that crashed at Havering-atte-Bower, visited the scene of the crash site in 1986 at the invitation of members of the Essex Historical Aircraft Society. The site was excavated in his presence and in the photograph we see him inspecting parts of his aircraft he hastily parted company from in February 1944.

(Below)

The crash site itself, south of Bower House, Orange Tree Hill. Members of the Essex Historical Aircraft Society excavate the site with the help of a mechanical digger.

163

fire. The two engines buried themselves deep into the ground. Surrounding the wreckage were scattered small cardboard containers that were the unused marker flares. Of more concern was an unexploded 50kg bomb found amongst the wreckage and it could not be certain that this was the only one. Forty-two years later members of the Essex Historical Aircraft Society organised a dig at the crash site. Helmut Neidack, then 64, was invited over from West Berlin to witness the remains of his Junkers Bomber being exhumed. At the dig he was reunited with air raid warden Len Butcher who had captured him all those years before. At the reunion Mr. Butcher returned Herr Neidack's flying helmet and life-jacket he had appropriated the last time they had encountered one another. Both were still stained with the blood of his wartime injuries.

The dig yielded various parts of corroded airframe, but of most interest was the damaged radio receiver that Helmut Neidack had once operated. A bomb disposal expert stood by, just in case there were any unexpected discoveries.

■ 6/4/45   17:00   British Mustang Crashed in Cranham.

Whilst on an anti-aircraft co-operation flight with the Royal School of Artillery at Laindon, Flying Officer J.N Kokaj flying his P51 Mustang reported the presence of fumes in his cockpit. He circled his base and it became apparent that the aircraft was on fire. It then crashed at high speed near Lambkins Farm, Cranham, where it exploded on impact. The pilot was buried at St. Andrews Church, North Weald.

Day by Day
Record of Bombing

I feel I should perhaps preface the following twelve pages by introducing a slight note of caution. The tables are as accurate as remaining documents will allow, for unfortunately many of the most detailed bombing records for the area have apparently either been destroyed or lost. Whilst all the major incidents are hopefully recorded, I am aware that some minor ones, and in particular those where bombs fell in rural areas, may well have been overlooked. I have tried to reduce these omissions to an absolute minimum by cross referencing wherever possible.

Perhaps the following will help put the situation into perspective. On discussing the poor state of records with one former A.R.P. official, he interjected dryly,

"When bombs are falling down all around, you are more concerned about your posterior than posterity!"

I trust the reader will keep this sentiment in mind!

■ H.E. = High Explosive Bomb	■ P. M. = Parachute Mine
■ U.X.B. = Unexploded Bomb	■ A. A. = Anti-Aircraft Shell
■ Incs. = Incendiaries	■ Oil = Oil Incendiary Bomb

MAY / AUGUST

DATE	TIME	DISTRICT	LOCALITY	BOMB	DAMAGE & CASUALTIES
MAY					
22/5/40	03:54	Rain	Berwick Rd	Plane	British bomber
AUGUST					
1/8/40	01:50	H.Wood	Harold Wood nr station.	35 inc	
24/8/40	16:14	N.Ock	Fairclay Field Clay Tye Hill	Plane	Heinkel 111
	15:47	Rain	Rainham	12 HE	4 houses demolished in Glenwood Av & 1 house set on fire in Berwick Road. Many U.X.B.s
	15:45	Horn	Horn. Aerodrome	7 HE	1 house demolished
	15:42	Horn	Minster Way	20 HE	1 house demolished
	15:45	Horn	Briscoe Rd. }		1 house damaged
			Cherry Tree Lane }	17 HE	2 houses demolished
			Edmund Road }		2 houses damaged
			Philip Road }		
			Mardyke Av }		
26/8/40	15:15	Upm	Upminster	Plane	Hurricane
	15:25	Elm Pk.	Benhurst Av.	1 HE	No. 55 demolished
	15:25	Rain	Upminster Rd.	inc	74 Upminster Rd.
	15:25	Horn	High St. Horn.	inc	
27/8/40	23:08	Rom	Jubilee Av.	1 HE	Crater in road.
	23:04	Horn	Hornchurch	inc	
28/8/40	22:30	Rain	Rainham Marshes	1 HE	
	22:30	Rain	Ferry Lane	incs	
	22:30	Rain	Ayletts Farm	incs	
	23:55	Horn	Hornchurch	incs	
	22:40	Rom	In field	incs	
	23:55	Rom	Junct. of Clock-House Lane & Pinewood Av.	1 HE	
30/8/40	12:10	Rain	Damyns Hall Fm.	Plane	Spitfire
	12:45	Rain	Bridge Rd	Plane	Me 109
	22:22	Rain	Cowper Rd.	1 HE	3 houses demolished
31/8/40	13:15	Horn	Park Lane	HE's	Houses demolished Two fatalities.

(continued) / SEPTEMBER

DATE	TIME	DISTRICT	LOCALITY	BOMB	DAMAGE & CASUALTIES
31/8/40	13:15	Horn	Southend Rd.	HE's	Houses demolished. One fatality.
			King Edward Rd }		
	13:21	Rom	Hearn Rd }	7 HE	40 houses damaged 8 casualties, 3 fatal
			Randall Rd. }		
			Richmond Rd }		
	13:30	Wenn	Wennington Marsh	Plane	British pilot killed
	17:40	Horn	Hacton Lane	1 HE + inc	1 house demolished
SEPTEMBER					
1/9/40		Horn	Hornchurch	incs	
2/9/40	16:35	Horn	Lancaster Dr.	HE	1 house demolished
	16:35	Horn	Herbert Rd.	HE	2 houses demolished
	16:35	Horn	Parkstone Av.	HE	Several damaged
	16:35	Horn	High St. Horn.	HE	
	16:35	Horn	Stanley Rd.	HE	
	16:35	Horn	Abbs Cross Lane.	HE	
	16:00	Horn	Farm Way	HE	
	16:00	Horn	The Avenue	HE	
	16:00	Upm	Eversleigh Gdns.	HE	
	16:00	Cran	Cranham P.O	HE	
	16:00	Rain	W. of Berwick Rd.	6 HE's	
4/9/40	23:45	Rain	N.Ockendon	incs	Barley field & haystack set on fire
5/9/40	23:50	Rom	Lawnsway	HE	House demolished
	23:50	Rom	Clockhouse Lane & Lynwood Drive	HE	
6/9/40	22:00	Elm Pk.	Elm Park	HE	
	22:15	N.Ock	Pea Lane	1 HE	
7/9/40	15:50	Rain	Rainham	Plane	British bomber crashed.
	17:10	Upm	Hacton Lane	Plane	German fighter
	17:10	Horn	Rainsford Way	UXB	
	17:50	Rom	Gallows Cnr	HE	
	18:10	Rom	Gallows Cnr	Oil inc	
8/9/40	18:00	H.Wood	Avenue Rd.	HE	
	18:00	Rom	Waverley Crescent	HE	
	00:42	Rom	Noak Hill	incs	Fires
	00:55	Horn	Rainham Rd.	HE	

DATE	TIME	DISTRICT	LOCALITY	BOMB	DAMAGE & CASUALTIES
13/9/40	00:20	Rom	Btwn Main Road & Lodge Avenue	HE	
	09:45	Horn	Jersey Rd. & Princes Pk. +	HE & UXB	1 house demolished
			Argents Farm	incs	Barn wrecked
	21:35	Rom	Main Rd/Links Av	HE	
14/9/40	02:50	Rom	Strange & Co. Flour factory rear N. St.	UXB	
	03:40	Rom	282 Rush Green Rd.	UXB	
	03:40	Rom	Clayton Rd.	UXB	
	12:50	N.Ock	Clay Tye Rd.	AA UX	
	12:50	Horn	Kingsley Gdns	AA UX	
15/9/40	14:15	Rom	Lodge Lane	Plane	British pilot safe
	14:45	Rain	Castle Av.	HE	1 house demolished
	21:40	Rain	Blacksmiths Lane	HE	5 houses demolished 13 wounded
16/9/40	02:10	N.Hill	Near Priory	HE's	
	15:41	N.Ock	E. of Ock. Rd.	100 incs	
			N. of Fen Lane	2 Oil incs	
	23:40	Rain	New Rd. Rainham	HE	One fatality. 2 houses demolished & 100 damaged
	23:40	Horn	Edmund Rd.	HE	
	23:40	Rain	Ferry Lane. Rear of Starch wks.	2 PM	
17/9/40	00:05	Rom	Collier Row Lane	4 HE	2 houses demolished. 1 fatality
	00:15	Rom	Park End Road	HE	2 houses demolished
	00:15	Rom	Cross Road	HE	
	04:50	Rom	Mawney Rd/Eastn Av	HE	
17/9/40	04:50	Rom	N.of London Rd.	HE's	
	05:00	Rom	Nr. Town Hall	incs	
	04:55	Rom	Lynwood Drive & Clockhouse Lane	2 UXB	
	21:20	Rain	Murex Wks. Rain. Park Fm.	HE & incs	Fire
	21:20	Cran	Ellis Av. &	incs	
	21:20	Rain	37 Findon Gdns	HE & incs	1 house demolished
	21:20	Rain	W. Moor Hall Fm.	UX PM	One fatality

DATE	TIME	DISTRICT	LOCALITY	BOMB	DAMAGE & CASUALTIES
9/9/40	02:40	Rom	35 Parkside Av.	HE	
10/9/40	02:11	Rom	Jnct. of N. St. & Eastern Av.	HE	
	02:00	Cran	Broadfields Fm	HE	2 cottages damaged
	02:00	Rain	59 Wentworth Wy	HE	
	02:00	Rain	13 Ingrebourne Rd	HE	
	02:00	Upm	Cranston Pk. Av.	UXB	
	02:28	Rain	Murex Wks.	incs	
	02:28	Upm	Pooles Fm	incs	Barn set on fire
	03:40	Rom	St. John's Road	HE	2 houses demolished
	04:23	Rom	Pinewood Road	HE	
	20:15	N.Hill	Village Road	HE	
	20:15	Rom	Cedric Av.	HE	1 house demolished
	20:15	Rom	Highfield Road	HE	3 houses damaged
	20:15	Rom	Erith Crescent	HE	
	22:04	Rom	Hill Grove	HE	No.9,11,13,17 demolished
	22:04	Rom	Pettits Lane	Oil inc	
	22:04	Rom	Pettits Lane	2 UXBs	No. 102 & 122
	22:04	Rom	83 Dorset Av.	UXB	
	22:15	Rom	On A12	UXB	
	22:43	Rom	Main Rd.	UXB	
	23:10	Rom	Goosehays Fm.	HE	
	23:15	Rom	Pinewood Road	HE's	
	23:15	Rom	St. John's Road	HE's	
	23:15	Rom	Bower Farm	HE's	
	23:30	Rom	54 Chase Cross Rd.	HE	
11/9/40	03:20	Upm	Upminster	HE & incs	
	03:55	Horn	Hornchurch	incs	
	23:00	Rom	171b Chase Cross	UXB	
12/9/40	04:15	Horn	Albany Rd.	incs	
	17:30	Wenn	Wennington Rd ..	HE	1 house demolished Stanham Terraces
	22:50	Rom	Straight Rd.	UXB	
	22:50	Rom	Main Rd.	UXB	
	22:50	Rom	Shaftesbury	UXB	
	23:57	Rom	Victoria Rd.	HE	210,212,214 demolished 3 killed, 2 wounded.
	23:57	Rom	Carlton Rd & Stanley Av	HE	
	21:41	Horn	Woodhall Cres.	Oil inc	
13/9/40	00:05	Rom	Nr. Waverley Cres.	HE	

DATE	TIME	DISTRICT	LOCALITY	BOMB	DAMAGE & CASUALTIES
18/9/40	02:00	Rom	Victoria Rd.	incs	
	02:00	Rom	Pretoria Rd/ Marks Rd.	Oil	
	02:00	Rom	Wheatsheaf Rd/ Eastern Road	Oil	
	20:45	Elm Pk.	Benhurst Av.	HE	2 houses demolished
	20:50	Elm Pk.	Warren Drive	UXB	
	20:15	Rom	Straight Rd/ Lower Bedfords Rd	HE	
	20:15	Rom	Broxhill Road	HE	
19/9/40	01:15	Rom	Straight Rd. & Lower Bedfords Rd.	6 UXB	
	01:20	Rom	Bower Farm	HE's	
	00:01	Rom	On Maylands	HE'S	
	20:35	Wenn	Wennington	250 inc	
	20:35	Horn	Emerson Pk	UXB	
	21:50	Horn	Abbs Cross Lane	HE	1 house demolished 5 wounded, 2 fatally.
	23:05	Horn	Cottage Home	UXB	2 houses demolished
	23:05	Horn	Patricia Drive	HE	2 killed and 3 wounded
	23:05	Horn	Lyndhurst Drive	HE	
	22:00	Rom	E. Gallows Cnr.	HE	
	22:04	Rom	Near Heath Drive	HE	
	21:30	Rom	Collier Row Fm.	HE	Farm Buildings Wrecked
20/9/40	22:22	Rom	Straight Rd.	incs	
	23:50	Rom	Oaklands Av	HE	1 house demolished
	23:50	Rom	Kingston Rd.	HE	
	23:50	Rom	Carlton Parade	HE	
	23:50	Rom	Main Road	HE	
	23:50	Rom	Havering Drive	HE	4 fatal casualties 2 houses demolished
21/9/40	23:35	Rom	Carlton Rd. & Stanley Av.	PM	100 houses damaged 8 wounded
	24:00	Rom	Essex Rd.	UXB	
22/9/40	00:20	Horn	Chepstow Av.	3 HE's	
	00:20	Horn	Harrow Drive	3 HE's	
	00:20	Horn	Goodwood Av	HE	1 house demolished
	00:20	Cran	Bird Lane	UXB	

DATE	TIME	DISTRICT	LOCALITY	BOMB	DAMAGE & CASUALTIES
22/9/40	20:50	Rain	Berwick Pond	20 incs	
	20:59	Rom	Hornchurch Rd.	HE & incs	3 houses demolished 1 fatality
	20:50	Rom	Oldchurch Rd.	HE	
	22:50	Rom	Heaton Av. HE		
23/9/40	00:51	Rom	Lower Bedfords Rd/ Straight Rd.	HE	
	01:10	Upm	Corbets Tey Rd.	HE & UXB	4 houses demolished & 14 damaged
	03:40	Rom	Beauly Way	HE	2 houses demolished 1 fatality
	08:54	Rom	Oldchurch Rd.	UXB	
	21:40	N.Hill	Noak Hill	incs	
	23:30	Rom	Birkbeck Rd.	UX PM	Quarter mile radius evacuated
	22:40	Horn	Harrow Lodge		
			Elmhurst Drive		
			Abbs Cross Lane. }	incs	
			Bruce Av. }		
			High Street }		
			Kings Head. }		
	19:50	Horn	Plumpton Av.	AA UX	
	19:50	Upm	Woodside Cott.		
			Upm. Common	AA UX	
	23:59	Rom	Nr. Crichton Gdns	HE's	
24/9/40	01:15	Upm	St. Mary's Lane	HE	4 cottages demolished 2 fatalities.
	20:30	Elm Pk.	73 Spring Gdns.	HE	1 fatality.
	20:30	Cran	Monks Farm	PM & 2 HE	5 cottages demolished
	20:30	Upm	Upm. Golf Course	2 HE	
	20:40	Horn	Ardliegh Grn Rd.	UXB	
	21:50	Rom	Straight Rd	UXB	
25/9/40	05:40	H.Wood	Harold Wood	UXB	
	05:45	Horn	Lilliputt Fm	HE	
	05:45	Horn	Wingletye Lane	HE	
	05:45	Rain	Stephens Garage,	HE	
26/9/40	21:40	Rain	Berwick Pond Fm.	PM	
	21:40	Cran	Cranham,400yds N.W of Rectory	HE	
27/9/40	12:00	Wenn	Wennington	Plane	Spitfire crashed.

DATE	TIME	DISTRICT	LOCALITY	BOMB	DAMAGE & CASUALTIES
27/9/40	22:40	Horn	Randall Drive	HE	7 houses demolished 2 killed, 6 wounded
	22:45	Horn	Junct of Ascot Gdns & Goodwood Av.	UXB	
28/9/40	00:45	Horn	Junct. of A125 & Dagenham Rd.	HE	
29/9/40	17:55	Rom	135 Brentwood Rd.	AA UX	
	18:35	Rom	20 Hog Hill Rd.	AA UX	
	22:07	Rain	Upminster Rd.	3 HE & UXB	
	23:55	Rom	Clockhouse Lane	Oil Bombs	
30/9/40	22:50	Rom	Bedfords Park	HE's	

OCTOBER

DATE	TIME	DISTRICT	LOCALITY	BOMB	DAMAGE & CASUALTIES
1/10/40	02:00	Horn	Suttons Fm.	PM	40 houses in Elm Park damaged
	04:45	Horn	Wych Elm Rd.	UXB	
	04:40	Horn	E.of Lilliputt Fm	2 UXB	
	05:00	Horn	N.E Wingletye Ln	UXB	
	05:00	Horn Nr.	Beltinge Rd.	UXB	
3/10/40	05:10	Rom	Erith Crescent	HE	2 houses demolished
	05:10	Rom	Faircross Av.	HE	
	05:10	Rom	Hulse Avenue	HE	2 houses demolished
	05:10	Rom	White Hart Lane	HE	1 house demolished
	12:30	Horn	Beverley Gdns	AA UX	
	12:30	Horn	Wingletye Lane	AA UX	
	16:00	N.Ock	N.O. Hall Farm	HE	1 fatality
4/10/40	02:00	Rain	Refuse Tip	HE	
	17:30	H.Wood	Cnr. Athelstan Rd & Squirrel Heath Rd	HE	
	17:32	H.Wood	Nr. Redden Ct Sch.	4 HE	
	17:32	N.Hill	The Mount	incs	
	21:20	Rom	Bedfords Pk.	3 Oil incs	
	21:20	Rom	Pyrgo Park	HE'S	
5/10/40	01:15	Rom	½ mile south of Gallows Corner	UXB	
	07:00	Wenn	Wennington Rd.	HE	No. 3,4,5 demolished
	20:30	Rom	Rush Green Rd.	Oil inc	

DATE	TIME	DISTRICT	LOCALITY	BOMB	DAMAGE & CASUALTIES
5/10/40	22:50	Rom	Pammer Av.	HE	3 houses demolished
	22:50	Rom	Junct. of East. Av & Ashmour Gdns	UXB	
	22:50	Rom	Fontayne Avenue	HE	Fires started
	21:20	Elm Pk.	Elm Park	incs	
	21:20	Upm	Upminster	incs	
	21:20	Upm	Park Corner Fm., Hacton Lane	HE or PM	6 buildings damaged
	21:20	Upm	Hacton White Hart	HE	
6/10/40	00:40	Rom	N.of Lodge Lane	HE's	
	01:05	Upm	Bush Farm, Aveley Rd	1 UXB	
	01:05	Rain	Ford Fm, Rainham	3 UXB & HE	
	01:05	Rain	Rothbury Av	AA UX	
	01:15	Rom	Romford Station	HE	Damage to station
	01:17	Rom	Gidea Pk Station	UXB	
	01:17	Rom	Woodfield Drive	HE	4 houses demolished
	01:17	Rom	Lodge Avenue	HE	
	01:17	Rom	Kingston Rd.	HE	
	01:17	Rom	Romford Gas Works	AA UX	
	01:17	Rom	Maylands Golf Crse	UXB	
	15:00	Rom	NE of Gidea Pk Stn	HE	
	15:00	Rom	Crossways	HE	
	15:00	Rom	Compton Avenue	HE	2 houses demolished
8/10/40	03:00	Rain	Junct. of Pinewood Av. & Hawthorn Av	UXB	No. 23 Hawthorne Av damaged.
	01:30	Rain	Findon Gdns	UXB	
	20:00	Rom	Maylands & Dagnam	HE'S	
	20:15	H.Park	Ingreway	HE & UXB	
	20:15	Cran	Jnct of Warley St. & St Mary's Lane	Oil inc	
	20:49	Rom	Brick Fields, E.Av	HE	
	21:03	Rom	Nr. Hainault Rd.	HE	
	21:10	Rom	Nr.Collier Row	HE	
9/10/40	00:27	N.Hill	Paternoster Row	HE	
	03:17	N.Hill	Peek's Farm	HE	
	20:10	Rom	Eastern Av	UXB	
	20:20	Rom	London Rd.	HE	Hit First Aid post School & houses in Spring Gdns damaged.
	20:45	Rain	Leonard Arms	HE	1 wounded
	19:20	Elm Pk	Heath Rd. Elm Pk.	UXB	

DATE	TIME	DISTRICT	LOCALITY	BOMB	DAMAGE & CASUALTIES
10/10/40	05:10	Horn	Westland Av.	HE	
	05:10	Horn	Cnr.of North St & Burnway	HE	
	05:10	Horn	Butts Grn Rd. & Bertha Rd.	HE	
	05:10	Horn	Rear Utd Dairies	HE	
	05:10	Horn	Westland Av. up North Street	10 HE	4 houses demolished
	08:50	Rom	Marlborough Rd. Woodland Av	HE	
	20:30	Rom	N.of Town Hall	HE	1 house demolished
	20:40	Rom	62 Larchwood Av.	AA UX	
	20:40	Rom	Victoria Road	HE	
	20:40	Rom	The Chase	HE	2 houses demolished
	20:40	Rom	Eastern Av.	HE	1 house demolished, 1 fatality.
	20:40	Rom	Ashmour Gdns.	HE	2 houses demolished
	20:40	Rom	Horndon Rd.	HE	
	20:40	Rom	Lodge Lane	HE	
	22:50	Rom	Broxhill Road	HE	
	22:50	Rom	Bedfords Park	HE	
	23:58	Rom	Btwn. Broxhill Rd. & Orange Tree Hill	HE	
	23:45	Horn	40 Harrow Drive	AA UX	
11/10/40	14:30	Rain	Noak Cafe, Rainham	UXB	
	20:45	Rom	Near Clockhouse Lane School	HE	
	22:45	Rom	Rear of St.Edwards School	HE	
12/10/40	16:40	Horn	Globe Road	Plane	Spitfire crashed
	15:00	H.Wood	Avenue Rd.	AA UX	
	20:00	Rain	Melville Rd	HE	No. 78 demolished 1 fatality.
13/10/40	21:10	Horn	Sewage Fm,Brettons	4 HE	
	21:10	Upm	Tawny Av	HE	2 wounded
	21:10	Horn	Cnr. Station Lane & Suttons Av.	HE	1 house demolished
	21:10	Upm	Cnr.Parkland Av & Clayton Av.	HE	3 houses demolished
	20:45	Rom	Collier Row	Oil inc & HE	
	21:15	Rom	Town Hall	HE & incs	
	21:35	Rom	Oldchurch Hosp.	Oil inc	

DATE	TIME	DISTRICT	LOCALITY	BOMB	DAMAGE & CASUALTIES
13/10/40	21:15	Rom	North St.	HE	Haysoms furniture store burnt out.
	21:15	Rom	The Brewery	Oil inc	
	21:40	Rom	Netherpark Drive	HE's	3 houses demolished
	21:45	Rom	Horndon Rd.	UXB	
14/10/40	22:30	Elm Pk.	Rainham Rd. & Elm Park Av.	HE	Gas main alight
	22:30	Elm Pk.	St. Andrews Av.	3 HE's	
15/10/40	20:00	Rom	George St	Oil inc	5 houses demolished
	20:00	Rom	A118 between Balgores Lane & Pettits Lane	UXB	
	22:00	Rom	Randall Rd.	HE	4 houses demolished
	22:00	Rom	Kingston Rd.	HE	2 houses demolished
	22:00	Rom	Richmond Rd.	HE	
	20:16	Rain	Manser Rd.	HE	
	20:15	Rain	Parsonage Rd.	Oil inc	
	20:15	Cran	Moor Lane	HE	6 wounded
	20:15	Cran	Open country by Fairholme Gdns & Moor Lane	10 HE's	
	22:15	Rom	Nr. Lodge Av	HE's	
	22:35	Rom	Sheila Close	HE	
	22:35	Rom	Carter Drive	HE	
	22:35	Rom	Ramsden Drive	HE	
	22:35	Rom	Lynwood Drive	HE	
	22:35	Rom	Larchwood Av.	HE	
	22:35	Rom	Dominion Drive	HE	1 house demolished
	22:35	Rom	Riversdale Rd.	HE	3 houses demolished
	22:35	Rom	Collier Row Rd.	HE	
	22:35	Rom	White Hart Lane	HE	
16/10/40	01:00	Rain	Ford Fm.	HE	
	01:00	N.ock	Whitechapel Fm.	4 HE	
	01:00	Rain	Albion P.H.	HE	
	19:35	Rom	Pettits Lane	HE	
	19:30	Rom	Havering Green	HE	
	19:30	Rom	Havering Village	incs	
	19:40	Rom	Havering Village	2 PM	
	20:10	Rom	The Drive	HE	5 fatalities
	20:15	Rom	Lawnsway	UXB	
	21:30	Horn	Brettons Sewage Fm.	PM	
	21:30	Cran	Cranham	PM	

DATE	TIME	DISTRICT	LOCALITY	BOMB	DAMAGE & CASUALTIES
16/10/40	21:30	Horn	Squirrels Heath Rd	UX PM	
	21:30	Rain	Ferry Lane	2 HE	
	21:30	Upm	Hall Lane	UX PM	
	22:00	Cran	Moor Lane	HE	
	23:30	Rom	Cottons Rec. Ground	HE	Shelter hit. 5 killed 2 wounded
	23:30	Rom	Richards Av.	HE	1 house demolished
	23:30	Rom	Recreation Av.	HE	5 houses demolished
	23:30	Rom	Knightsbridge Gdns.	HE	
	23:30	Rom	London Road	HE	
17/10/40	04:44	Rom	Allens Garage	HE	
	10:20	Rom	Risebridge Farm	HE	
	10:20	Rom	1 Risebridge Chase	4 Oil incs	
	21:00	N. Ock	Manor Farm	UXB	
18/10/40	01:25	N. Ock	Bays Farm, Ock. Rd	HE	
	02:20	Cran	E & N of Moorings	2 HE	
	19:00	Rom	Maylands Aero	Plane	British plane down
	19:00	Rom	64 Poplar St.	AA UX	
	20:10	Rom	S. of Lower Bed. Rd.	HE's	
20/10/40	05:44	Horn	Cedar Rd.	inc	
	01:00	Upm	Butts Fm, Aveley Rd	UXB	
	20:00	Upm	Cranborne Gdns	HE	No.22 & 24 demolished. 1 fatality.
	20:00	Upm	Tudor Gdns.	HE	No. 34 demolished. 1 fatality.
	20:00	Upm	Champion Rd.	HE	
	20:00	Upm	Sunnyside Gdns	HE	No. 22
	20:00	Upm	Derham Gdns	HE	No. 82 badly damaged
	20:00	Upm	Waldegrave Gdns	HE	No. 31 badly damaged
	20:00	Upm	St. Mary's Lane	HE	
	21:54	Upm	Upminster Common	incs	
	21:54	Rain	Melville Rd	3 HE's	
	21:50	H.Pk.	Harold Pk.	incs	
	22:04	Rom	Elm Walk & Heath Drive	2 HE & incs	1 house demolished & 2 wounded
	22:10	Rom	Gidea Close	HE	
	22:15	Rom	W. Mawney Rd. & Eastern Av.	HE & Oil inc	
	22:15	Rom	Park Boulevard	2 HE & Oil	1 casualty
	22:25	Rom	Beauly Way	2 HE	
	22:15	Rom	Pettits Lane	incs	
	22:15	Rom	Birkbeck Rd	2 HE	
	23:45	Rain	Wennington Road	HE	One Warden killed
	23:45	Rom	N. of Carter Drive	HE's	

DATE	TIME	DISTRICT	LOCALITY	BOMB	DAMAGE & CASUALTIES
20/10/40	23:50	Rom	Wolseley Rd.	HE	
21/10/40	00:35	Rom	Pyrgo Park	HE	
	19:45	Rom	Havering	HE's	
	21:50	Rom	Brooks Timber Yd Hornchurch Rd.	HE	
	21:47	. Horn	29 Clydesdale Rd.	HE	3 fatalities. 1 house demolished
22/10/40	02:30	Rom	Brooks & Co. Chase Cross Rd.	inc	
	00:25	Horn	Roneo Works	3 HE	
	23:15	Horn	Hacton Lane	HE	2 bungalows demolished, 3 wounded
23/10/40	22:45	Rom	London Rd.	UXB & HE	2 houses demolished
	22:45	Rom	Weald Way	HE	
	22:45	Rom	High Street	HE	
	22:45	Rom	Petley Gdns.	HE	
	22:45	Rom	Marina Gdns.	HE	
	22:45	Rom	Rear of Marks Rd.	HE	
24/10/40	01:30	Rom	Crow Lane	HE	
	01:51	Horn	Brentwood Rd.	HE	County High School
	05:25	N.Ock	N.Ockendon	2 HE	
	20:20	Rom	Chase Cross Rd.	HE & Oil	6 houses damaged. 2 fatalities
	20:20	Rom	Berkeley Avenue	HE	
	20:20	Rom	Lawnsway	HE	1 house demolished
	20:20	Rom	Hillfoot Av	HE	
	20:20	Rom	Erith Crescent	HE	
25/10/40	12:07	Rom	Woodstock Av.	Plane	Spitfire. Pilot injured.
	20:10	Horn	Wood Lane & Rainham Rd.	HE	4 houses damaged.
	20:10	Horn	Abbs Cross Lane	HE	
	21:00	Cran	Between Bury Farm & St. Mary's Lane	3 UXB	
26/10/40		Rom	Allotment rear of 234 London Road	UXB	
27/10/40	22:00	N. Ock	Manor Farm	8 HE's	
28/10/40	19:20	Rom	Collier Row	HE & Oil	
	23:15	H. Wood	Harold Wood	HE	A.R.P. Depot damaged.

DATE	TIME	DISTRICT	LOCALITY	BOMB	DAMAGE & CASUALTIES
3/11/40	15:50	Upm	Hall Lane	2 UXB	300 yd S. of Bird Lane.
4/11/40	19:35	Wenn	Wennington Rd.	HE	
	19:35	Wenn	East Hall Lane	HE	Kates Cotts. 1 fatality
	19:35	Horn	Shirley Gdns	HE	
	19:35	Horn	Abbs Cross Lane	HE	
	19:35	Horn	Suttons Av. & Belmont Av.	HE	
	19:35	Horn	Hacton Lane	incs	
	19:55	Rom	In line from Lodge Av. to Crow Lane	19 UXB	
5/11/40	03:45	Rom	Bedfords Park	HE's	
	05:00	Rom	Upper Bedfords Fm	HE'S	
	05:20	Rom	Nr. Straight Road	HE's	
	19:10	Rain	Sunningdale Av.	HE	
6/11/40	19:05	Rom	Recreation Av.	HE	
	23:15	Rom	Yew Tree Gardens	HE	
	23:20	Rom	Rush Green Road	HE	
	23:20	Rom	Romford Cemetery	HE	
	23:20	Rom	Gas Works	UXB	
	22:25	Elm Pk.	Cnr. Hartland Rd. & Saunton Rd.	HE	
	22:30	Upm	Gaynes School	3 incs	
	22:50	Horn	Melton Gdns.	HE	No. 14 & 16 demolished. 1 fatality
	22:50	Horn	Hubert Road	HE & UXB	30 houses damaged
8/11/40	18:50	Rain	Damyns Hall Fm	HE	
	18:50	Rain	Aylett Fm.	HE	
	20:38	H.Wood	13 The Ridgeway	HE	1 wounded
	20:40	Horn	Methodist Church	HE	3 wounded
	20:40	Upm	Gaynes School	HE	
	20:40	H.Park	5 Bryant Av.	2 HE	
	20:40	Upm	1 Hall Lane	HE	4 wounded
	20:37	Upm	Lilliputt Fm.	HE	
	20:40	Horn	15 Ashburnham Gdns	HE	
	20:33	Rom	N. side Colc. Road	HE	2 houses damaged
9/11/40	02:00	Rom	Dagnam Park	13 UXB's	
	18:25	Elm Pk.	Benhurst Av.	AA UX	
	20:00	Rom	Upper Bedfords Fm	HE	

DATE	TIME	DISTRICT	LOCALITY	BOMB	DAMAGE & CASUALTIES
29/10/40	19:25	Rom	Gallows Cnr.	incs	
30/10/40	02:10	Rom	Chase Cross Road	HE & Incs	
	02:50	Horn	17 & 19 Beulah Rd.	HE & UXB	5 houses demolished.
	02:50	Horn	67 Randall Drive	Oil	
	19:55	Elm Pk.	Suttons Av.	HE	
	19:55	Elm Pk.	Warren Drive	HE	6 houses demolished 5 wounded
	19:55	Horn	Harrow Lodge Pk	incs	
	19:55	Upm	Upminster Common	incs	
	21:51	Rom	Rush Green	incs	
	21:25	N.Hill	Noak Hill	HE	
	21:50	Rom	Marks Rd.	HE	4 houses demolished
	21:50	Rom	Richards Avenue	HE	
	21:50	Rom	Oak Street	HE	
	22:00	Rom	Wolseley Road	HE	
	22:00	Rom	Rush Green Rd.	HE	
31/10/40	07:50	Rom	Carter Drive	HE's	
	19:46	Rom	Bower House	Fm incs	
			Larchwood Av. & Carter Drive	HE	

NOVEMBER

DATE	TIME	DISTRICT	LOCALITY	BOMB	DAMAGE & CASUALTIES
1/11/40	03:30	Horn	Alma Av.	HE	
	03:20	Horn	Goodwood Av.	HE	
	03:30	Horn	Nr. Kempton Av.	HE	
	03:20	Rain	Rainham Lodge Fm.	incs	
	19:00	Rom	Mashiters Walk	HE	1 house demolished
	19:00	Rom	Btwn. Beauly & Eastern Av.	HE	
	19:00	Rom	Pettits Lane Sch.	Oil inc	
	21:30	Rom	Heath Drive	HE & Oil	1 fatality. 1 house demolished
	21:30	Rom	Park Boulevard	HE	
	21:40	Rom	Heath Drive	incs	
	21:45	Horn	Matlock Gdns	Plane	Heinkel 111 Bomber Two German crew & three civilians killed.
2/11/40	20:03	Rom	Waverley Crescent & Straight Rd.	9 HE's	
3/11/40	12:45	Horn	Lingfield Av.	15 UXB's	Over 100 yd radius.

DATE	TIME	DISTRICT	LOCALITY	BOMB	DAMAGE & CASUALTIES
10/11/40	19:50	Rom	Nr. Links Av.	HE's	
	20:00	Rom	Heaton Close	HE	2 houses demolished.
	20:00	Rom	Tennyson Road	HE	
	20:00	Rom	Straight Road	HE	
	22:25	Rom	Noak Hill	HE's	
	23:00	Rom	Havering Pk. Fm.	HE & Oil	
12/11/40	20:30	Horn	Wolburn Av.	HE	
		Horn	Elm Park Av.	UXB	Exploded next day
			Between Elm Pk. hotel & Wolburn Av		1 fatality, 2 wounded
13/11/40	18:55	Rom	Hamilton Av.	HE	2 houses demolished
		Rom	Ashmour Gdns.	HE	
		Rom	Eastern Av.	HE & Oil	
		Rom	North St.	HE	
		Rom	Havering Rd. Sch	HE	
14/11/40	21:47	Horn	Wood Lane	2 UXB	
	21:47	Horn	Rainham Road	2 AA UX	
15/11/40	20:05	Horn	82/84 Cecil Av.	HE & PM	5 fatalities, 55 wounded 3 houses demolished
	20:05	Horn	Redden Ct. Rd.	UX PM	
	23:39	Upm	Argyle Gdns.	5 HE & 1 Oil	
	22:55	Rom	Nr. Hog Hill Rd.	HE	
	22:55	Rom	Nr. Collier Row Rd	HE	
16/11/40	19:30	Rom	N.of Colchester Rd	HE	
		Cran	Broadfields Fm	UXB	
	22:05	Horn	Lacronoids Fact.	2 PM	Factory demolished & damage to many houses. 5 casualties.
	22:35	Rom	Havering Pk Farm	2 PM	Farm buildings damaged
	22:35	Rom	Bower Farm	1 PM	
20/11/40	05:30	Wenn	Kettle Lane, Wenn.	4 HE	
	05:30	N.Hill	Nr. Church Rd.	HE's	
	06:10	Rom	Bower Fm	HE's	
	06:10	Rom	Clockhouse Lane	HE's	
21/11/40	05:00	Upm	Upminster Common N. Nags Head Lane	PM	2 houses demolished 5 casualties, 1 fatal.
	05:00	Upm	48 Tawny Av.	HE	

DATE	TIME	DISTRICT	LOCALITY	BOMB	DAMAGE & CASUALTIES
23/11/40	03:15	Upm	Tylers Common	8 HE	
	04:30	Rain	Cory's Refuse Tip	HE	
24/11/40	18:38	Horn	Nr.Catholic Church	HE	23 casualties, 5 fatal 10 houses demolished
	21:15	Rom	Cedric Avenue	PM	
26/11/40	19:59	N.Ock	North Ockendon	9 HE & 1 Oil inc	
27/11/40	06:50	Rom	Crow Lane	1 inc	
29/11/40	19:10	Rom	Lynwood Drive & Edgeway	incs	
	18:59	Nk.Hill	Noak Hill	4 incs	
	18:55	H.Wood	Shepherds Hill	2 incs	
	19:05	H.Wood	Avenue Rd.	3 incs	
	19:10	N.Ock	Hall Farm	HE	
30/11/40	00:05	Rom	Romford Golf Course	HE	4 houses demolished 2 casualties
	00:05	Horn	Park Lane	HE	4 houses damaged. 1 casualty
	00:09	Horn	Harwood Av.	HE	2 houses damaged
	00:04	H.Wood	Shepherd & Dog	HE	12 houses demolished
	00:05	Horn	Jnct. of Park Lane & Clifton Road.	HE	4 casualties
	00:05	Horn	Oak Glen	HE	3 houses demolished. 2 casualties
DECEMBER					
3/12/40	20:25	Rom	Between London Rd. & Collier Row Rd.	10 HE's	1 house demolished. 4 casualties
	21:20	Horn	Devonshire Rd.	HE	1 house demolished
	21:20	Horn	Wayside Av.	HE	
	21:20	Horn	Albany Rd.	HE	
	21:20	Horn	Maylands Pk.	HE	
8/12/40	19:35	Rain	Ayletts Fm.	7 HE's	400 houses damaged 39 casualties, 1 fatal.
	23:14	H.Wood	Avenue Rd/Arundel Rd	PM	
	22:50	Rom	Havering Pk. Fm.	HE	8 casualties, 2 fatal
	23:00	Rom	Oldchurch Rd.	PM	2 houses, mortuary & civil defence post all demolished.

Left table:

DATE	TIME	DISTRICT	LOCALITY	BOMB	DAMAGE & CASUALTIES
8/12/40	23:00	Rom	Beechfield Gdns	HE	
	23:00	Rom	Gas Works	HE	1 house demolished
	23:10	Rom	Grosvenor Rd.	HE	2 fatalities, 2 shops
	23:10	Rom	Exchange Street	PM	& Telephone Exchange demolished.
	23:10	Rom	Jubilee Avenue	HE	
	23:10	Rom	Cromer Rd.	HE	
	23:14	Rom	N. of Colc. Road	PM	
	23:15	Rom	Sheringham Av.	HE	
	23:15	Rom	Rush Green Rd.	Oil	
	23:10	Rom	South St.	HE	2 shops burned
	23:15	Rom	Cemetery	HE	
9/12/40	00:05	Rom	St. Johns Rd.	HE	
	00:05	Rom	Clockhouse Lane	HE	
	01:00	Rom	Belle Vue Rd.	UX HE	
	01:00	Rom	Mount Pleasant Rd.	UX HE	
	01:10	Rom	Stanley Av.	HE	
	01:10	Rom	Woodfield Drive	HE	
	01:10	Rom	Collier Row Lane	HE	
	01:10	Rom	Collier Row Rd.	UX HE	
	01:10	Rom	Carlton Rd.	UX HE	
	01:20	Rom	Havering Pk. & Clockhouse Lane Sch.	incs	
	01:55	Rom	Meadow Road	HE	2 houses demolished. 2 fatalities
11/12/40	20:50	H.Wood	Shepherd & Dog Hill	2 HE's	
	20:50	H.Park	4 Court Av.	2 HE's	4 houses damaged 14 casualties, 1 fatal.
	20:50	Upm	Hall Lane	2 HE's	
	20:50	H.Wood	Church Rd School	2 HE's	Farm damaged
15/12/40	20:45	N.Ock	North Ockendon	6 HE's	
20/12/40	11:45	Upm	Ock. Rd. B1421	Machine Gunning	Done by two Spitfires
	11:30	Horn	Rainham Rd. AA		
22/12/40	17:50	Rom	W. of Meadow Rd.	HE	
23/12/40	19:10	Elm Pk.	Eyhurst Av.	AA	No.55 & 57 damaged. 1 fatality.
27/12/40	20:00	Rom	Hillfoot Rd.	HE	4 houses damaged
	20:03	Rom	47 Balgores Lane	PM	7 houses demolished, 13 casualties

Right table:

DATE	TIME	DISTRICT	LOCALITY	BOMB	DAMAGE & CASUALTIES
27/12/40	20:15	Rom	Gidea Pk Allotments	UX PM	
	22:00	Rom	North Street	Oil inc	
	20:38	Cran	Co.Op Factory	incs	Fire
29/12/40	19:20	Upm	Corbets Tey	24 incs	
	19:40	Rom	305 London Rd.	HE's	

1941

JANUARY

DATE	TIME	DISTRICT	LOCALITY	BOMB	DAMAGE & CASUALTIES
5/1/41	19:05	Rain	By Arterial Rd.	Oil & HE	
	19:05	Upm	Corbets Tey	Incs	Farmhouse & Haystack set on fire.
	21:35	Rain	Berwick Pond Fm.	HE	
	19:45	Rom	Pinewood Road	HE's	
	20:30	Rom	Upper Bedfords Fm	HE's	
	21:10	Rom	Nr. Heaton Av.	HE	
	21:25	Rom	Beech Street	HE	
	21:25	Rom	Cedar Road	HE	
	21:25	Rom	Western Rd.	HE	
	21:25	Rom	South Street	HE	
	21:30	Rom	Albert Road	HE	
	21:30	Rom	Milton Road	HE	
	21:30	Rom	Linden Street	HE	
	21:30	Rom	Como Street	HE	2 houses demolished
	21:30	Rom	Linden St/Mawney Rd.	HE	
7/1/41	00:40	Rom	Between Rush Green Rd. & Crow Lane	3 UX HE	
12/1/41	19:28	Horn	Southend Rd	HE	3 houses demolished
	19:28	Rain	Betterton Rd & Frederick Rd	incs	
	19:55	Rain	Murex Works	2 HE's	
	21:10	Wenn	The Green	HE	3 houses demolished
	20:31	H.Wood	Nr Woodlands Rd.	5 HE	
	21:30	Rom	Maylands Golf Course	HE	
	21:30	Rom	Oldchurch Rd. Pits	HE	2 houses damaged
	21:30	Rom	Colchester Rd.	HE	2 houses demolished
19/1/41	23:25	Cran	Broadfields Fm.	2 HE's	

DATE	TIME	DISTRICT	LOCALITY	BOMB	DAMAGE & CASUALTIES
29/1/41	19:47	N.Hill	Wrightsbridge Road	HE	
30/1/41	16:45	Rom	Lilliput Road	UX HE	
	16:05	Horn	Abbs Cross Lane	3 HE's	on allotments
	16:25	Horn	Diban Av	8 HE's	
FEBRUARY					
5/2/41	20:36	Horn	Northumberland Av.	incs	
	20:30	Rom	Gidea Pk.	HE	1 house demolished. 5 casualties
	20:40	Rom	Lodge Av	incs	
	20:25	Rom	59 Pettits Lane	HE	
	20:25	Rom	Balgores Lane	incs	
	20:30	Rom	Woodlands Road	HE	2 houses demolished
	20:30	Rom	Lowshoe Lane	HE	
14/2/41	22:50	Horn	Globe Rd.	AA	2 fatalities
17/2/41	22:55	Horn	Brooklands Gdns.	2 HE's	25 houses damaged. 26 casualties
	23:10	Horn	Hill Crescent	HE	
	23:10	Horn	Northumberland Av.	HE	Rear of No.35
26/2/41	21:45	Rom	Pettits Lane/Heather Gardens	HE	
	22:30	Rom	Gooshays Fm	UX HE	
MARCH					
4/3/41	19:40	Rain	Rothbury Av. } East Hall }- Wennington Fm. }	9 HE's	
	19:40	Upm	Ock. Road } Sunnings Lane }- Corbets Tey Rd }	12 HE's	
8/3/41	20:55	Rom	Salmons Farm	incs	
9/3/41	04:30	Rain	Wentworth Way	2 AP	
	21:00	Upm	St Mary's Lane	UX HE	
	21:10	Rom	Wolseley Road	HE	4 houses demolished 14 houses damaged 10 casualties, 5 fatal

DATE	TIME	DISTRICT	LOCALITY	BOMB	DAMAGE & CASUALTIES
9/3/41	22:19	Rom	Waverley Crescent	HE	
13/3/41	00:05	Horn	Patricia Drive } Westland Av. }- High Street }	12 HE & incs	3 houses in Westland Av. demolished. 8 casualties, 2 fatal.
15/3/41	20:50	Rom	Over wide area S. of A118	incs	
	22:50	Rom	Oldchurch Hospital	3 HE's	Doctors block demolished
	22:40	Rom	Romford Cemetery	HE	
	22:45	Rom	Coombewood Drive	HE	
	20:45	Horn	Longfield Av.	HE	
	21:30	Rain	Rainham Marshes	UX HE	
	20:48	Horn	Hylands Rec. Ground	HE	1 casualty
	21:00	Horn	Claremont Rd } Clifton Rd. }- Brentwood Rd. }	incs	Houses set on fire
19/3/41	04:20	Rom	Carter Drive } Carter Close }- Riversdale Rd }- Collier Row Rd } Lodge Lane }	28 HE's	150-200 houses damaged 1 fatality
	03:55	Upm	Rushmere Av.	HE or AA	
	20:40	Rom	6 Hayden Way	UX AA	
	20:58	Cran	E of Wantz Bridge	4 HE's	
	23:15	Rain	Upminster Rd.	PM	6 houses demolished 100 houses damaged, 12 fatalities
	23:25	Horn	Suttons Lane	UX AA	
	23:15	Upm	Bramble Lane	200 incs	
	23:05	Rain	Ayletts Farm	HE	
20/3/41	01:30	Rain	E. of River Beam	PM	
	01:30	Rain	S. of New Road	PM	
APRIL					
16/4/41	22:19	Horn	Jersey Road	HE	
	22:20	Horn	Gainsborough Road	HE	
	22:40	Horn	Southend Rd	4 HE's	
	23:00	Rain	Launders Lane	HE	
	22:15	Rain	S. of Victor Eng Wks	PM	
	21:30	Upm	Hall Lane	2 HE's	
	21:30	Rain	Nr. Eastwood Drive	2 UX HE's	

1941

DATE	TIME	DISTRICT	LOCALITY	BOMB	DAMAGE & CASUALTIES
17/4/41	01:45	Horn	Rainham Road	2 PM	Damage to houses
	01:09	Rain	Nr. Victor Eng Wks	3 HE'S	
	01:30	Wenn	New Road	PM	1 casualty
	03:05	Rain	Nr. LMS bridge	PM	
	03:05	Elm Pk.	Broadway	PM	
19/4/41	21:40	Rom	Essex Road	PM	38+ fatalities 17 houses demolished
	21:45	Rom	Netherpark Drive	HE's	4 houses demolished
	22:15	Rom	Hillfoot Av.	PM	6 fatalities, 22 houses demolished
	22:30	Rom	Between Carlisle Rd. & Princes Rd.	PM	35 houses demolished
	22:45	Rom	Pettits Lane	PM	15 houses demolished
	23:00	Rom	Crown Cott.London Rd	PM	
	22:30	Rain	AA Battery, Ferry Ln.	PM & HE	
	22:25	Rain	Victory Road	PM	houses demolished
	23:00	Horn	Brentwood Rd & Claremont Road	12 HE	6 houses demolished, 10 fatalities.
	22:30	Horn	Stanley Road	HE	1 fatality, 3 houses demolished
	22:30	Horn	Highfield Crescent	HE	5 casualties, 3 houses demolished
20/4/41	00:30	Rom	Havering Park Farm	HE	
	02:20	Rom	Nr. White Hart Lane	PM	
	02:20	Rom	Nr.Eastern Av (west)	PM	
	03:00	Rom	Nr. Lodge Lane	PM	
MAY					
10/5/41	19:30	H.Wood	Harold Court School	UX HE	
11/5/41	00:35	Rom	Castellan Avenue	PM	1 fatality, 8 houses demolished
	00:47	Rom	Upper Brentwood Rd.	PM	Direct hit on All Saints Church. 16 houses demolished
	02:20	Rom	Harrow Crescent	HE	1 house demolished
	04:10	N.Hill	Dagnam Park	3 HE's	
13/5/41	00:10	Rom	Rush Green	incs	
	00:11	H.Wood	Harold Wood	3 HE's	
JULY					
28/7/41	02:45	Rom	Catherine Road & Hamilton Road	4 HE'S	1 fatality, 4 houses demolished
	03:05	Horn	½ m.N.of Newtons Cnr	HE	
	08:45	Horn	Hacton Lane	UX HE	

1942

DATE	TIME	DISTRICT	LOCALITY	BOMB	DAMAGE & CASUALTIES
SEPTEMBER					
4/9/42	17:15	Rain	Hawthorn Av.	UXB Exploded	2 killed, 6 wounded all military personnel 4 houses demolished
DECEMBER					
7/12/42	23:10	Upm	Rushmere Av.	AA	
	23:10	N.Ock	Ockendon Rd.	AA	

1943

DATE	TIME	DISTRICT	LOCALITY	BOMB	DAMAGE & CASUALTIES
MARCH					
12/3/43	07:40	Hornchurch & Romford		Machine Gunning by enemy planes	1 casualty
14/3/43		Rain	Rainham Marshes	10 HE's	
		N.Ock	North Ockendon	8 HE'S	
MAY					
19/5/43	03:20	Rain	Ayletts Farm	HE	
JUNE					
15/6/43	01:50	Rom	Park Fm. Havering	2 HE's	
SEPTEMBER					
14/9/43	16:42	Horn	W. of Rainham Rd.	Plane Mustang. Pilot injured	
OCTOBER					
7/10/43	22:00	Rom	Romford Golf Course	HE's	

DATE	TIME	DISTRICT	LOCALITY	BOMB	DAMAGE & CASUALTIES
8/10/43	20:30	Rain	Berwick Ponds	10 HE's	
	20:40	Cran	Warley Street	HE	
	20:40	Wenn	Wennington	6 HE's	
18/10/43	02:39	Horn	27 Rockingham Av.	HE	5 casualties, 1 fatal
21/10/43	01:05	Cran	Between St Mary's Lane and Codham Hall	14 HE's	

NOVEMBER

DATE	TIME	DISTRICT	LOCALITY	BOMB	DAMAGE & CASUALTIES
5/11/43	13:00	Rain	Southend Arterial	Plane	British fighter
8/11/43	22:41	Rom	Nr. Pinewood Road & Wellingtonia Av.	HE's	1 house demolished
26/11/43	21:25	Rom	Between Lodge Lane & Carter Drive	HE	
20/11/43	06:04	Wenn	Wennington Marshes	HE	

1944

JANUARY

DATE	TIME	DISTRICT	LOCALITY	BOMB	DAMAGE & CASUALTIES
15/1/44	19:45	Rom	Chase Cross Rd.	AA	
21/1/44	21:30	Horn	Rear of Harlow Rd.	PM	20 casualties 200 houses damaged
	21:12	Rain	Rainham	incs	10 casualties
22/1/44	05:20	Rom	Albert Rd/Victoria Rd	incs	1 fatality
	05:20	Rom	Romford Brewery	incs	Bottling Dept. damaged
	05:15	Upm	Howard Rd	AA	3 casualties
	05:05	N.Ock	Church Lane	2 HE's	N.O Hall damaged
29/1/44	20:30	Rom	Mawney Rd.	AA	1 fatality (seizure)
	21:30	Rom	14 Ascension Rd	HE	1 fatality

FEBRUARY

DATE	TIME	DISTRICT	LOCALITY	BOMB	DAMAGE & CASUALTIES
4/2/44	05:35	H.Wood	Harold Wood	PM	Extensive damage, 3 casualties
	05:45	Upm	Cedar Av.	HE	1 fatality (warden)
	05:45	Upm	St Mary's Lane	HE	
	05:45	Upm	Bush Fm. Aveley Rd.	HE	

DATE	TIME	DISTRICT	LOCALITY	BOMB	DAMAGE & CASUALTIES
13/2/44	21:16	Rom	Havering Road N.	Plane	JU 88
	21:15	Upm	Park Farm	incs	
	21:07	Upm	Corbets Tey	incs	
	21:07	Upm	Aveley Rd.	incs	
	21:06	Rain	Between Willow Fm & Moor Hall	incs	
19/2/44	01:09	Rom	North Rd, Havering	HE & incs	
	01:05	H.Wood	Harold Wood	Explo. incs	
	01:05	Horn	Boscombe Av.	AA	
20/2/44	22:05	Rom	Rosedale Rd.	HE	
	22:05	Rom	Erroll Rd.	AA	
	22:05	Rom	Dagenham Rd.	AA	
	22:05	Rom	Lodge Lane & Havering Park Fm	HE's	
23/2/44	00:15	Rom	Collier Row	HE	
	00:50	Horn	W.D. Property	HE	2 soldiers wounded
	00:45	Horn	A.M. Property	8 HE's	
	00:45	Upm	261 Corbets Tey Rd.	HE	
	00:45	Upm	Byron Mansions	HE	
	00:45	Horn	Hillcrest Rd.	HE	
24/2/44	22:00	Rom	Collier Row Road	HE	
	22:00	Rom	Lynwood Drive	HE	

MARCH

DATE	TIME	DISTRICT	LOCALITY	BOMB	DAMAGE & CASUALTIES
14/3/44	23:05	Horn	Avelon Rd & Gainsborough Rd.	6 HE's & incs	
	23:20	H.Wood	Harold Wood	incs	
22/3/44	01:05	N.Ock	White Post Fm.	incs	
24/3/44	22:09	Upm	The Grove	AA	3 casualties

APRIL

DATE	TIME	DISTRICT	LOCALITY	BOMB	DAMAGE & CASUALTIES
19/4/44	01:05	Rom	Over wide area	incs	Fires- Brewery, Rise Pl...

V-1 Doodlebugs

District	Date	Time	Location and Damage
Rainham	16/6/44	02:10	N.E. of Moor Hall Rainham.
Rainham	16/6/44	02:10	Eastwood Drive, Rainham. One fatality.
Romford	16/6/44	02:25	Collier Row Road (near Whalebone Lane).
Rainham	16/6/44	02:40	On Rainham Marshes. Murex plant damaged.
Upminster	16/6/44	02:55	South of Upminster.
Romford	16/6/44	03:30	Rush Green Hospital. 6 fatalities (nurses & patients). On Dagenham and Romford border.
Romford	16/6/44	03:30	Barton Av. Seven people killed and seven seriously injured. Six houses demolished and 16 beyond repair.
Rainham	17/6/44	23:40	East Hall Lane, Wennington. East Hall & two cottages seriously damaged. Outbuildings destroyed.
Cranham	17/6/44	23:35	St. Mary's Lane, Cranham.
Romford	18/6/44	05:27	Lodge Lane. One fatality. 12 houses demolished.
Romford	20/6/44	05:00	Hainault Road. Three fatalities and 18 seriously wounded. 15 houses demolished. 100 shops and houses seriously damaged.
Hornchurch	21/6/44	14:52	Hornchurch Station. 100 houses damaged & 10 serious casualties (1 maternity)
Elm Park	22/6/44	03:45	74 houses damaged.
Romford	22/6/44	04:10	Heaton way. One casualty & 100 houses damaged.
Romford	23/6/44	06:52	Parkland Av. Three casualties & 100 houses damaged.
Hornchurch	23/6/44	07:03	Hornchurch Aerodrome. No damage.
Honchurch	23/6/44	21:00	Ascot Gardens. Three serious casualties.
Rainham	24/6/44	06:30	Rainham Starch Works Factory. West of Ferry Lane. Fire broke out. Salamons factory and Briggs Bodies factory both 50% demolished. One fatality.
Romford	25/6/44	01:50	Fowlers Farm, Collier Row Road. In open country.
Romford	25/6/44	21:50	Clockhouse Lane. Two fatalities and 10 houses demolished.
Rainham	29/6/44	03:50	Rainham Marshes. Superficial damage to Murex Works.
Rainham	30/6/44	03:46	Rainham Marshes. On Cory's dump.
Romford	30/6/44	20:15	On railway bank East of Romford Station. 34 casualties & 500 houses damaged.
Upminster	1/7/44	10:35	The Grove, on the corner with Tawny Av. Two serious casualties & 10 houses seriously damaged.
Romford	1/7/44	23:55	N.W. of Lodge Farm, Lodge Lane.
Rainham	3/7/44	19:55	N.W. of Chandlers Corner, Rainham. 27 houses damaged.
Romford	4/7/44	21:20	Between Eastern Av. & Marlborough Rd. 10 casualties.
Hornchurch	7/7/44	23:51	Rainham Road, Near Roneo Corner. 13 casualties. Six houses demolished & 300 damaged.
Romford	8/7/44	00:25	Mawney Road/Percy Road. One fatality & 11 houses demolished.
Cranham	9/7/44	21:18	St. Marys Lane, Cranham. Pub & 60 houses slightly damaged. Eleven people wounded including 3 military personnel.
Rainham	20/7/44	10:55	Rainham Marshes. Railway wires cut. Superficial damage to 50 houses. One casualty.

District	Date	Time	Location and Damage
Rainham	21/7/44	06:25	In River Thames east of Murex jetty. Damage to plant and sea wall.
S.Hornchurch	21/7/44	21:40	Jersey Road/ Elmer Gardens. Two fatalities. Slight damage to 200 houses.
Upminster	22/7/44	01:42	Springfield Gardens. Two fatalities and 12 other casualties. Serious damage to 6 houses, mild damage to 300-400 houses.
Hornchurch	22/7/44	21:40	Harrow Lodge Park, in field. Severe damage to library. Superficial damage to 300 houses.
Romford	23/7/44	00:30	North of Gallows Corner. Damage to Police Station & 100 houses.
Harold Park	24/7/44	04:40	Harold Park. 100 houses superficially damaged. Messers Denco seriously damaged.
Wennington	26/7/44	02:55	Wennington, slight damage to houses.
Wennington	27/7/44	01:30	Wennington.
Romford	27/7/44	15:40	South of junction of Havering Road & Lower Bedfords Road. 55 houses & 1 wardens post damaged.
Harold Wood	29/7/44	00:14	Superficial damge to 50 houses and E.C.C. Sanatorium.
S.Hornchurch	1/8/44	09:55	Danbury road. 7 casualties, 1 fatal. 6 houses demolished.
Great Warley	3/8/44	02:40	Bird Lane. Damage to Great Tomkyns & cottages.
Romford	5/8/44	07:16	Between Gorseway & Rush Green Road. Five fatalities & 16 houses demolished
Elm Park	6/8/44	03:30	St. Andrew's Avenue. Two fatalities & 24 casualties. 4 houses demolished & 15 seriously damaged.
Romford	6/8/44	23:20	Junction of Hillfoot Road and Collier Row Road. One fatality & 14 houses demolished.
Upminster	7/8/44	06:30	By Hall Lane. Chapel & 3 cottages demolished. One fatality.
Romford	7/8/44	07:30	Bower Farm, Havering.
S.Hornchurch	8/8/44	06:00	Betterton Road. Superficial damage to nearby houses.
Wennington	8/8/44	23:06	Wennington. Some damage to 15 houses.
Noak Hill	12/8/44	06:25	North of Noak Hill Road. Farmhouse demolished.
Rainham	15/8/44		Frog Island. Slight damage to Murex Works.
Rainham	15/8/44		Gerpins Lane, in sandpit. Grass fire caused.
Rainham	20/8/44	09:03	Between Leonard Arms & Chandlers Corner. 3/4 acre of rhubarb & 1/2 acre of marrows destroyed.
Romford	28/8/44	12:59	Havering Park Farm.
S.Hornchurch	28/8/44	15:30	Gainsborough Road. Six serious casualties. Ten houses seriously damaged.
Hornchurch	19/9/44	04:20	Crystal Avenue. Six fatalities and eleven other serious casualties. 6 houses demolished and 30 severely damaged.
Hornchurch	19/9/44	04:29	Great Gardens Road. 11 fatalities & 6 serious casualties. 6 houses demolished. & 50 severely damaged.
Noak Hill	5/10/44	19:58	Benskins Lane, Noak Hill. One bungalow seriously damaged.
Great Warley	11/11/44	01:45	Codham Hall.
Rainham	11/11/44	23:15	Burst on impact with trees 100 feet south of Berwick Pond Farm. No crater. Farm buildings demolished. Two trees set on fire.

V-2 Rockets

District	Date	Time	Crater	Launch Site	Location and Damage
Noak Hill	16/944	22.42	16'x3'	The Hague	Noak Hill in field of corn stubble at Hill Farm 121' N. of centre of Wrightsbridge Road. Unthrashed corn rick set on fire by fragments. Four cottages damaged.
N. Ockendon	11/10/44	05:15	41'x13'	The Hague	Whitepost Farm, North Ockendon. In potato field 864 yards E. of North Ockendon Road and 70 yards N. of Fen Lane. 1 hay and 2 straw stacks set on fire.
Hornchurch	3/11/44	00:58	40'x10'	Unknown	In open field ¼ mile S.E. of Bretton Hall Farm and 600' East of Romford-South Hornchurch Road. No damage.
Romford	4/11/44	21:42	34'x12'	Unknown	In field W. of Cross Road, Collier Row. One casualty.
Hornchurch	5/11/44	12:45	50'xWater	The Hague	¼ mile S.E. of Albyns Farm, Rainham. On W. edge of River Ingrebourne
Romford	12/11/44	02:35	45'x12'	The Hague	In field 400' S. of Harold Hill Farm. D damage for 800' radius.
Great Warley	13/11/44	04:35	26'x7'	The Hague	Great Warley. In field rear of houses in St. Mary's Lane. 400 yards S.W. of Monks Farm. C damage to 8 houses. Four casualties.
Romford	15/11/44	05:12	36'x10'	The Hague	Ainsley Avenue. Fell at side of railway. 8 houses demolished. 15 casualties.
Romford	16/11/44	07:40	41'x12'	The Hague	Rear gardens of houses of junction of Collier Row Lane and Rosedale Road. 13 fatal casualties. 32 people seriously wounded. 21 houses demolished.
Hornchurch	17/11/44	21:37	41'x7'	The Hague	In clover field 300' N. of Dovers Farm, W. side of Rainham Road. Slight blast damage.
Wennington	21/11/44	05:35	Airburst	E. of Hague	Over Wennington Marshes. ½ mile north of River Thames.
Great Warley	25/11/44	11:34	46'x12'	Monster Area	Great Warley. In field 150 yards W. of Great Warley Hall. C & D damage to farm and houses.
S. Hornchurch	26/11/44	11:02	38'x8'	Monster Area	Victory Road. 25 houses seriously damaged. Three fatalities and 30 serious casualties.
Cranham	26/11/44	17:49	32'x7'	Monster Area	Cranham. Fell on waste ground 500 yards S.S.W of Folkes. Slight D damage. Two casualties.
Hornchurch	1/12/44	13:01	37'x11'	The Hague	Fell on allotments W. side of Elmhurst Road. C& D damage to houses. 33 slightly wounded.

District	Date	Time	Crater	Launch Site	Location and Damage
Rainham	3/12/44	06:13	38'x7'	E. of Hague	Near Lake Avenue. 600 yards S.W. of Berwick House. 25 casualties. Four houses seriously damaged.
Wennington	3/12/44	07:41	44'x11'	E. of Hague	On rubbish dump ¾ mile N. of Great Coldharbour.
Hornchurch	9/12/44	04:50	34'x7'	E. of Hague	Hornchurch Aerodrome. ¼ mile S.W. of Suttons. Blast damage to windows. Crater in runway.
Romford	21/12/44	01:45	Airburst	The Hague	Airburst between Bear Inn and Harold Hill Farm. Ventura of rocket found at map Ref 107/979118. Slight damage to houses.
Romford	31/12/44	02:48	34'xWater	Wassenaar	Rush Green. In field off Rush Green Road, near Meadow Road. No damage.
Noak Hill	31/12/44	03:40	22'x9'	E. of Hague	Noak Hill. Fell S.W. corner of wood that is N.E. of Church adjoining Hill Farm. Near Chequers Road.
Harold Wood	9/1/45	22:20	41'x12'	N.E. of Hague	600yards E. of Harold Court Sanatorium. No damage.
Hornchurch	13/1/45	14:10	33'x3'	Vasseaar/Voorburg	Mardyke Farm. D damage to 50 houses.
Rainham	15/1/45	23:15	Direct hit	Naaldwijk/Naajdijk	51 Penerly road, Rainham. A damage to 5 houses, b damage to 4 houses and C & D to 400 houses. 14 fatalities & 41 other casualties.
Romford	16/1/45	02:59	35'x9'	Monster/Naaldwijk	Havering-atte-Bower.In field 1 mile W. of Harold Hill Farm and ¾ mile S.W Widdrington Farm. C damage to 2 bungalows.
Upminster	20/1/45	01:14	39'x Water	N. of Voorburg	In field rear of houses in Argyle Gardens, 400' west of Cranham Hall. Blast damage of C grade to 24 houses and D damage to 150 houses. Three serious casualties.
Noak Hill	21/1/45	15:17	43'x15'	Hague/Hoorn	In meadow 100 yards S.E. of Priory , Noak Hill. Two houses & farm buildings seriously damaged. Two serious casualties.
Rainham	21/1/45	18:52	53'x11'	Hague/Loosduinen	On Corys rubbish dump 400yards E. of Ford's Works. 8 houses and 2 shops slightly damaged.
Hornchurch	26/1/45	09:45	53'x 25'	Unknown	Rear gardens N. side of Staffords Avenue. 420' E.from junction with Ashlyn Grove then 100' N at right angles. Lacranoids factory badly damaged. 8 houses demolished & 15 seriously damaged. Three fatalities & 36 serious casualties.
Cranham	26/1/45	10:00	Airburst	Unknown	Burst in mid air between Clay Tye Farm and Whitepost Farm. Venturi found ½ mile S.W of Cranham Hall.
Hornchurch	4/2/45	23:50	48'x12'	E. of Voorburg/Delft	Rear gardens of houses on E. side of Ernest Road, north of Junction with Parkstone. 120 houses damaged. Eight casualties.

District	Date	Time	Crater	Launch Site	Location and Damage
Romford	11/2/45	01:05	46'x Water	Naaldwijk	Gobions Farm. 1500' S. from bridge in Collier Row Road. D damage to 60 houses & 6 shops.
Harold Wood	13/2/45	18:50	25'x Water	Poeldijk/Naaldwijk	In David Drive (E. Side). 180' N. of Church Road. 12 fatalities and 36 serious casualties.
Cranham	14/2/45	03:02	41'x14'	Voorburg	In field of pasture by St. Mary's Lane. ¼ mile S. of Franks Farm. Severe damage to Franks farm Cottages.
Romford	14/2/45	15:00	36'x15'	Kerkehout/Voorburg	In pasture land of Pyrgo Park, Havering. ½ mile S. of Ashton Farm. C damage to 20 houses. Two minor casualties.
Romford	14/2/45	17:00	46'x20'	Wassenaar/Westeing	Pasture of Bedfords Parkland. 400 yards N. of Bedfords Mansion.
Upminster	20/2/45	11:15	53'x14'	Unknown	In field on Aylens Farm, 300 yards E. of Hall Lane and ¾ mile S. of Tylers Common. Slight damage to 10 houses.
Rainham	20/2/45	13:20	Airburst	E. of Hague	Directly over Rainham Village. No damage.
Romford	20/2/45	20:35	31'x10'	N.E. of Hague	In rear gardens of Fairholme Av. (north side). A damage to 4 houses, B damage to 3 houses. 12 fatalities.
Romford	22/2/45	21:05	40'x12'	Wassenaar/Voorburg	In field adjoining W. side of Cross Road, opposite west end of Birch Rd. D damage for 600'.
Romford	2/3/45	02:20	31'x10'	Monster/Hoorn	In field E. side of pathway running N. of Clock House. ½ mile S.E. of Parks Farm
Romford	4/3/45	01:30	40'x10'	Monster/Naaldwijk	Havering-atte-Bower. E. of Bowers Farm, W. side of North Road. 900' S.W. of Liberty Cottage. 1 House demolished.
Rainham	5/3/45	22:40	50'x Water	Waalsdorperlaan	In field 200' off S.E. end of Wilfred Av. Two casualties.
Rainham	6/3/45	03:10	Direct Hit	E. of Hook	Ferro Road (E. side). A damage to 2 houses, B damage to 2 houses and severe C damage. Venturi found 200' away. Six fatalities.
Harold Wood	8/3/45	21:51	49'x12'	Hook of Holland	In wheat field on edge of woods ½ mile E. of Gooshays.
Upminster	12/3/45	00:25	35'x13'	Hague/Duindigt	Front Garden of No. 59 Waldegrave Gdns. A damage to 4 houses, B damage to 7 houses and D damage for 400'. Five fatalities.
Hornchurch	12/3/45	05:10	32'x12'	The Hague	In Hylands Park. By Hillcrest Road and 250' S. of Osborne Road Gate. D damage for 1200'. 8 casualties.
Romford	14/3/45	00:39	26'x7'	Hook of Holland	Havering-atte-Bower. In meadow 300 yards S. of Park Farm. D damage to farmhouse.
S. Hornchurch	14/3/45	21:25	Direct Hit	Monster Area	Direct hit on 7-9 Manser Road. A damage to 6 houses, B damage to 4 houses. Eight fatalities.

District	Date	Time	Crater	Launch Site	Location and Damage
Hornchurch	15/3/45	22:25	50'x13'	Hook of Holland	On waste ground ¼ mile S. of Lilliputts. D damage to 350 houses. 9 minor casualties.
Upminster	17/3/45	00:15	37'x7'	Hague/Haagschebosch	In cabbage field 400'E of Brambles. Slight damage to Farm
Hornchurch	17/3/45	00:55	44'x11'	Hook of Holland	In meadow on Mount Pleasant Farm. N. side of Eastern Avenue and W. of River Ingrebourne.
Wennington	17/3/45	03:34	Direct Hit	Hook of Holland	Direct hit on 22 ton steam engine. 1/4 mile E. of Gt. Coldharbour Lighthouse, 54' from waters edge. Damage to jetty, buildings and machinery.
Cranham	18/3/45	01:30	Airburst	S'Gravenzande	Burst in air ½ mile N. of Cranham. D damage to 6 houses.
Hornchurch	19/3/45	01:35	52'x Water	Hague/Houtrust	On waste ground ½ mile S. of Brettons. Some D damage. 14 minor injuries.
Hornchurch	20/3/45	05:40	Nil UX	Hague/Zorgvliet	Heath Park. In garden of No. 45 Northumberland Av. Failed to explode.
Romford	21/3/45	18:45	Airburst	Hague/Zorgvliet	Over junction of Colchester Road and Southend Arterial Rd. Turbine and other parts fell in Ferguson Avenue, Edward Close and near Harrow Crescent.
Hornchurch	26/3/45	04:42	37'x8'	Hook of Holland	Ravenscourt Grove (south side). Three killed and eight seriously wounded. 3 houses demolished, 44 seriously damaged and 1000 superficially damaged.
Romford	26/3/45	19:05	Airbreak	Hague/Zorgvliet	Broke up in air. Warhead fell in centre of Mawney Road, on the corner with Forest Road. 16 houses demolished. Two fatal casualties and 34 hospital cases.
Romford	26/3/45	22:35	31'x12'	Hague/Haagschebosch	In field N. side of Navestock and Noak Hill Road. 700' S.E. of Church. Victory Hut demolished.

Key to Damage

◆ **A - Totally Destroyed**

◆ **B - Demolition Necessary**

◆ **C - Seriously Damaged**

◆ **D - Slightly Damaged**

ROLL OF HONOUR 1939 – 1945

The pages that follow testify to the great price paid by the citizens of this Borough in defeating the tyranny of Nazi Germany. It is fitting that these names are now enrolled in Westminster Abbey, among the most illustrious of the nation's dead, where they form part of the National Roll of Honour of civilians killed in the United Kingdom. It is from these volumes that these tables have been extracted and supplemented wherever possible when omissions were discovered. In order to keep family, friends and neighbours as they were in life and ultimately in death - together, the original alphabetical order has been forsaken for a chronological arrangement.

CIVILIAN FATAL CASUALTIES

NAME	AGE	LOCATION	DATE
LEWIS, John Richard	32	Hornchurch Aerodrome	24th Aug 1940
BEATTIE, Arthur Moffatt	16	Randall Road, Romford	31st Aug 1940
DIBLEY, Constance May	46	10 Randall Road, Romford	31st Aug 1940
PEARSON, Walter Joseph	33	10 Richmond Road, Romford	31st Aug 1940
BOUCHARD, Kathleen Elise	32	117 Park Lane, Hornchurch.	31st Aug 1940
BOUCHARD, Letitia	59	117 Park Lane, Hornchurch	31st Aug 1940
WHITE, Marjorie Enid	13	488a Southend Road, Hornchurch	31st Aug 1940
PLUMMER, Catherine	75	212 Victoria Road, Romford	13th Sept 1940
PLUMMER, Herbert Walter	70	212 Victoria Road, Romford	13th Sept 1940
PLUMMER, Elise Phyllis	36	212 Victoria Road, Romford	13th Sept 1940
GREEN, Lilian Eileen	17	Isabel Villa, New Road	16th Sept 1940
TRIMNELL, William Arthur	45	70 Park End Road, Romford	17th Sept 1940
CHAMBERS, Mary Ellen	57	37 Findon Gdns., Rainham	18th Sept 1940
RIDGWELL, Florence Grace	19	5 Willowdene Cott., Abbs Cross Lane	19th Sept 1940
STEANE, Gwendoline Mary	23	5 Willowdene Cott., Abbs Cross Lane	19th Sept 1940
RYCRAFT, Walter George	53	42 Havering Drive, Romford	20th Sept 1940
RYCRAFT, Kathleen Mary	51	42 Havering Drive, Romford	20th Sept 1940
RYCRAFT, Gerald Bernard	19	42 Havering Drive, Romford	20th Sept 1940
RYCRAFT, Peter Bernard	15	42 Havering Drive, Romford	20th Sept 1940

BURCHNALL, William	46	142 Hornchurch Road , Romford	22nd Sept 1940
COPPING, Edward Parker	42	11 Beauly Way, Romford	23rd Sept 1940
EVANS, Gladys Maria	35	73 Spring Gardens, Elm Park	24th Sept 1940
MORTLOCK, Fanny Rebecca	70	Victoria Row Cottages, St. Mary's Lane	24th Sept 1940
MORTLOCK, Robert William	70	Victoria Row Cottages, St. Mary's Lane	24th Sept 1940
QUARTERMAN, Edward	36	14 Suttons Lane, Hornchurch	27th Sept 1940
QUARTERMAN, Sarah	38	14 Suttons Lane, Hornchurch	27th Sept 1940
CRABB, Alfred Stewart	30	Eastern Avenue, Romford	10th Oct 1940
PATERSON, William Henry	31	78 Melville Road, Rainham	12th Oct 1940
CHIPP, John William	30	76 The Drive, Romford	17th Oct 1940
CHIPP, Charlotte Maud	24	76 The Drive, Romford	17th Oct 1940
CHIPP, Jean Dorothy	4	76 The Drive, Romford	17th Oct 1940
CHIPP, Ann Elizabeth	2	76 The Drive, Romford	17th Oct 1940
CHIPP, Alan	11 mths	76 The Drive, Romford	17th Oct 1940
COLE, Edith	33	Cottons Recreation Ground Shelter, Rom.	17th Oct 1940
COLE, Terence Henry	5	Cottons Recreation Ground Shelter, Rom.	17th Oct 1940
COLE, Alan Christopher	12 mths	Cottons Recreation Ground Shelter, Rom.	17th Oct 1940
ELLIS, Walter Charles	28	Cottons Recreation Ground Shelter, Rom.	17th Oct 1940
ELLIS, Arthur Charles	4	Cottons Recreation Ground Shelter, Rom.	17th Oct 1940
MINTER, Arthur Henry	10	Cottons Recreation Ground Shelter, Rom.	17th Oct 1940
PARKER, Irene	55	22 Cranborne Gdns., Upminster	20th Oct 1940
TIPPING, Ethel Maude	60	34 Tudor Gardens , Upminster	20th Oct 1940
WINN, William Henry	34	Wardens' Post, Wennington Road	20th Oct 1940
RUDDELL, John Joseph	62	29 Clydesdale Road, Hornchurch	21st Oct 1940
RUDDELL, Florence	61	29 Clydesdale Road, Hornchurch	21st Oct 1940
RUDDELL, Ivy	34	29 Clydesdale Road, Hornchurch	21st Oct 1940
WARREN, James Walter	61	Chase Cross Farm, Chase Cross	24th Oct 1940
WARREN, Sarah Elizabeth	62	Chase Cross Farm, Chase Cross	24th Oct 1940
WHITE, Alice May	69	Clayton Farm, White Hart Lane	30th Oct 1940
BIRD, William James	29	12 Matlock Gdns., Hornchurch	1st Nov 1940
BIRD, Margaret Catherine	26	12 Matlock Gdns., Hornchurch	1st Nov 1940
BIRD, Joyce Margaret	2	12 Matlock Gdns., Hornchurch	1st Nov 1940
GONELLA, Margarita Giovanna	31	74 Main Road, Romford	2nd Nov 1940
BATTERSBY, Esther	77	4 Kates Cott., Abbs Cross Lane	4th Nov 1940
BYNOM, George Henry	78	14 Melton Gardens, Hornchurch	6th Nov 1940
GENTLEMAN, Elsie May	35	259 Elm Park Avenue	13th Nov 1940

EKE,	Arthur James	41	84 Cecil Avenue, Ardleigh Green	15th Nov 1940
EKE,	Violet Maude	39	84 Cecil Avenue, Ardleigh Green	15th Nov 1940
EKE,	Ronald Alfred	13	84 Cecil Avenue, Ardleigh Green	15th Nov 1940
SMITH,	James William	17	82 Cecil Avenue, Ardleigh Green	15th Nov 1940
SMITH,	Alfred William	42	82 Cecil Avenue, Ardleigh Green	15th Nov 1940
BELLETT,	Nelly	73	48 Tawny Avenue, Upminster	21st Nov 1940
ATKINSON,	Cedric	37	12 Cedric Avenue, Romford	24th Nov 1940
ATKINSON,	Donald	34	12 Cedric Avenue, Romford	24th Nov 1940
ATKINSON,	Elly	30	12 Cedric Avenue, Romford	24th Nov 1940
BARKER,	Mabel Irene	35	10 Cedric Avenue, Romford	24th Nov 1940
BARKER,	William Henry	38	10 Cedric Avenue, Romford	24th Nov 1940
POLLARD,	John Robert	48	Oldchurch Hospital, A.R.P. Depot.	8th Dec 1940
STEVENS,	Frederick	5	Oldchurch Hospital, A.R.P. Depot.	8th Dec 1940
VANGO,	Percy Alfred	27	South Street, Romford	8th Dec 1940
FLEMING,	Edward	42	Telephone Exchange, Romford	8th Dec 1940
PAGE,	Melitia Lillian	55	35 Arundel Road, Harold Wood.	8th Dec 1940
SMITH,	Ada	32	128 Bell House Road, Romford	9th Dec 1940
SMITH,	Ann Patricia	2	128 Bell House Road, Romford	9th Dec 1940
SMITH,	Helen	78	4 Court Avenue, Harold Park	10th Dec 1940
PEARCE,	William Henry	46	57 Eyehurst Avenue, Elm Park	23rd Dec 1940
BISHOP,	George	45	79 Globe Road, Hornchurch	14th Feb 1941
BISHOP,	Isabella Winifred	43	79 Globe Road, Hornchurch	14th Feb 1941
JOLLEY,	Daisy Margaret	26	47 Wolseley Road, Romford	9th March 1941
MAYES,	Edith Elizabeth	31	45 Wolseley Road, Romford	9th March 1941
MAYES,	Donald Arthur	4	45 Wolseley Road, Romford	9th March 1941
MAYES,	John	2	45 Wolseley Road, Romford	9th March 1941
RIDINGTON,	Leslie William	10 mths	38 Wolseley Road, Romford	9th March 1941
BONE,	Hylda	38	Westlands, Westlands Av., Hornchurch	13th March 1941
BONE,	Robert Sydney	40	Westlands, Westlands Av., Hornchurch	13th March 1941
SIMMONS,	Elizabet Ivy	32	Ramsden Drive, Collier Row	19th March 1941
BIGGS,	Violet Elizabeth	2	2 Brights Cott., Upminster Road, Rain.	19th March 1941
CRAIG,	James Talbot	49	'Elan Villa', Upminster Road, Rain.	19th March 1941
GREGORY,	Rosina Gladys	39	1 Brights Cott., Upminster Road, Rain.	19th March 1941
HENDRY,	Harriet Emma	45	Hawthorn House, Upminster Road, Rain.	19th March 1941
JACOBS,	Ernest Wilfred	41	'Florence', Upminster Road, Rainham	19th March 1941
JACOBS,	Bertha	30	'Florence', Upminster Road, Rainham	19th March 1941
JACOBS,	Denice	3	'Florence', Upminster Road, Rainham	19th March 1941
MIDDLEDITCH,	William John	60	'June Villa', Upminster Road, Rainham	19th March 1941
MIDDLEDITCH,	Lucy Emily	40	'June Villa', Upminster Road, Rainham	19th March 1941
SAUNDERS,	Derek William	6	'Mayfair', Upminster Road, Rainham	19th March 1941
SAUNDERS,	William George	30	'Mayfair', Upminster Road, Rainham	19th March 1941
TYLER,	Horace George	35	Cycling Past, Upminster Road, Rainham	19th March 1941
POTTER,	Robert Henry	53	31 Sutton's Lane, Hornchurch	20th March 1941

BARCLAY, Mary Beatrice	48	107 Essex Road, Romford	19th April 1941
BARCLAY, Phyllis	18	107 Essex Road, Romford	19th April 1941
BARCLAY, John Stanley	14	107 Essex Road, Romford	19th April 1941
BARCLAY, Ernest Harold	12	107 Essex Road, Romford	19th April 1941
BARCLAY, Gordon	8	107 Essex Road, Romford	19th April 1941
BEAN, Joan	16	107 Essex Road, Romford	19th April 1941
CARTER, Elizabeth	38	103 Essex Road, Romford	19th April 1941
CARTER, Vera Patricia	10	103 Essex Road, Romford	19th April 1941
CHESTER, Georgina Mary	4	105 Essex Road, Romford	19th April 1941
CHESTER, Mary Ann	42	105 Essex Road, Romford	19th April 1941
DENNIS, Elsie	14	105 Essex Road, Romford	19th April 1941
DENNIS, Lily	16	105 Essex Road, Romford	19th April 1941
HOBBS, Rosina	69	103 Essex Road, Romford	19th April 1941
HOLLANDS, Charles James	37	109 Essex Road, Romford	19th April 1941
LEWIS, Florence Irene	20	115 Essex Road, Romford	19th April 1941
LIMEHOUSE, Edwin	35	115 Essex Road, Romford	19th April 1941
LIMEHOUSE, Maud Alice	35	115 Essex Road, Romford	19th April 1941
LIMEHOUSE, Beryl	11	115 Essex Road, Romford	19th April 1941
LIMEHOUSE, Edwin	10	115 Essex Road, Romford	19th April 1941
LIMEHOUSE, Barbara	5	115 Essex Road, Romford	19th April 1941
QUINCEY, Violetta	27	113 Essex Road, Romford	19th April 1941
QUINCEY, David Robert	12 mths	113 Essex Road, Romford	19th April 1941
RATCLIFFE, Pathaney	67	101 Essex Road, Romford	19th April 1941
REEKS, Rhoda Annie	40	113 Essex Road, Romford	19th April 1941
REEKS, Rosina Rebecca	9	113 Essex Road, Romford	19th April 1941
TRACEY, Josephine	27	100 Essex Road, Romford	19th April 1941
TRACEY, Margaret	35	100 Essex Road, Romford	19th April 1941
WILSON, Thomas Stanley	35	117 Essex Road, Romford	19th April 1941
WILSON, Winifred Ada	34	117 Essex Road, Romford	19th April 1941
WILSON, Joyce Ada	7	117 Essex Road, Romford	19th April 1941
WILSON, Roy Stanley	5	117 Essex Road, Romford	19th April 1941
WOOD, Robert	26	111 Essex Road, Romford	19th April 1941
WOOD, Doris Helen	25	111 Essex Road, Romford	19th April 1941
WOOD, James Charles	6	111 Essex Road, Romford	19th April 1941
WOOD, Henry Robert	4	111 Essex Road, Romford	19th April 1941
KNOWN ONLY TO GOD		Essex Road, Romford	19th April 1941
KNOWN ONLY TO GOD		Essex Road, Romford	19th April 1941
KNOWN ONLY TO GOD		Essex Road, Romford	19th April 1941
GILL, George	64	144 Brentwood Road, Hornchurch	19th April 1941
GILL, Adelaide May	39	144 Brentwood Road, Hornchurch	19th April 1941
GILL, Joyce Rosemary	11	144 Brentwood Road, Hornchurch	19th April 1941
GILL, George John	9	144 Brentwood Road, Hornchurch	19th April 1941
GILL, John William	7	144 Brentwood Road, Hornchurch	19th April 1941
GILL, Mary Winifred	6	144 Brentwood Road, Hornchurch	19th April 1941
GILL, Adelaide Doris	5	144 Brentwood Road, Hornchurch	19th April 1941
GILL, Edward Richard	3	144 Brentwood Road, Hornchurch	19th April 1941
GILL, Pamela Mary	1	144 Brentwood Road, Hornchurch	19th April 1941
FROST, Sarah	57	140 Brentwood Road, Hornchurch	19th April 1941
BEDFORD, Richard Archibold	57	Hillfoot Road, Romford	19th April 1941
DUNCAN, George William	30	Hillfoot Avenue, Romford	19th April 1941
ELLIS, Louisa	69	11 Hillfoot Avenue, Romford	19th April 1941
THOMAS, Ernest Howard	57	8 Hillfoot Avenue, Romford	19th April 1941
WALLING, May Emma	39	11 Hillfoot Avenue, Romford	19th April 1941
WALLING, Carol Ann	2	11 Hillfoot Avenue, Romford	19th April 1941

186

NASH, Herbert George	73	64 Stanley Road, Sth. Hornchurch	19th April 1941
DURRANT, Robert Samuel	28	Rainham	21st April 1941
WHITTAKER, Walter Harry	60	59 Castellan Avenue, Gidea Park	11th May 1941
BIXBY, Francis George	12	Margaret Road, Romford	28th July 1941
MANN, Frederick Charles	41	27 Rockingham Avenue, Hornchurch	18th Oct 1943
FULCHER, Harold	68	50 Albert Road, Romford	22nd Jan 1944
COOK, George Hart	15	63 Ingrebourne Road, Rainham	23rd Jan 1944
SHARP, Alice Eliza	33	14 Ascension Road, Chase Cross	29th Jan 1944
GARWOOD, Frank William	56	A.R.P Post, Cedar Avenue, Upminster	4th Feb 1944
WALLACE, Queenie Elizabeth	26	5 James Square, St. Andrew's Road, Rom.	19th April 1944
HOWES, Alfred James	35	27 Eastwood Drive, Rainham	16th June 1944
CROWE, Beatrice Mary	62	15 Barton Avenue, Romford	16th June 1944
CROWE, Maureen Ellen	5	15 Barton Avenue, Romford	16th June 1944
CROWE, Barbara Jean	11 mths	15 Barton Avenue, Romford	16th June 1944
SARGEANT, George William	49	17 Barton Avenue, Romford	16th June 1944
SARGEANT, Emily Isobel	49	17 Barton Avenue, Romford	16th June 1944
SARGEANT, Eileen Pamela	9	17 Barton Avenue, Romford	16th June 1944
TIZZARD, Alice Louise	44	19 Barton Avenue, Romford	16th June 1944
SELLEN, Annie Harriet	70	22 Lodge Lane, Collier Row	18th June 1944
LITTLE, Arthur George	54	154 Hainault Road, Romford	21st June 1944
LITTLE, Susannah Elizabeth	49	154 Hainault Road, Romford	21st June 1944
MOORHOUSE, Alexandra	42	156 Hainault Road, Romford	21st June 1944
STARKEY, Eva	83	Half Way House, Ferry Lane, Rainham	24th June 1944
CRAY, Beatrice	43	62 Clockhouse Lane, Collier Row	25th June 1944
HARBURN, Kenneth William	42	56 Clockhouse Lane, Collier Row	25th June 1944
WEMBRIDGE, Edith Emily	58	345 Mawney Road, Romford	8th July 1944
SMITH, Norman Frank	16	27 Jersey Road, Sth. Hornchurch	21st July 1944
SMITH, Gordon Kenneth	7	27 Jersey Road, Sth. Hornchurch	21st July 1944
WELCH, Lilian Olive	56	51 Springfield Gardens, Upminster	22nd July 1944
WELCH, Kathlyn Celia	22	51 Springfield Gardens, Upminster	22nd July 1944
BARNES, Beatrice	39	27 Gorseway, Rush Green	5th Aug 1944
BARNES, Alan Charles	7	27 Gorseway, Rush Green	5th Aug 1944
ELLIOTT, May Evelyn	45	29 Gorseway, Rush Green	5th Aug 1944
ELLIOTT, Anthony	12	29 Gorseway, Rush Green	5th Aug 1944
KINCH, Clara Graham	74	25 Gorseway, Rush Green	5th Aug 1944
NEWHAM, Edith Annie	53	49 St. Andrew's Avenue, Elm Park	6th Aug 1944
NEWHAM, Frederick	54	49 St. Andrew's Avenue, Elm Park	6th Aug 1944

TUBBY, Charles	30	202 Collier Row Lane, Romford	6th Aug 1944
HOLMAN, Mary	75	Tyes Cottage, Hall Lane, Upminster	7th Aug 1944
ASHDOWN, Rose Beatrice	65	35 Crystal Avenue, Hornchurch	19th Sept 1944
EDMUNDS, Ivy Maud	29	37 Crystal Avenue, Hornchurch	19th Sept 1944
EDMUNDS, Raymond David	3	37 Crystal Avenue, Hornchurch	19th Sept 1944
ENGWELL, Doris Irene	21	37 Crystal Avenue, Hornchurch	19th Sept 1944
NORTHOVER, Daisy Isabella	35	33 Crystal Avenue, Hornchurch	19th Sept 1944
NORTHOVER, Valerie Daisy	5	33 Crystal Avenue, Hornchurch	19th Sept 1944
BONNER, Agnes Ida	79	77 Great Gardens Road, Hornchurch	19th Sept 1944
CHUMLEY, Alfred Thomas	41	75 Great Gardens Road, Hornchurch	19th Sept 1944
CHUMLEY, Gwenoline Kate	36	75 Great Gardens Road, Hornchurch	19th Sept 1944
CHUMLEY, Jean Frances	13	75 Great Gardens Road, Hornchurch	19th Sept 1944
CHUMLEY, Mary Joan	10	75 Great Gardens Road, Hornchurch	19th Sept 1944
CHUMLEY, Margaret Ann	5	75 Great Gardens Road, Hornchurch	19th Sept 1944
CHUMLEY, John Jeffrey	6 wks	75 Great Gardens Road, Hornchurch	19th Sept 1944
COLLYER, Ellen	64	77 Great Gardens Road, Hornchurch	19th Sept 1944
FOSTER, Mabel Alice	41	83 Great Gardens Road, Hornchurch	19th Sept 1944
JONES, Violet Eva	30	79 Great Gardens Road, Hornchurch	19th Sept 1944
PILBOROUGH, Hilda Mary	49	73 Great Gardens Road, Hornchurch	19th Sept 1944
KING, George Frederick	54	5 Hartland Road, Hornchurch	5th Nov 1944
ATTWOOD, Adeline	49	17 Collier Row Lane, Collier Row	16th Nov 1944
COPSEY, Florence Ada	35	15 Collier Row Lane, Collier Row	16th Nov 1944
COPSEY, Leonard Keith	8	15 Collier Row Lane, Collier Row	16th Nov 1944
EARL, Minnie	42	11 Collier Row Lane, Collier Row	16th Nov 1944
EARL, John Frederick	13	11 Collier Row Lane, Collier Row	16th Nov 1944
EARL, Ronald James	11	11 Collier Row Lane, Collier Row	16th Nov 1944
KEY, Ivy Edith Kathleen	33	15 Collier Row Lane, Collier Row	16th Nov 1944
KEY, Maureen Edith Sheila	6	15 Collier Row Lane, Collier Row	16th Nov 1944
MITCHELL, Lillian	57	19 Collier Row Lane, Collier Row	16th Nov 1944
MITCHELL, Betty	16	19 Collier Row Lane, Collier Row	16th Nov 1944
ROBERTS, John Edward	46	15 Collier Row Lane, Collier Row	16th Nov 1944
LARNER, Blanche Mary	48	54 Rosedale Road, Collier Row	16th Nov 1944
WHITEMAN, Lily Elizabeth	47	50a Rosedale Road, Collier Row	16th Nov 1944
BULL, Albert Arthur	39	6 Orion Cottages, South Hornchurch	26th Nov 1944
BULL, Brian Howard	5	6 Orion Cottages, South Hornchurch	26th Nov 1944
REVELL, Frederick William	50	10 Blue House Estate, South Hornchurch	26th Nov 1944
ANTHONY, David Francis	49	51 Penerley Road, Rainham	15th Jan 1945
ANTHONY, Bertha Elizabeth	44	51 Penerley Road, Rainham	15th Jan 1945
ANTHONY, John	9	51 Penerley Road, Rainham	15th Jan 1945
GOWER, Elsie Lucy	35	55 Penerley Road, Rainham	15th Jan 1945
GOWER, Royston Edward	11	55 Penerley Road, Rainham	15th Jan 1945
GOWER, Brian Edward,	4	55 Penerley Road, Rainham	15th Jan 1945
GOWER, Patricia Elsie	9 mths	55 Penerley Road, Rainham	15th Jan 1945
HOWELLS, Jehoyda Howard	40	49 Penerley Road, Rainham	15th Jan 1945
HOWELLS, Caroline Arianwen	39	49 Penerley Road, Rainham	15th Jan 1945
HOWELLS, Howard	15	49 Penerley Road, Rainham	15th Jan 1945
HOWELLS, Robert	18 mths	49 Penerley Road, Rainham	15th Jan 1945
MORRIS, Henry David	14	53 Penerley Road, Rainham	15th Jan 1945
MORRIS, Henry John	51	53 Penerley Road, Rainham	15th Jan 1945
MORRIS, Jessie Martha	51	53 Penerley Road, Rainham	15th Jan 1945

McLAUGHLIN, Phillip	36	Rainham		25th	Jan	1945
BROWN, Elsie Gladys	17	Staffords Avenue, Ardleigh Green		26th	Jan	1945
CRUTCHLEY, Ivy Rose	17	Staffords Avenue, Ardleigh Green		26th	Jan	1945
BARRETT, Joyce	20	Staffords Avenue, (WAAF on Leave)		26th	Jan	1945
BETTS, Brian Christopher			David Drive, Harold Park	13th	Feb	1945
CURTIS, Minnie	53	48	David Drive, Harold Park	13th	Feb	1945
DAWKINS, Anthony Leonard	4	44	David Drive, Harold Park	13th	Feb	1945
DAWKINS, Marie Winifred	32	44	David Drive, Harold Park	13th	Feb	1945
HUSON, Jane Kate	69	46	David Drive, Harold Park	13th	Feb	1945
LEVERINGTON, Mabel Helen	35	52	David Drive, Harold Park	13th	Feb	1945
MELVILLE, Sydney Arthur	45	46	David Drive, Harold Park	13th	Feb	1945
MELVILLE, Eileen Dora	36	46	David Drive, Harold Park	13th	Feb	1945
MELVILLE, Pauline Illena	6	46	David Drive, Harold Park	13th	Feb	1945
MELVILLE, Michael Ian	4	46	David Drive, Harold Park	13th	Feb	1945
NEWLING, Arthur John	45	50	David Drive, Harold Park	13th	Feb	1945
NEWLING, Rose Miriam	39	50	David Drive, Harold Park	13th	Feb	1945
NEWLING, Iris Mary	17	50	David Drive, Harold Park	13th	Feb	1945
LEE, John Ewing	17		Church Road, Harold Park	13th	Feb	1945
BARNET, George	69	53	Fairholme Avenue, Gidea Park	20th	Feb	1945
BARTLEY, Sophia Elizabeth	70	53	Fairholme Avenue, Gidea Park	20th	Feb	1945
BARTLEY, William Frederick	35	53	Fairholme Avenue, Gidea Park	20th	Feb	1945
BARTLEY, Lilian lucy	33	53	Fairholme Avenue, Gidea Park	20th	Feb	1945
CARTER, Ellen	69	55	Fairholme Avenue, Gidea Park	20th	Feb	1945
HALLAS, Iris Mabel	43	59	Fairholme Avenue, Gidea Park	20th	Feb	1945
HUGHES, John Lloyd	47	53	Fairholme Avenue, Gidea Park	20th	Feb	1945
NORRIS, Arthur	46		Fairholme Avenue, Gidea Park	20th	Feb	1945
TURNER, Sidney George	53	55	Fairholme Avenue, Gidea Park	20th	Feb	1945
WEST, Barbara Anne	14	57	Fairholme Avenue, Gidea Park	20th	Feb	1945
WEST, John Laston	11	57	Fairholme Avenue, Gidea Park	20th	Feb	1945
WEST, David Hurst	7	57	Fairholme Avenue, Gidea Park	20th	Feb	1945
FROGLEY, Charles Henry	61	9	Ferro Road, Rainham	6th	March	1945
FROGLEY, Constance Evelyn	31	9	Ferro Road, Rainham	6th	March	1945
FROGLEY, Doris Ellen	43	9	Ferro Road, Rainham	6th	March	1945
MONTGOMERY, Peggy Anita	8	6	Ferro Road, Rainham	6th	March	1945
PAGE, Ethel Rose	42	10	Ferro Road, Rainham	6th	March	1945
PAGE, Martha Sarah	68	10	Ferro Road, Rainham	6th	March	1945
BROOKS, Ralph Rowley	58	65	Waldegrave Gardens, Upminster	12th	March	1945
BROOKS, Jessie Alexandra	56	65	Waldegrave Gardens, Upminster	12th	March	1945
LEWIS, Annie	41	61	Waldegrave Gardens, Upminster	12th	March	1945
LEWIS, Maxwell John	7	61	Waldegrave Gardens, Upminster	12th	March	1945
OAKES, William Richard	2	67	Waldegrave Gardens, Upminster	12th	March	1945
COLE, Charles John	67	9	Manser Road, South Hornchurch	14th	March	1945
COLE, Agnes Maud	61	9	Manser Road, South Hornchurch	14th	March	1945
GALE, Jane	58	11	Manser Road, South Hornchurch	14th	March	1945
GALE, William John	58	11	Manser Road, South Hornchurch	14th	March	1945
MOCKERADGE, Frances	66	5	Manser Road, South Hornchurch	14th	March	1945
MOCKERADGE, William	60	5	Manser Road, South Hornchurch	14th	March	1945
TURNER, Gladys	44	7	Manser Road, South Hornchurch	14th	March	1945
TURNER, Daintry Michael	11	7	Manser Road, South Hornchurch	14th	March	1945

RANDALL, Frances	58	'Highview, Ravenscourt Grove, Hornchurch	26th March 1945
TURNER, Frederick Harris	48	'Doma', Ravenscourt Grove, Hornchurch	26th March 1945
TURNER, Kathleen	45	'Doma', Ravenscourt Grove, Hornchurch	26th March 1945
HITCHCOCK, Lilian Emily	59	235 Mawney Road, Romford	26th March 1945
JONES, Keith David	18	256 Mawney Road, Romford	26th March 1945